METRO

A GRAPHIC NOVEL OF VERY DARK FANTASY

Writers
Brian Quinn and Cullen Bunn

Artist
Walt Flanagan

Inker
Phillip R. Williams Jr.

Color Artist
Wayne Jansen

Letterer
Marie Enger

Cover Artist
Francesco Francavilla

Metro Logo created by the Kucharek Brothers
Metro Book Design by Anton Kromoff

FOREWORD

There are hidden messages within these pages

Sure, sure. You'll see plenty of nods to Tell 'Em Steve-Dave, the podcast that stars my co-creators, but there's much more to it than that.

Herein, you'll find secrets.

There are codes and algorithms and formulae to be found in METRO. You'll need to search for them, and they will not be easy to find. They can be found in this volume, in its sequels, and in supplemental material. Even this foreword might hold a clue. The discovery of one might—and I must stress "might"—lead to another. And the order in which you discover these obscure bits of information will determine the very nature of the mysteries unlocked.

We will not provide hints. We will not even tell you if you're right about what you find. Our purpose was only to present this information, obscured though it may be. We were tasked, if you will, by our friends the Wide-Eyed Three.

Don't worry. You'll understand when you meet them.

In the meantime, I hope you enjoy the story for what it was meant to be—a very dark urban fantasy. Reading the book in that way—for simple enjoyment—is the first step to illuminating the deeper mysteries.

—Cullen Bunn
Writing from Snake Mountain

This is the key.

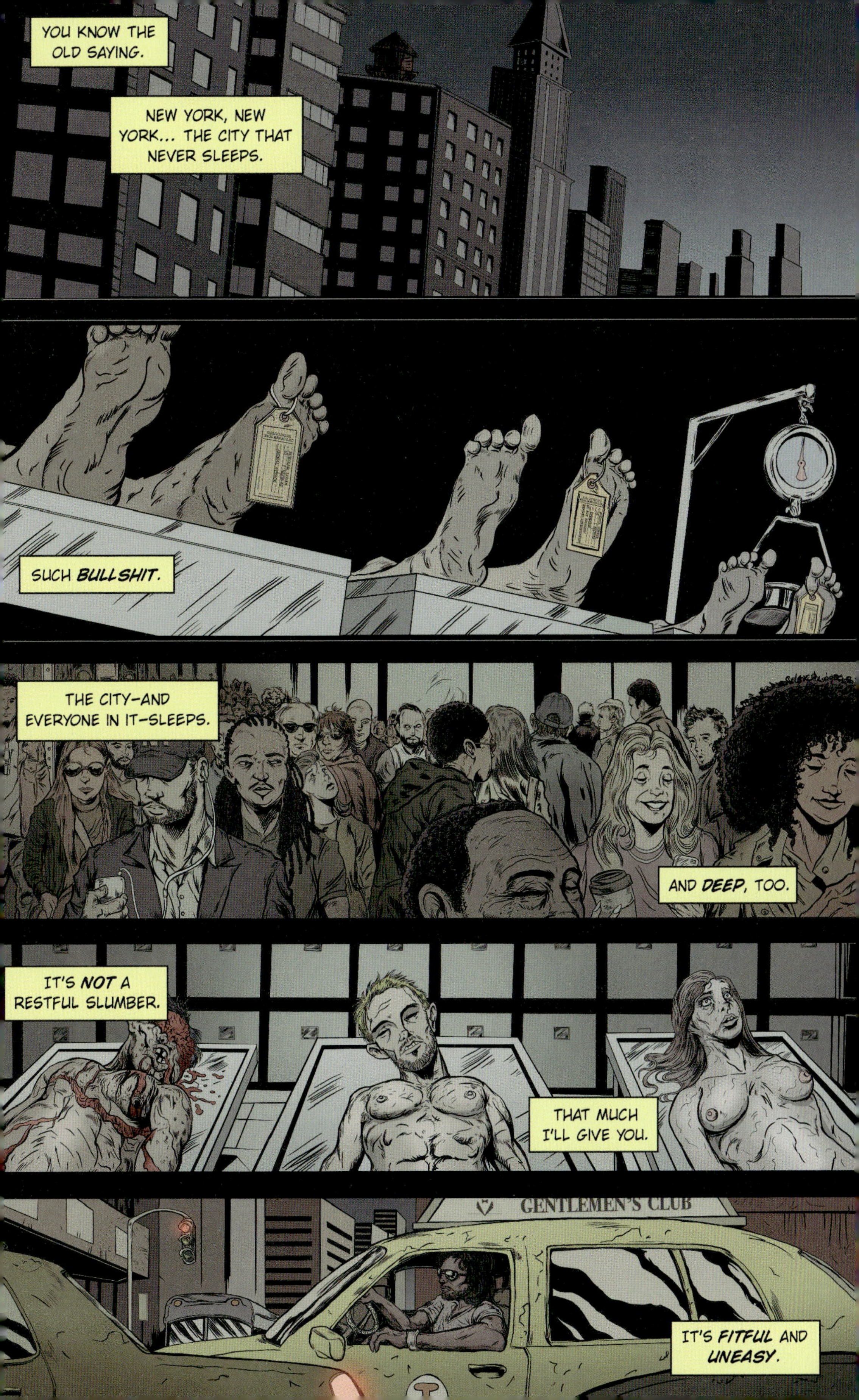
YOU KNOW THE OLD SAYING.
NEW YORK, NEW YORK... THE CITY THAT NEVER SLEEPS.
SUCH BULLSHIT.
THE CITY–AND EVERYONE IN IT–SLEEPS.
AND DEEP, TOO.
IT'S NOT A RESTFUL SLUMBER.
THAT MUCH I'LL GIVE YOU.
GENTLEMEN'S CLUB
IT'S FITFUL AND UNEASY.

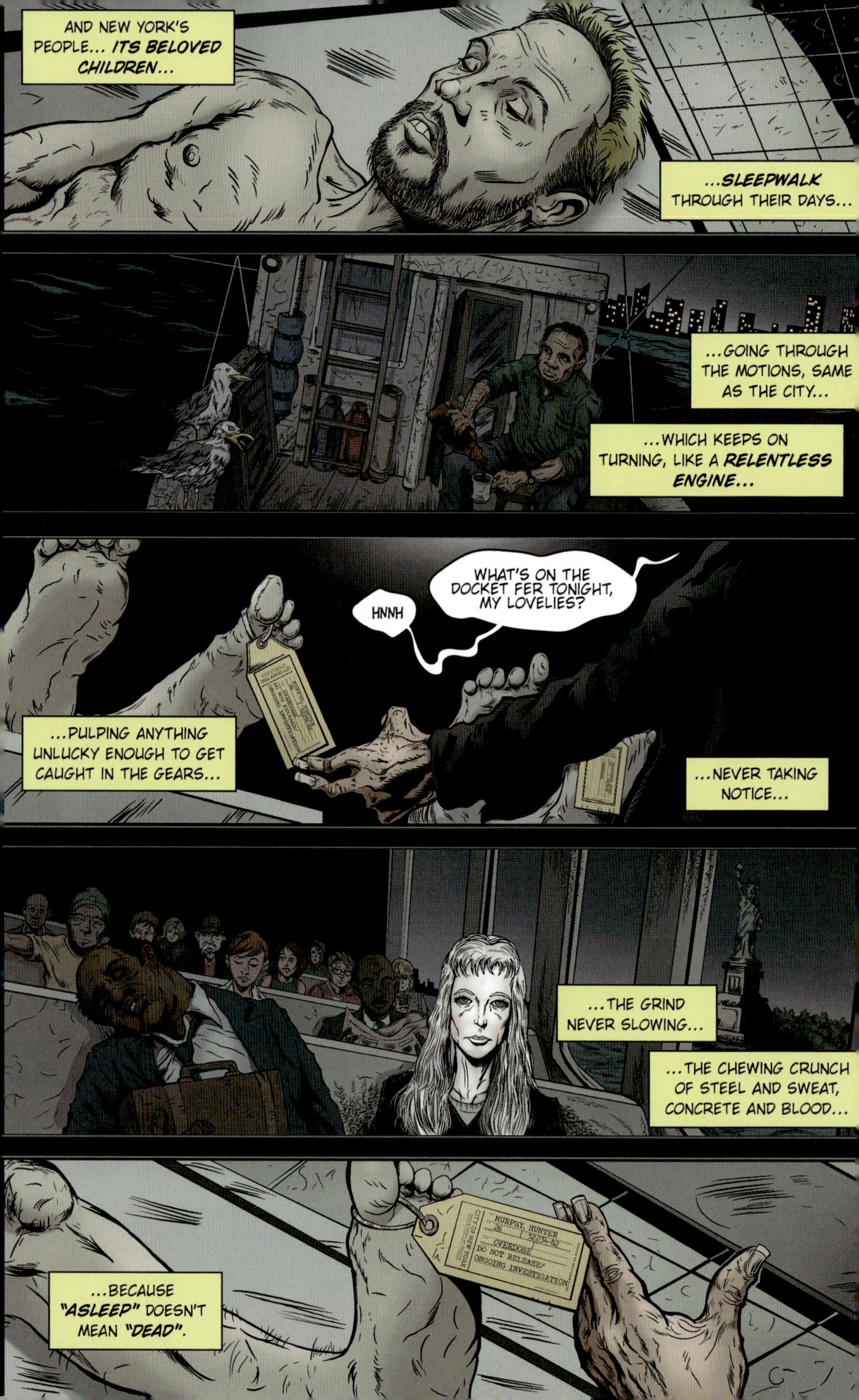
AND NEW YORK'S PEOPLE... *ITS BELOVED CHILDREN...*
...SLEEPWALK THROUGH THEIR DAYS...
...GOING THROUGH THE MOTIONS, SAME AS THE CITY...
...WHICH KEEPS ON TURNING, LIKE A *RELENTLESS ENGINE...*
HNNH
WHAT'S ON THE DOCKET FER TONIGHT, MY LOVELIES?
...PULPING ANYTHING UNLUCKY ENOUGH TO GET CAUGHT IN THE GEARS...
...NEVER TAKING NOTICE...
...THE GRIND NEVER SLOWING...
...THE CHEWING CRUNCH OF STEEL AND SWEAT, CONCRETE AND BLOOD...
CITY OF NEW YORK
MURPHY, HUNTER
26
52234-82
OVERDOSE
DO NOT RELEASE/
ONGOING INVESTIGATION
...BECAUSE *"ASLEEP"* DOESN'T MEAN *"DEAD"*.

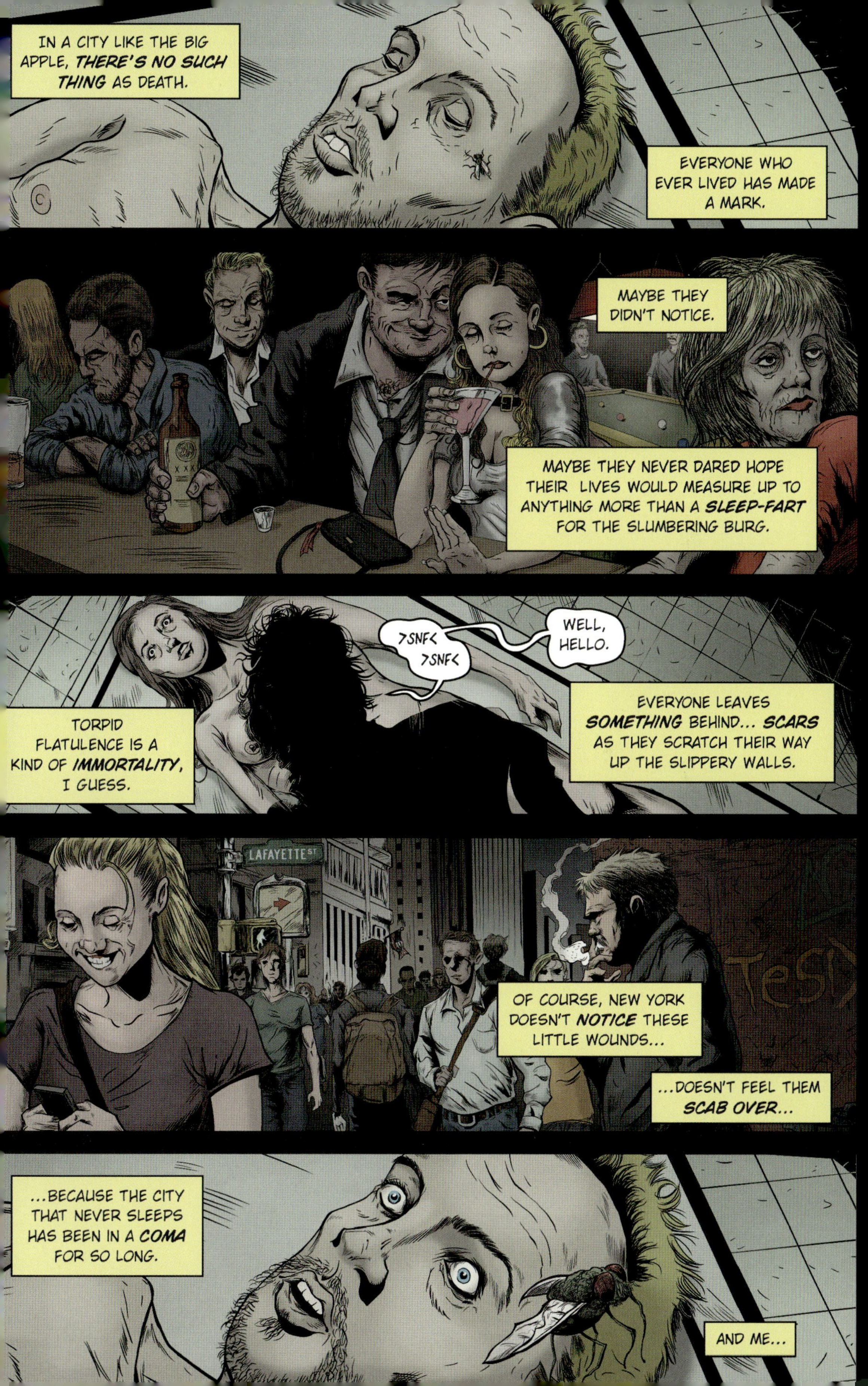

IN A CITY LIKE THE BIG APPLE, ***THERE'S NO SUCH THING*** AS DEATH.
EVERYONE WHO EVER LIVED HAS MADE A MARK.
MAYBE THEY DIDN'T NOTICE.
MAYBE THEY NEVER DARED HOPE THEIR LIVES WOULD MEASURE UP TO ANYTHING MORE THAN A ***SLEEP-FART*** FOR THE SLUMBERING BURG.
>SNF<
>SNF<
WELL, HELLO.
TORPID FLATULENCE IS A KIND OF ***IMMORTALITY***, I GUESS.
EVERYONE LEAVES ***SOMETHING*** BEHIND... ***SCARS*** AS THEY SCRATCH THEIR WAY UP THE SLIPPERY WALLS.
LAFAYETTE ST
OF COURSE, NEW YORK DOESN'T ***NOTICE*** THESE LITTLE WOUNDS...
...DOESN'T FEEL THEM ***SCAB OVER***...
...BECAUSE THE CITY THAT NEVER SLEEPS HAS BEEN IN A ***COMA*** FOR SO LONG.
AND ME...

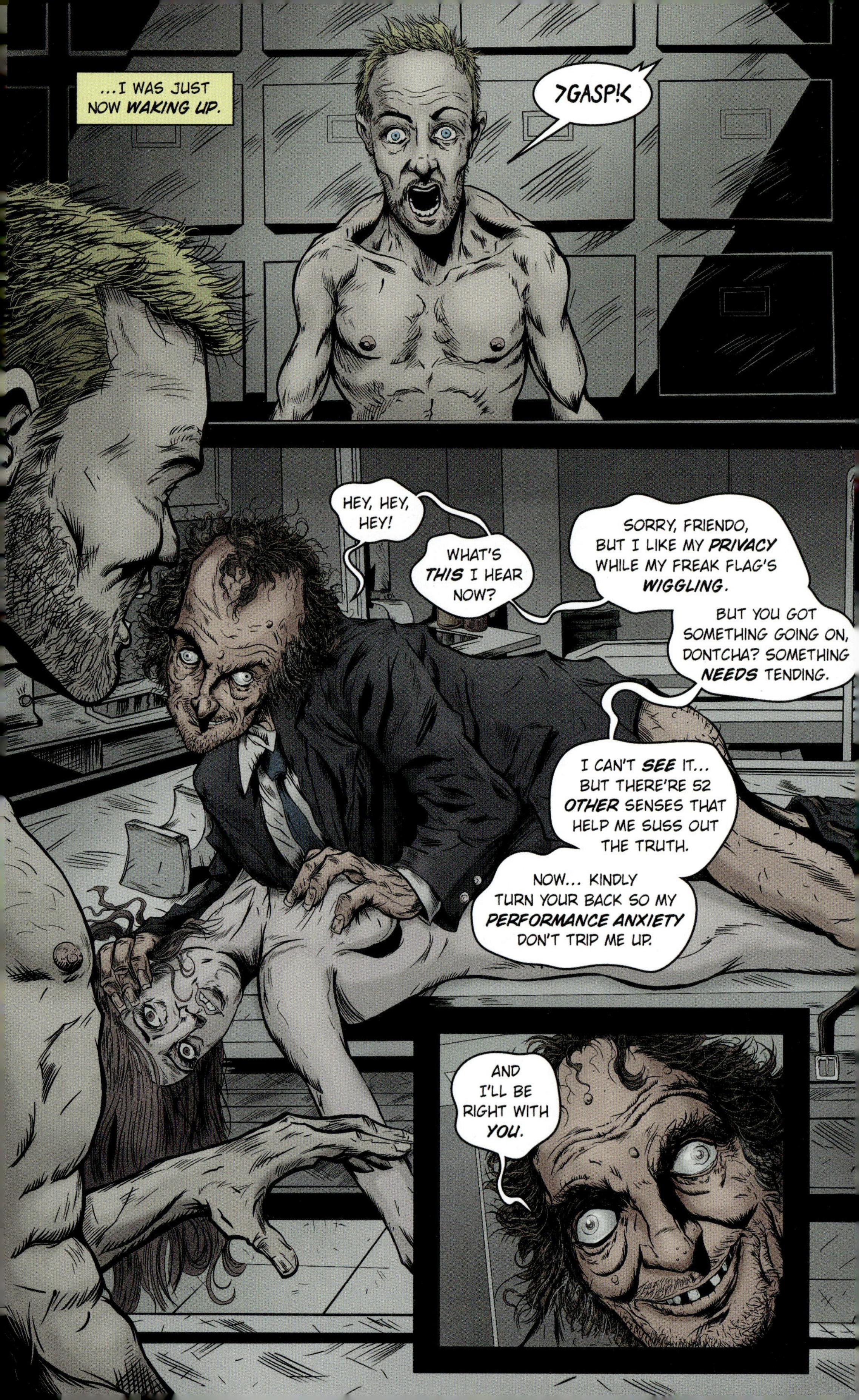
...I WAS JUST NOW WAKING UP.
>GASP!<
HEY, HEY, HEY!
WHAT'S THIS I HEAR NOW?
SORRY, FRIENDO, BUT I LIKE MY PRIVACY WHILE MY FREAK FLAG'S WIGGLING.
BUT YOU GOT SOMETHING GOING ON, DONTCHA? SOMETHING NEEDS TENDING.
I CAN'T SEE IT... BUT THERE'RE 52 OTHER SENSES THAT HELP ME SUSS OUT THE TRUTH.
NOW... KINDLY TURN YOUR BACK SO MY PERFORMANCE ANXIETY DON'T TRIP ME UP.
AND I'LL BE RIGHT WITH YOU.

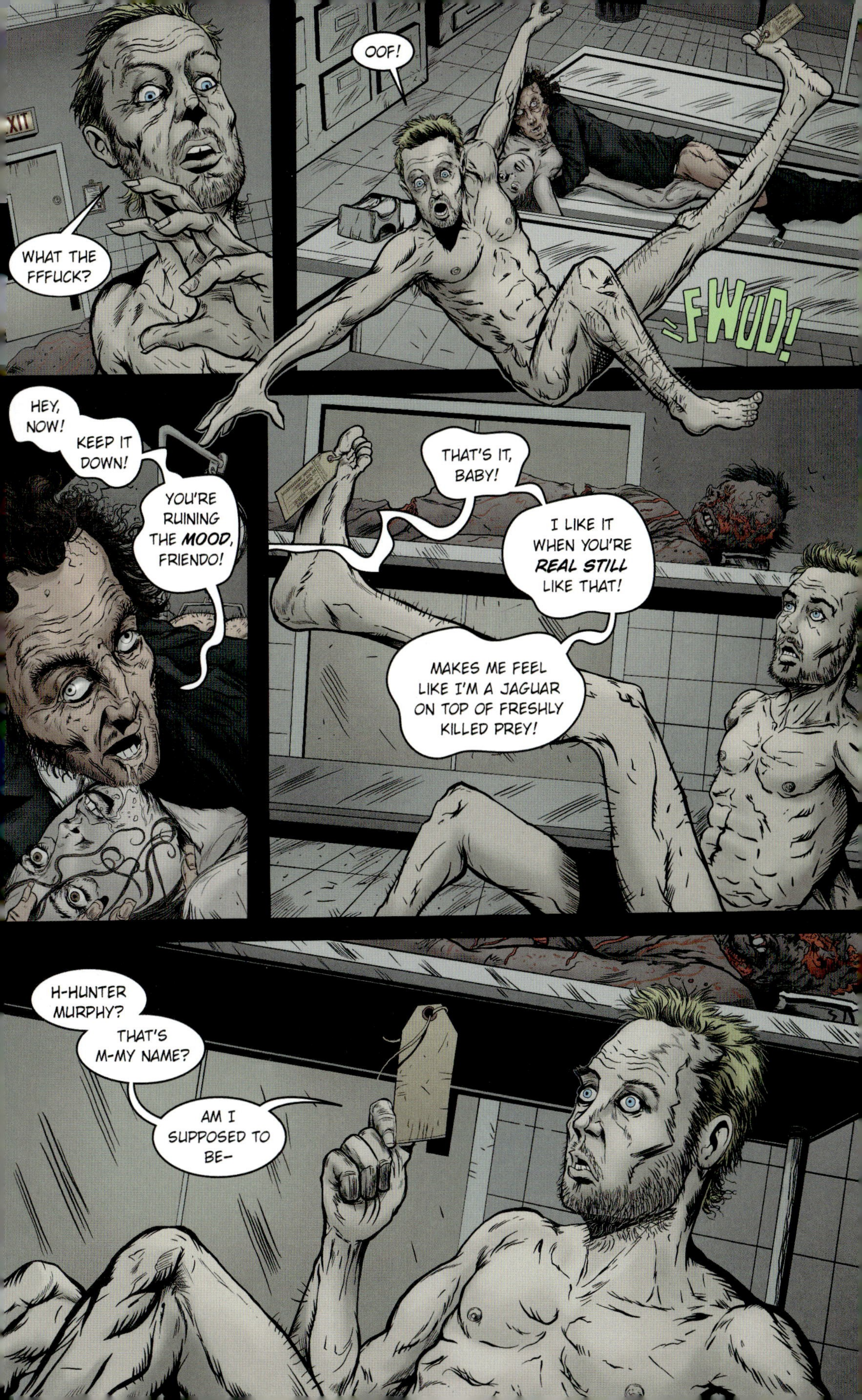
WHAT THE FFFUCK?
OOF!
FWUD!
HEY, NOW!
KEEP IT DOWN!
YOU'RE RUINING THE **MOOD**, FRIENDO!
THAT'S IT, BABY!
I LIKE IT WHEN YOU'RE **REAL STILL** LIKE THAT!
MAKES ME FEEL LIKE I'M A JAGUAR ON TOP OF FRESHLY KILLED PREY!
H-HUNTER MURPHY?
THAT'S M-MY NAME?
AM I SUPPOSED TO BE-

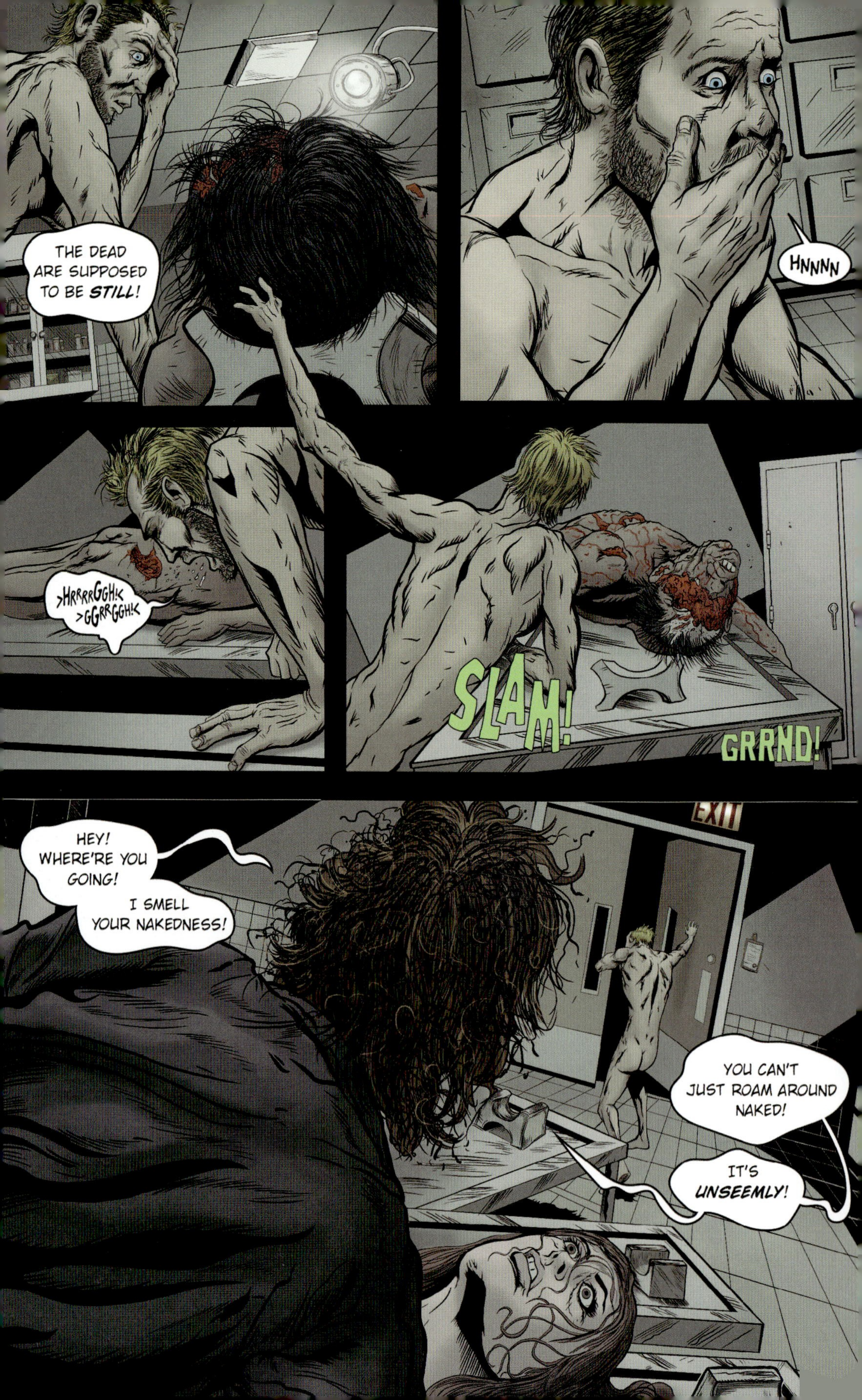
THE DEAD ARE SUPPOSED TO BE **STILL**!
HNNNN
>HRRRRGGHK<
>GGRRGGHK<
SLAM!
GRRND!
HEY! WHERE'RE YOU GOING!
I SMELL YOUR NAKEDNESS!
EXIT
YOU CAN'T JUST ROAM AROUND NAKED!
IT'S **UNSEEMLY**!

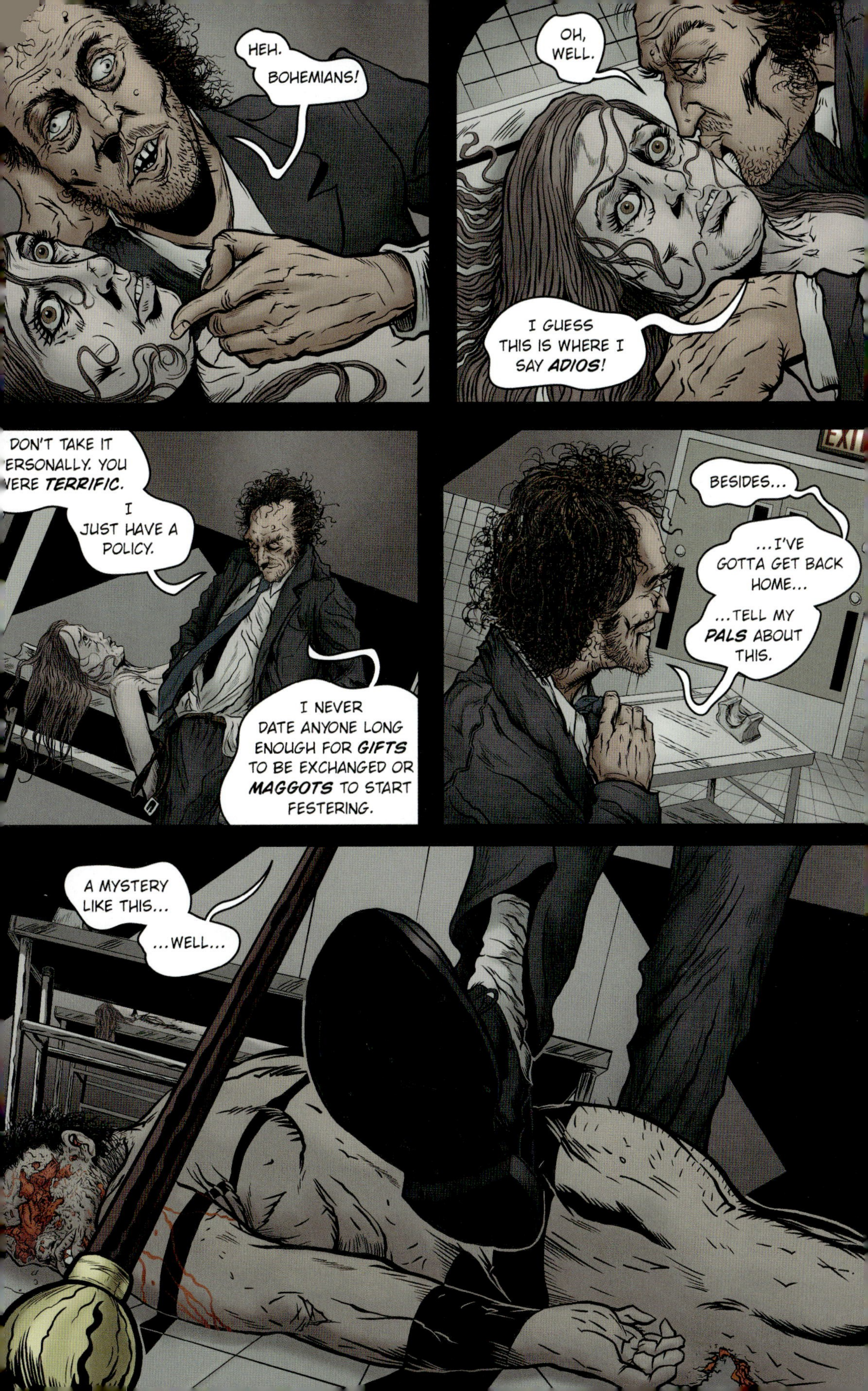

HEH.
BOHEMIANS!
OH, WELL.
I GUESS THIS IS WHERE I SAY *ADIOS!*
DON'T TAKE IT ERSONALLY. YOU VERE *TERRIFIC.*
I JUST HAVE A POLICY.
I NEVER DATE ANYONE LONG ENOUGH FOR *GIFTS* TO BE EXCHANGED OR *MAGGOTS* TO START FESTERING.
BESIDES...
...I'VE GOTTA GET BACK HOME...
...TELL MY *PALS* ABOUT THIS.
EXIT
A MYSTERY LIKE THIS...
...WELL...

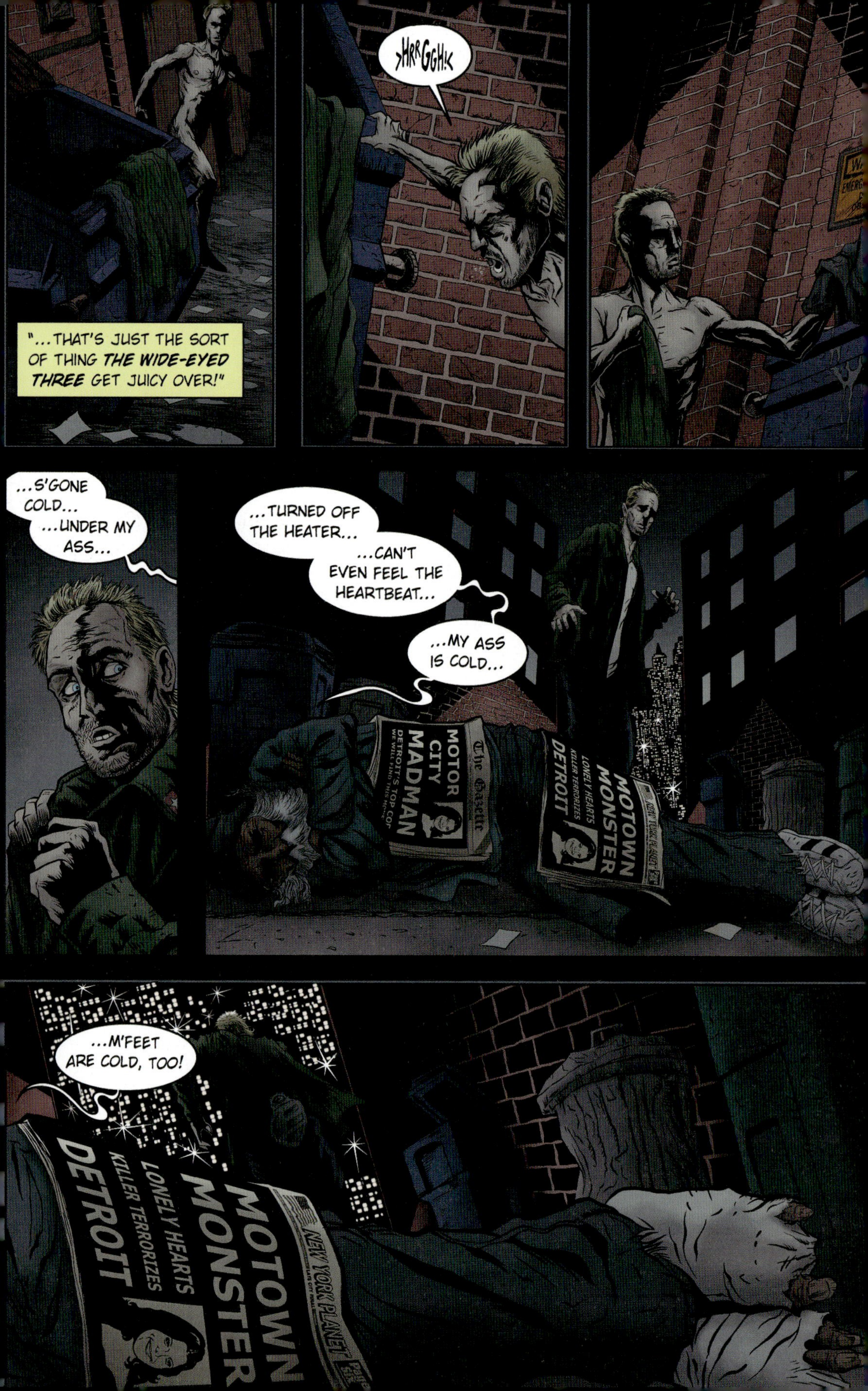
"...THAT'S JUST THE SORT OF THING THE WIDE-EYED THREE GET JUICY OVER!"
>HRRGGH!<
...S'GONE COLD...
...UNDER MY ASS...
...TURNED OFF THE HEATER...
...CAN'T EVEN FEEL THE HEARTBEAT...
...MY ASS IS COLD...
The Gazette
MOTOR CITY MADMAN
DETROIT'S TOP COP
NEW YORK PLANET
MOTOWN MONSTER
LONELY HEARTS KILLER TERRORIZES DETROIT
...M'FEET ARE COLD, TOO!
NEW YORK PLANET
MOTOWN MONSTER
LONELY HEARTS KILLER TERRORIZES DETROIT

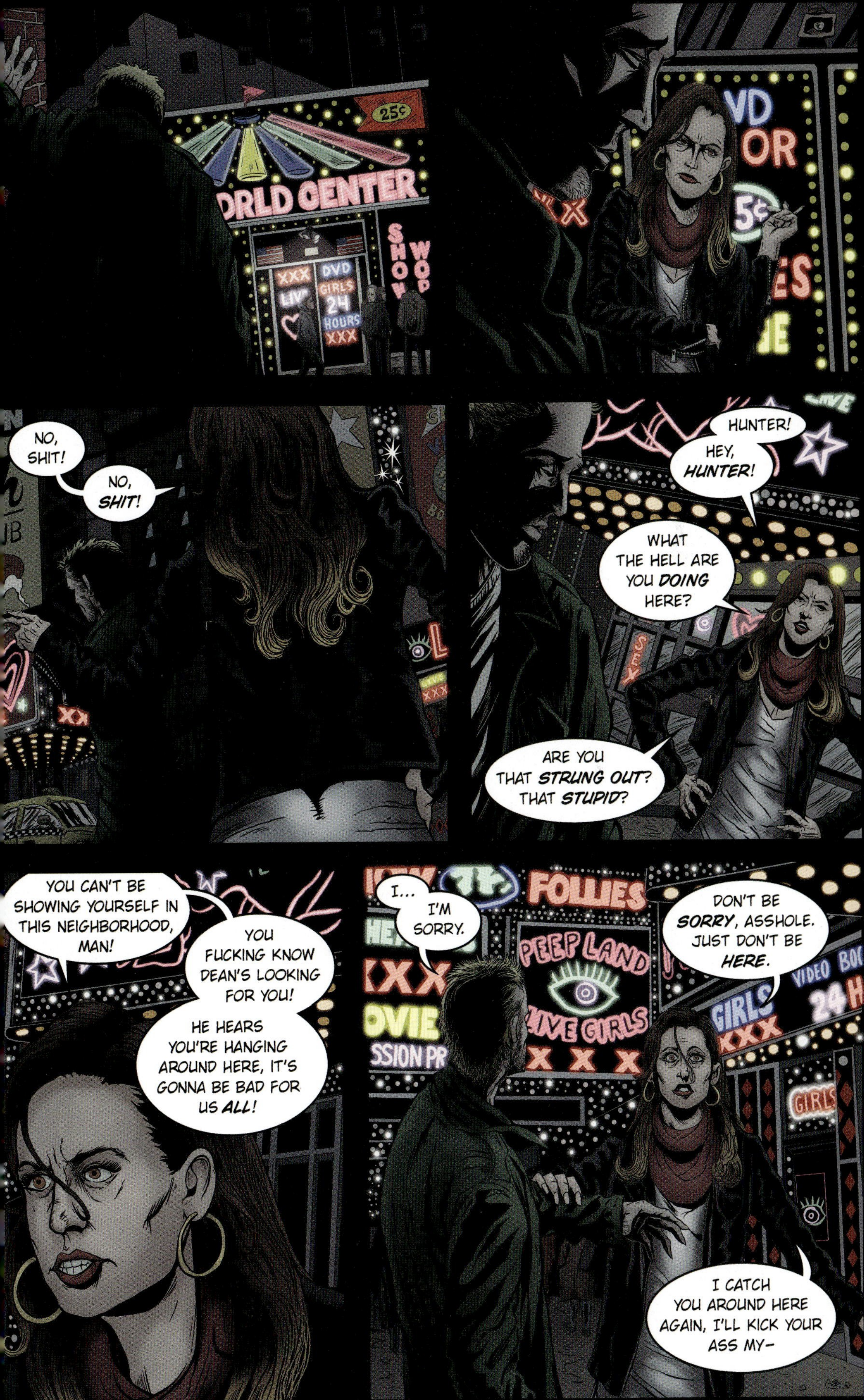
NO, SHIT!
NO, SHIT!
HUNTER!
HEY, HUNTER!
WHAT THE HELL ARE YOU DOING HERE?
ARE YOU THAT STRUNG OUT? THAT STUPID?
YOU CAN'T BE SHOWING YOURSELF IN THIS NEIGHBORHOOD, MAN!
YOU FUCKING KNOW DEAN'S LOOKING FOR YOU!
HE HEARS YOU'RE HANGING AROUND HERE, IT'S GONNA BE BAD FOR US ALL!
I... I'M SORRY.
DON'T BE SORRY, ASSHOLE. JUST DON'T BE HERE.
I CATCH YOU AROUND HERE AGAIN, I'LL KICK YOUR ASS MY–

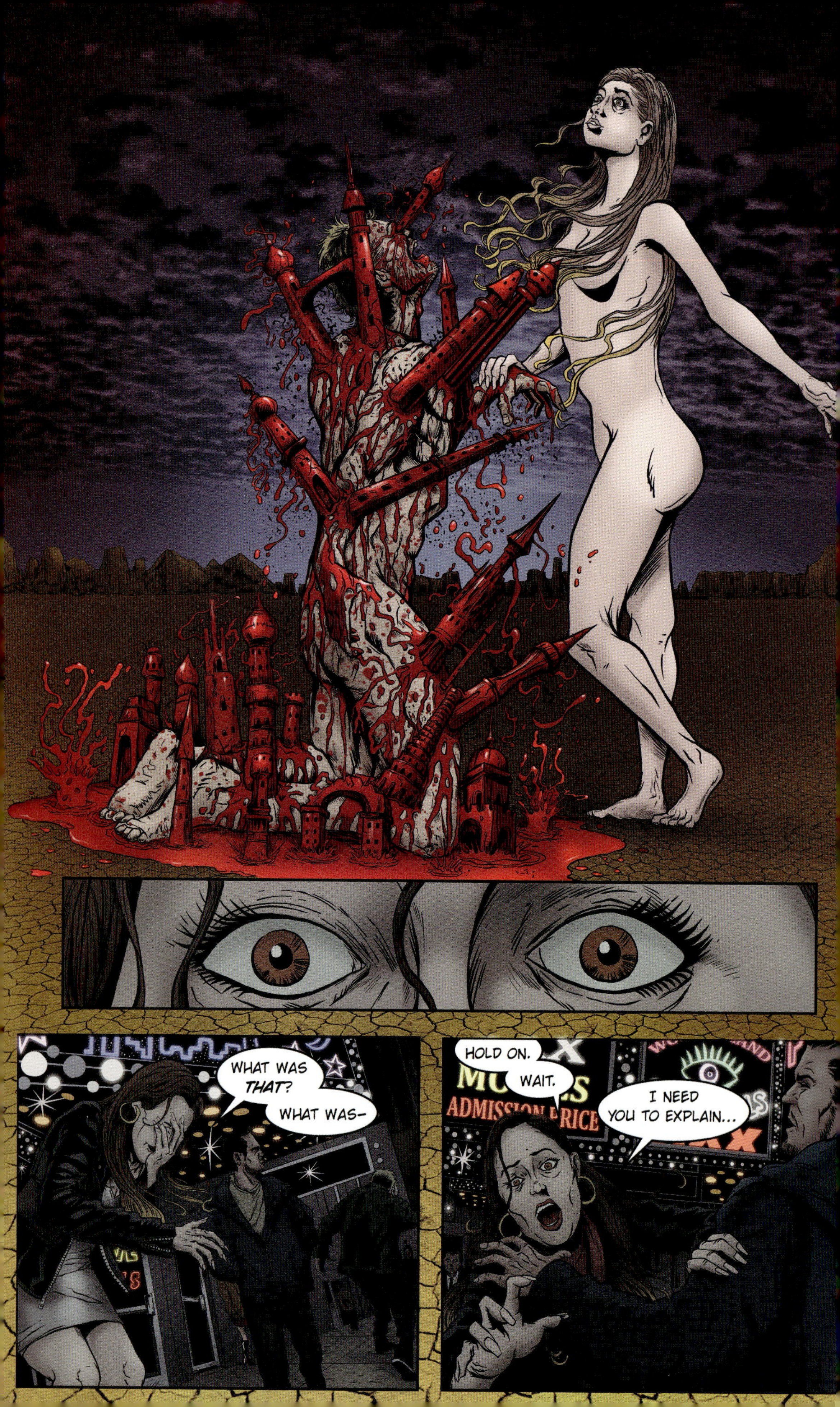
WHAT WAS *THAT*?
WHAT WAS-
HOLD ON.
WAIT.
I NEED YOU TO EXPLAIN...
ADMISSION PRICE

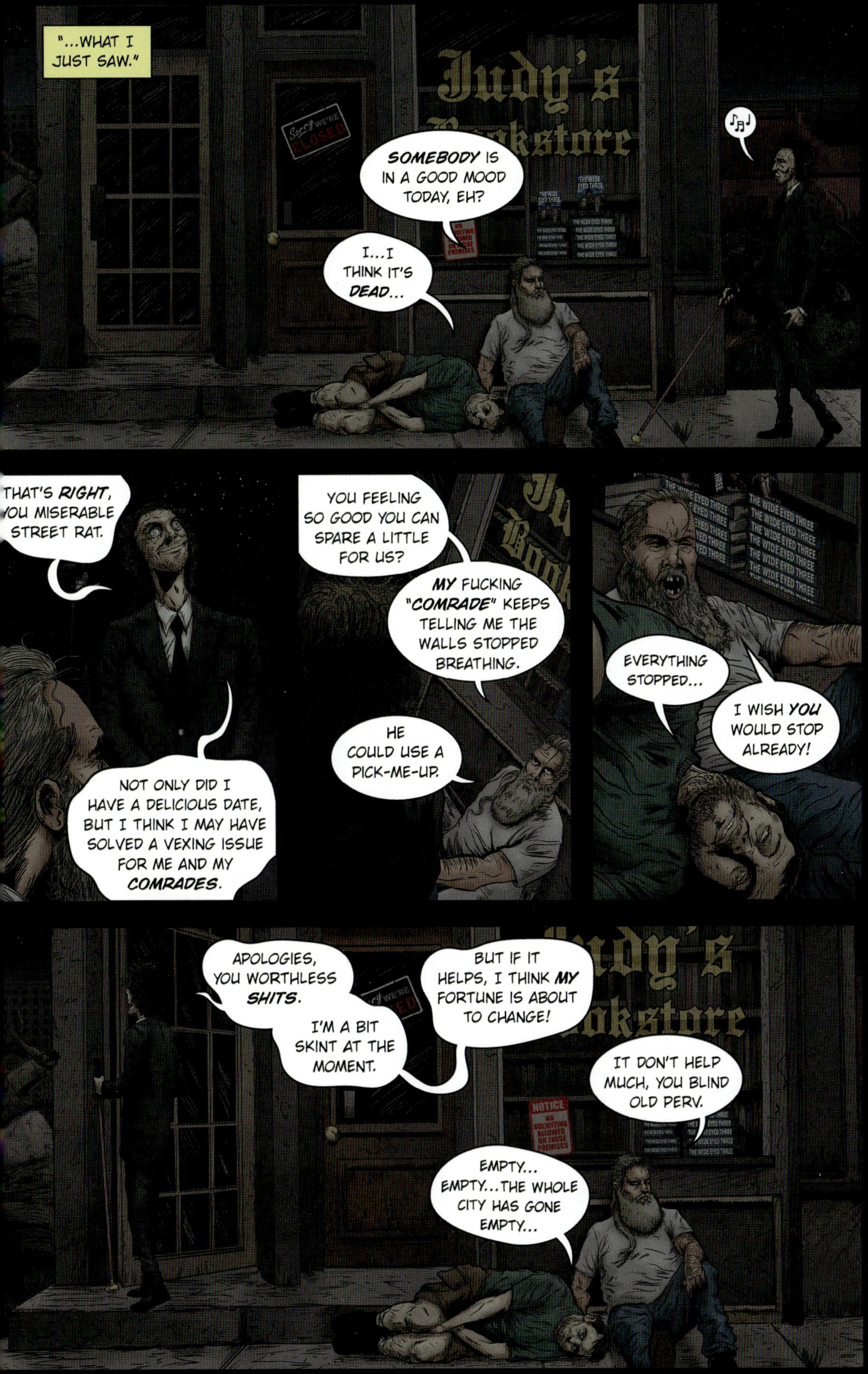
"...WHAT I JUST SAW."
Judy's Bookstore
Sorry WE'RE CLOSED
SOMEBODY IS IN A GOOD MOOD TODAY, EH?
I...I THINK IT'S DEAD...
THAT'S RIGHT, YOU MISERABLE STREET RAT.
NOT ONLY DID I HAVE A DELICIOUS DATE, BUT I THINK I MAY HAVE SOLVED A VEXING ISSUE FOR ME AND MY COMRADES.
YOU FEELING SO GOOD YOU CAN SPARE A LITTLE FOR US?
MY FUCKING "COMRADE" KEEPS TELLING ME THE WALLS STOPPED BREATHING.
HE COULD USE A PICK-ME-UP.
EVERYTHING STOPPED...
I WISH YOU WOULD STOP ALREADY!
APOLOGIES, YOU WORTHLESS SHITS.
I'M A BIT SKINT AT THE MOMENT.
BUT IF IT HELPS, I THINK MY FORTUNE IS ABOUT TO CHANGE!
IT DON'T HELP MUCH, YOU BLIND OLD PERV.
EMPTY... EMPTY...THE WHOLE CITY HAS GONE EMPTY...

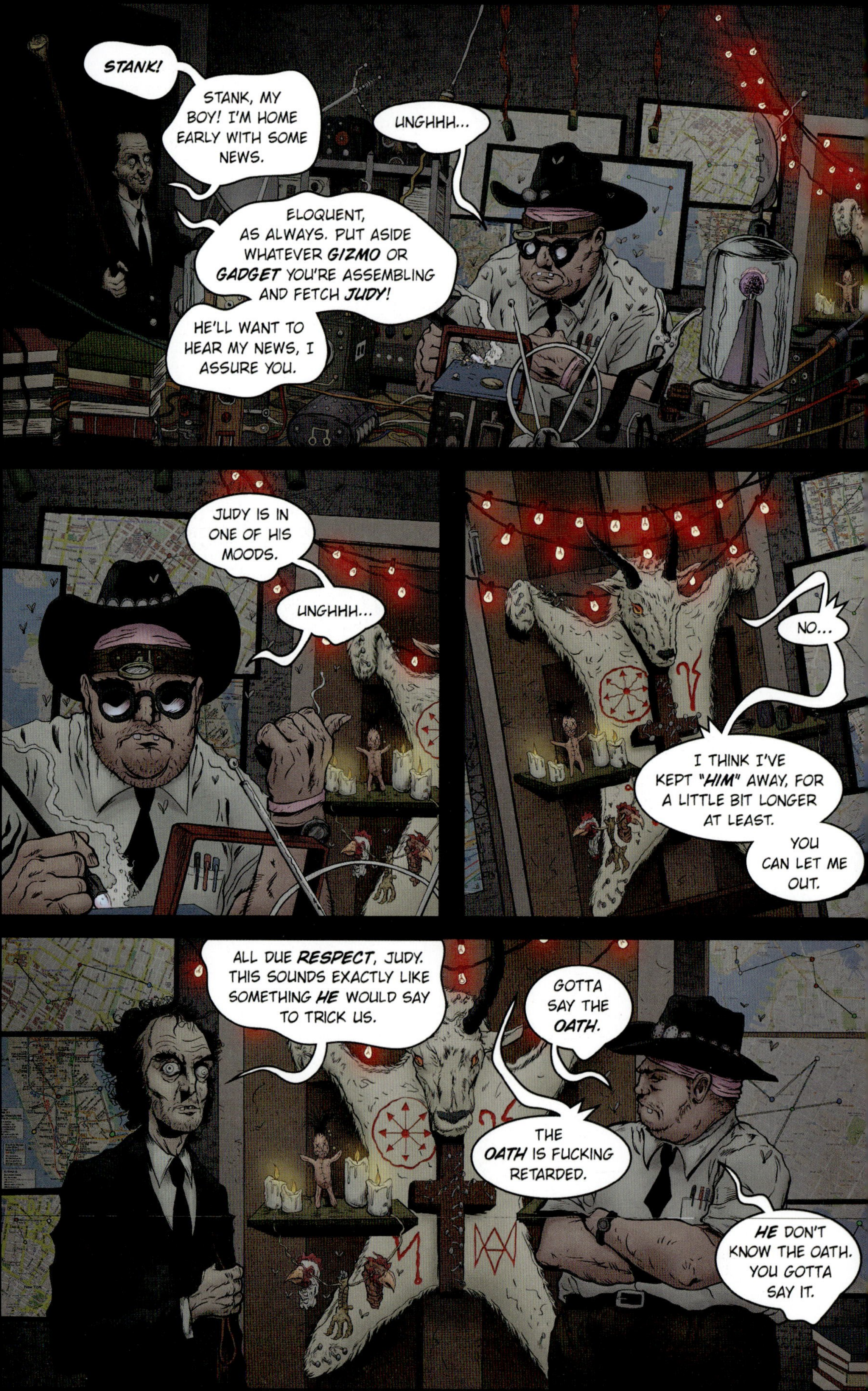

STANK!
STANK, MY BOY! I'M HOME EARLY WITH SOME NEWS.
UNGHHH...
ELOQUENT, AS ALWAYS. PUT ASIDE WHATEVER GIZMO OR GADGET YOU'RE ASSEMBLING AND FETCH JUDY!
HE'LL WANT TO HEAR MY NEWS, I ASSURE YOU.
JUDY IS IN ONE OF HIS MOODS.
UNGHHH...
NO...
I THINK I'VE KEPT "HIM" AWAY, FOR A LITTLE BIT LONGER AT LEAST.
YOU CAN LET ME OUT.
ALL DUE RESPECT, JUDY. THIS SOUNDS EXACTLY LIKE SOMETHING HE WOULD SAY TO TRICK US.
GOTTA SAY THE OATH.
THE OATH IS FUCKING RETARDED.
HE DON'T KNOW THE OATH. YOU GOTTA SAY IT.

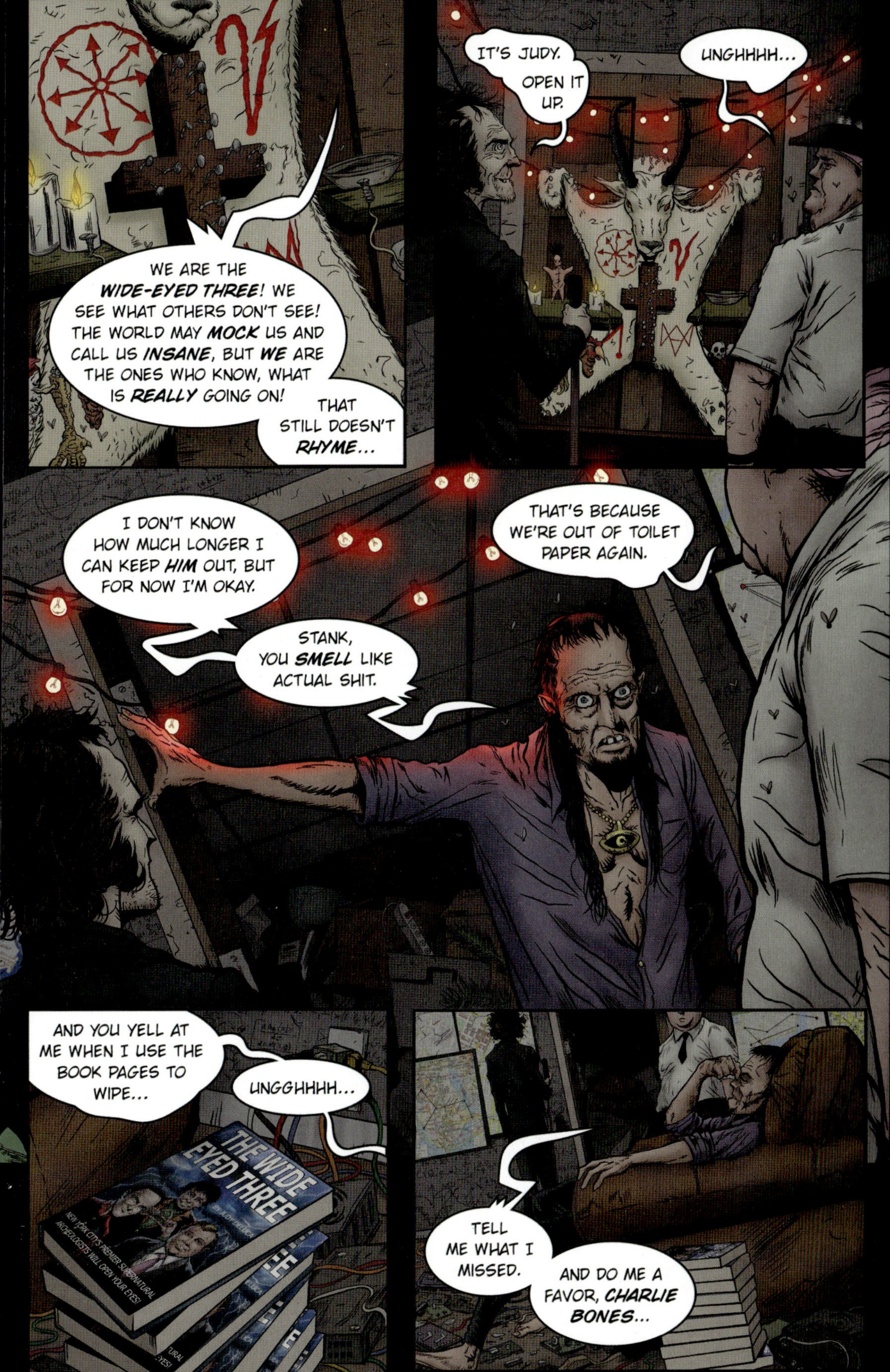

WE ARE THE **WIDE-EYED THREE**! WE SEE WHAT OTHERS DON'T SEE! THE WORLD MAY **MOCK** US AND CALL US **INSANE**, BUT **WE** ARE THE ONES WHO KNOW, WHAT IS **REALLY** GOING ON!
THAT STILL DOESN'T **RHYME...**
IT'S JUDY.
OPEN IT UP.
UNGHHHH...
I DON'T KNOW HOW MUCH LONGER I CAN KEEP **HIM** OUT, BUT FOR NOW I'M OKAY.
STANK, YOU **SMELL** LIKE ACTUAL SHIT.
THAT'S BECAUSE WE'RE OUT OF TOILET PAPER AGAIN.
AND YOU YELL AT ME WHEN I USE THE BOOK PAGES TO WIPE...
UNGGHHHH...
THE WIDE EYED THREE
TELL ME WHAT I MISSED.
AND DO ME A FAVOR, **CHARLIE BONES...**

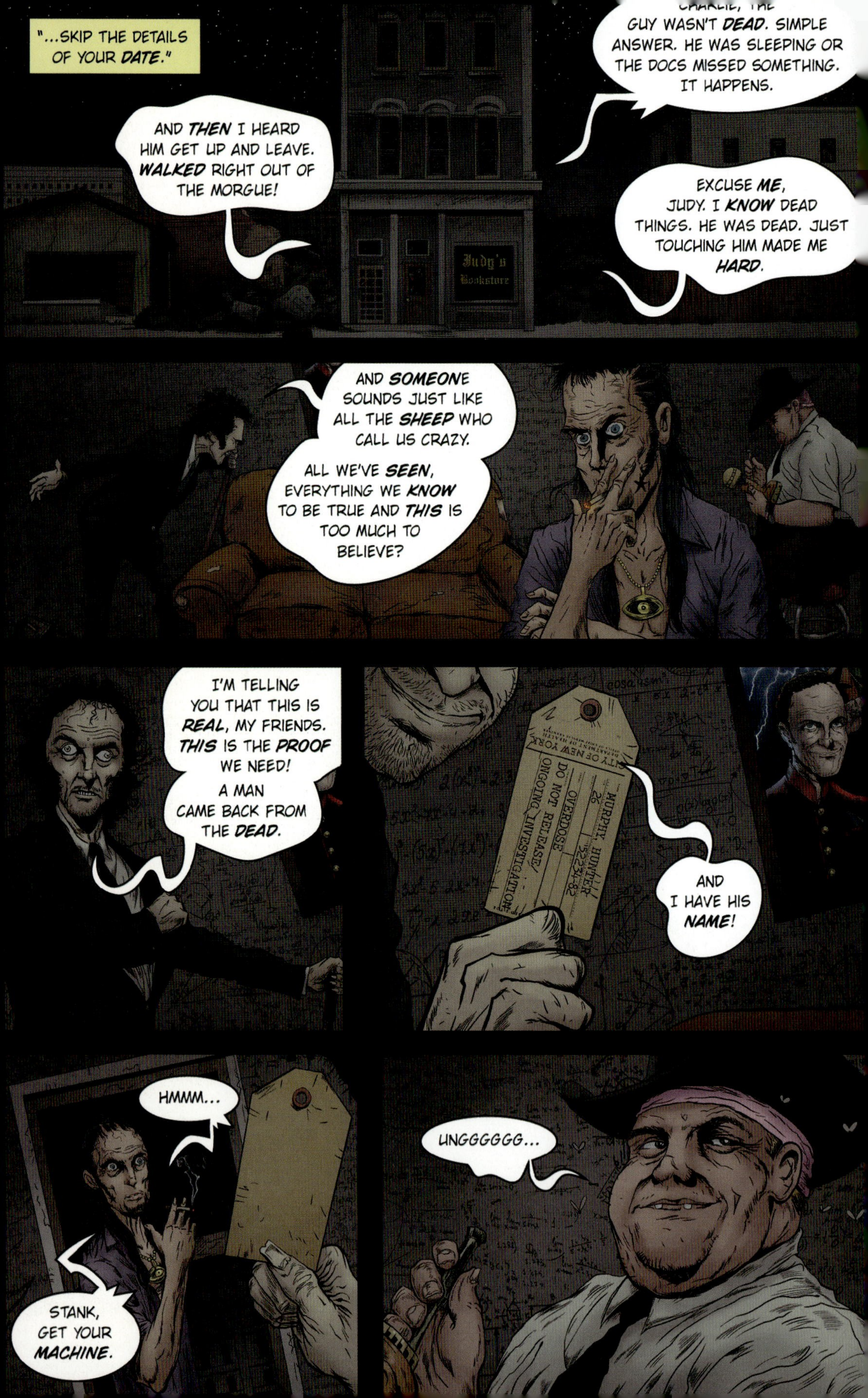
"...SKIP THE DETAILS OF YOUR DATE."
AND THEN I HEARD HIM GET UP AND LEAVE. WALKED RIGHT OUT OF THE MORGUE!
GUY WASN'T DEAD. SIMPLE ANSWER. HE WAS SLEEPING OR THE DOCS MISSED SOMETHING. IT HAPPENS.
EXCUSE ME, JUDY. I KNOW DEAD THINGS. HE WAS DEAD. JUST TOUCHING HIM MADE ME HARD.
Judy's Bookstore
AND SOMEONE SOUNDS JUST LIKE ALL THE SHEEP WHO CALL US CRAZY.
ALL WE'VE SEEN, EVERYTHING WE KNOW TO BE TRUE AND THIS IS TOO MUCH TO BELIEVE?
I'M TELLING YOU THAT THIS IS REAL, MY FRIENDS. THIS IS THE PROOF WE NEED!
A MAN CAME BACK FROM THE DEAD.
MURPHY, HUNTER
OVERDOSE
DO NOT RELEASE
ONGOING INVESTIGATION
AND I HAVE HIS NAME!
HMMM...
STANK, GET YOUR MACHINE.
UNGGGGGG...

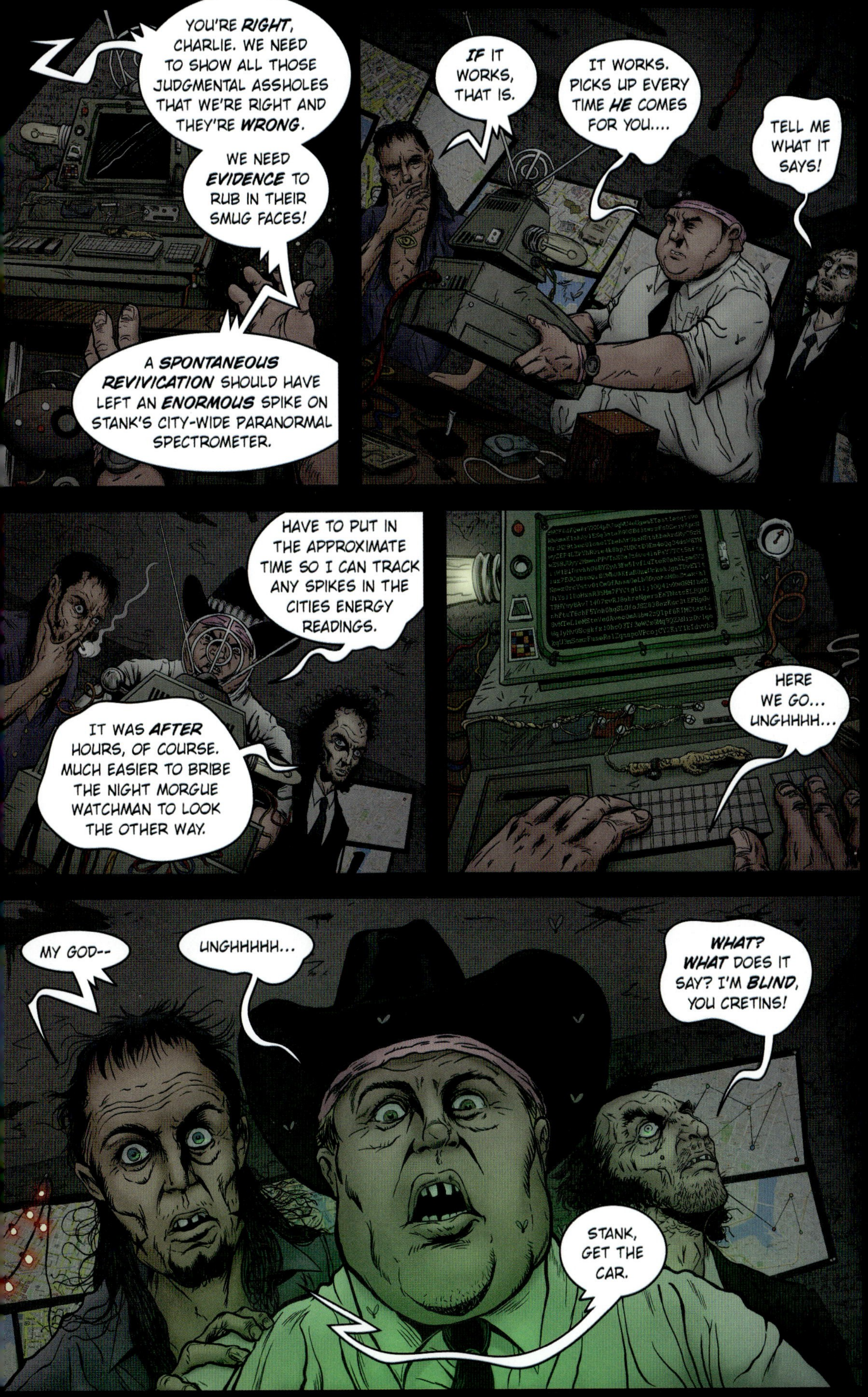
YOU'RE RIGHT, CHARLIE. WE NEED TO SHOW ALL THOSE JUDGMENTAL ASSHOLES THAT WE'RE RIGHT AND THEY'RE WRONG.
WE NEED EVIDENCE TO RUB IN THEIR SMUG FACES!
A SPONTANEOUS REVIVICATION SHOULD HAVE LEFT AN ENORMOUS SPIKE ON STANK'S CITY-WIDE PARANORMAL SPECTROMETER.
IF IT WORKS, THAT IS.
IT WORKS. PICKS UP EVERY TIME HE COMES FOR YOU....
TELL ME WHAT IT SAYS!
HAVE TO PUT IN THE APPROXIMATE TIME SO I CAN TRACK ANY SPIKES IN THE CITIES ENERGY READINGS.
IT WAS AFTER HOURS, OF COURSE. MUCH EASIER TO BRIBE THE NIGHT MORGUE WATCHMAN TO LOOK THE OTHER WAY.
HERE WE GO... UNGHHHH...
MY GOD--
UNGHHHHH...
WHAT? WHAT DOES IT SAY? I'M BLIND, YOU CRETINS!
STANK, GET THE CAR.

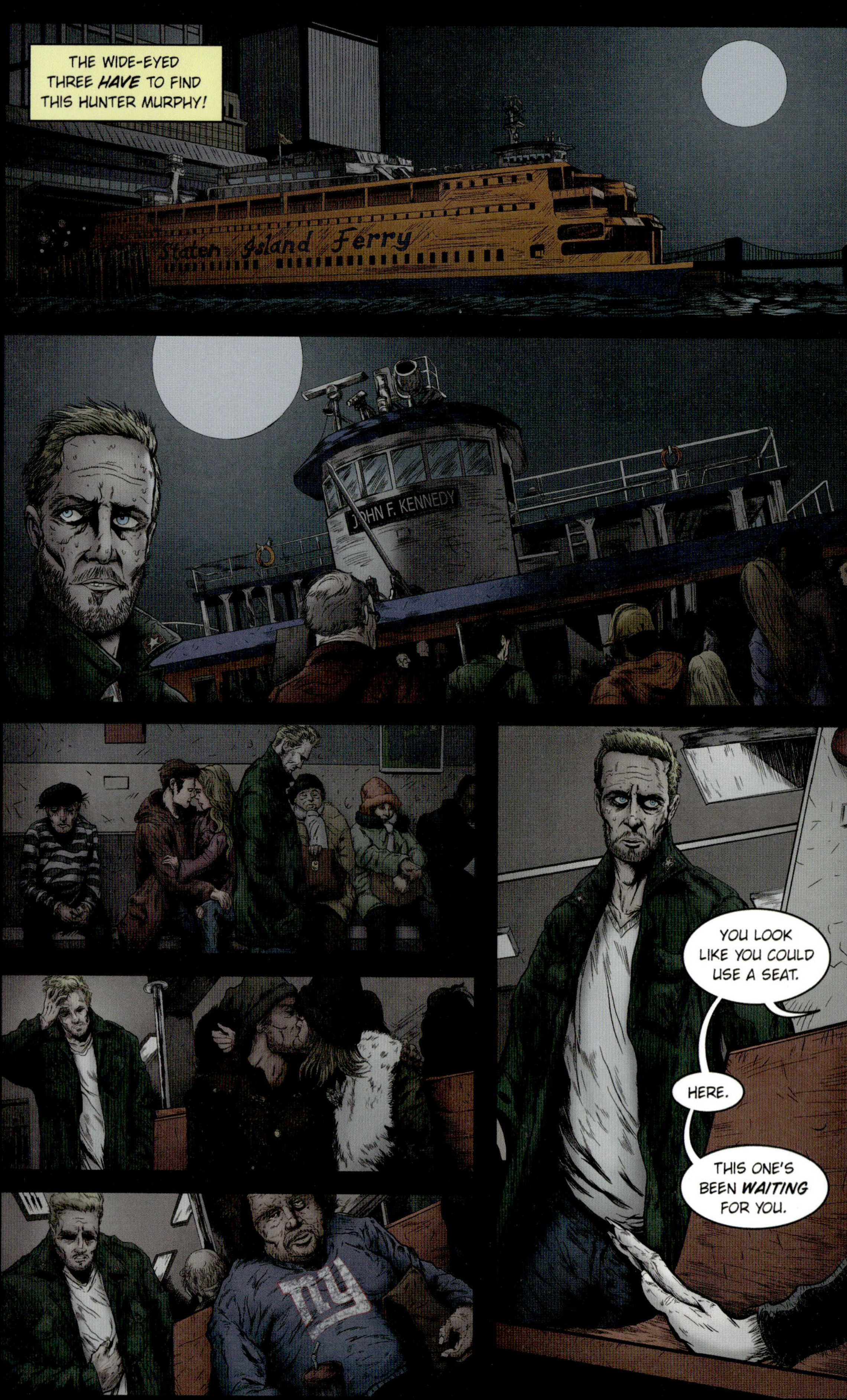
THE WIDE-EYED THREE HAVE TO FIND THIS HUNTER MURPHY!
Staten Island Ferry
JOHN F. KENNEDY
YOU LOOK LIKE YOU COULD USE A SEAT.
HERE.
THIS ONE'S BEEN WAITING FOR YOU.

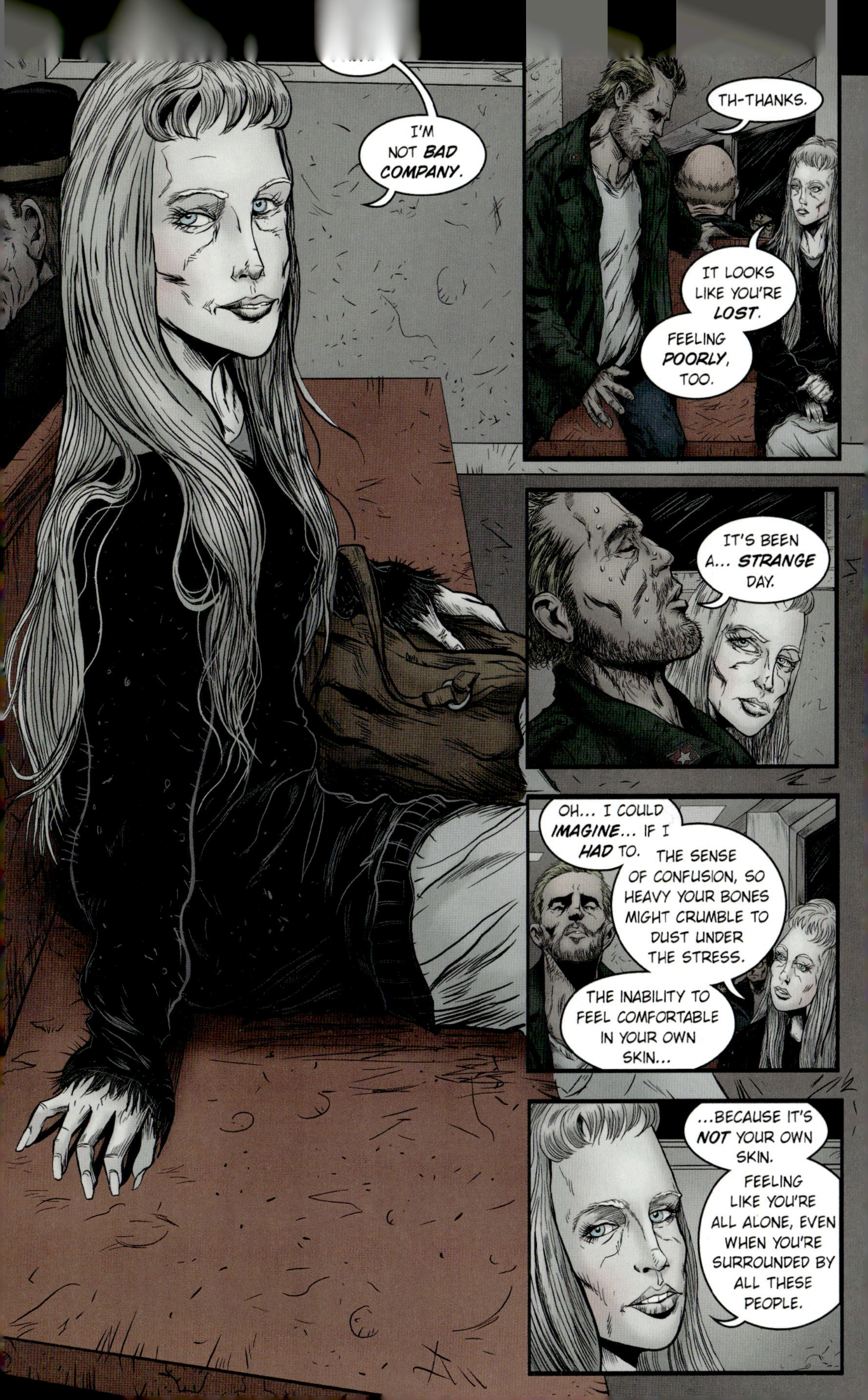
I'M NOT BAD COMPANY.
TH-THANKS.
IT LOOKS LIKE YOU'RE LOST.
FEELING POORLY, TOO.
IT'S BEEN A... STRANGE DAY.
OH... I COULD IMAGINE... IF I HAD TO.
THE SENSE OF CONFUSION, SO HEAVY YOUR BONES MIGHT CRUMBLE TO DUST UNDER THE STRESS.
THE INABILITY TO FEEL COMFORTABLE IN YOUR OWN SKIN...
...BECAUSE IT'S NOT YOUR OWN SKIN.
FEELING LIKE YOU'RE ALL ALONE, EVEN WHEN YOU'RE SURROUNDED BY ALL THESE PEOPLE.

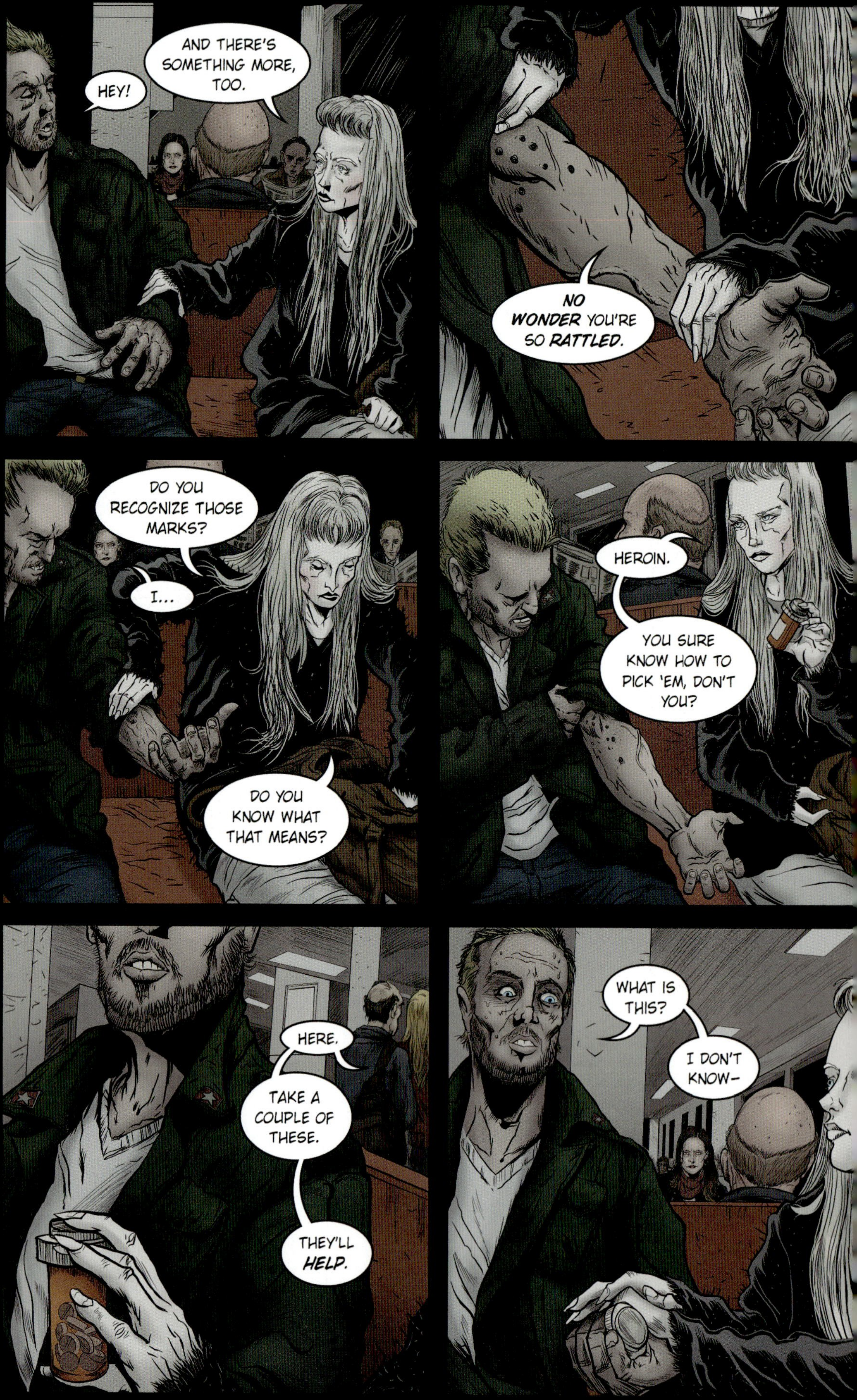
HEY!
AND THERE'S SOMETHING MORE, TOO.
NO **WONDER** YOU'RE SO **RATTLED.**
DO YOU RECOGNIZE THOSE MARKS?
I...
DO YOU KNOW WHAT THAT MEANS?
HEROIN.
YOU SURE KNOW HOW TO PICK 'EM, DON'T YOU?
HERE.
TAKE A COUPLE OF THESE.
THEY'LL **HELP.**
WHAT IS THIS?
I DON'T KNOW-

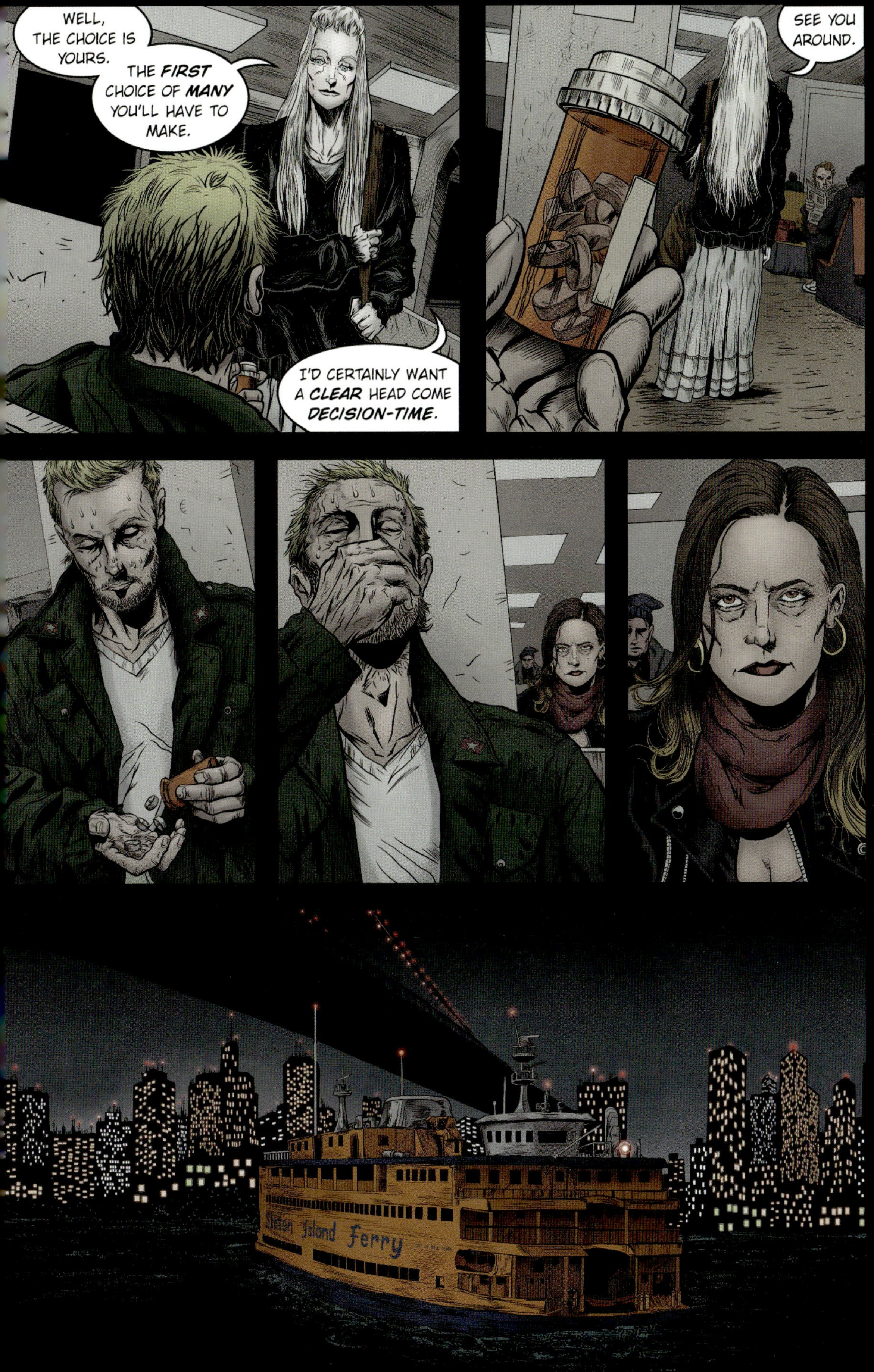
WELL, THE CHOICE IS YOURS.
THE FIRST CHOICE OF MANY YOU'LL HAVE TO MAKE.
I'D CERTAINLY WANT A CLEAR HEAD COME DECISION-TIME.
SEE YOU AROUND.
Staten Island Ferry

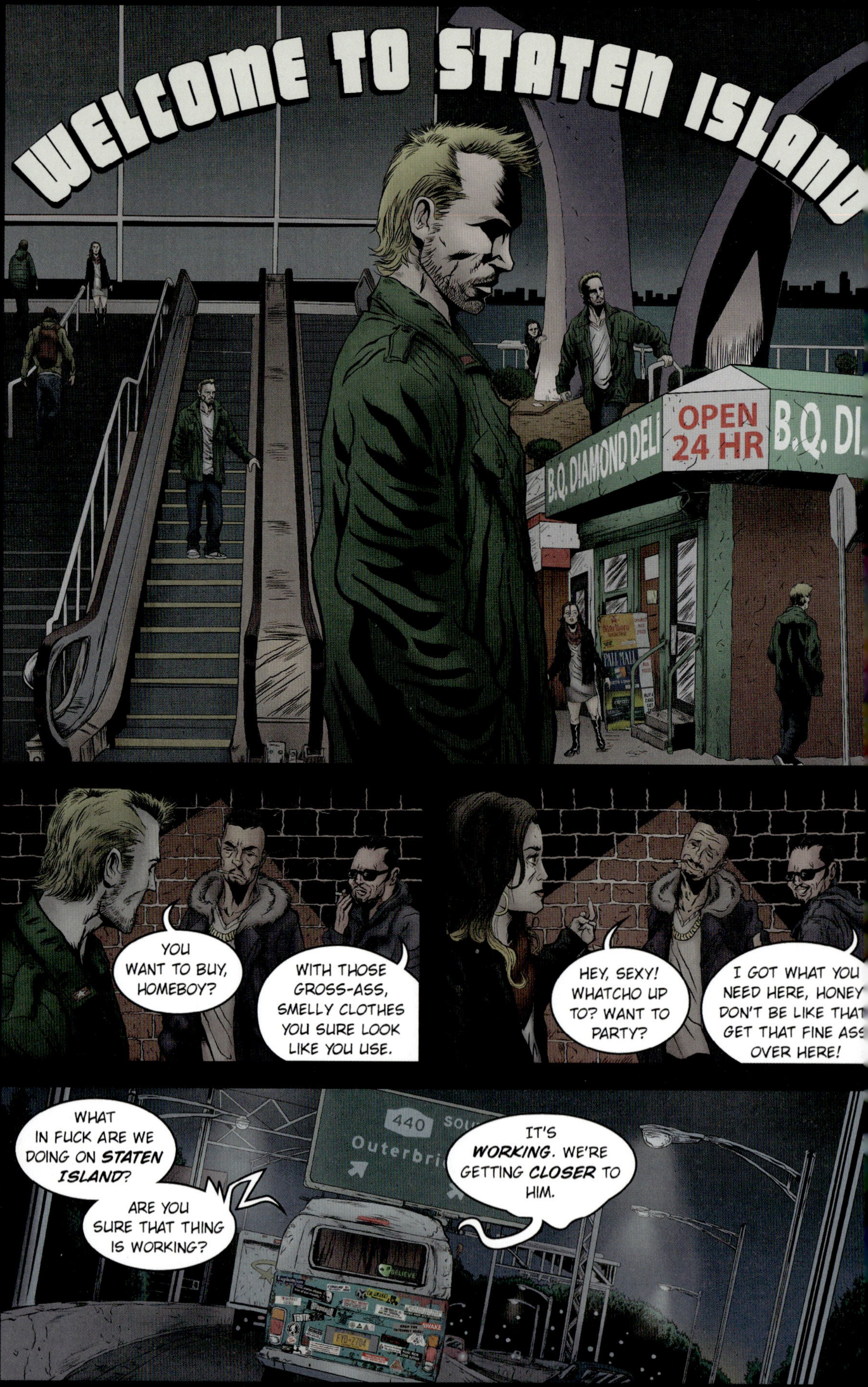
WELCOME TO STATEN ISLAND
OPEN 24 HR
B.Q. DIAMOND DELI
YOU WANT TO BUY, HOMEBOY?
WITH THOSE GROSS-ASS, SMELLY CLOTHES YOU SURE LOOK LIKE YOU USE.
HEY, SEXY! WHATCHO UP TO? WANT TO PARTY?
I GOT WHAT YOU NEED HERE, HONEY DON'T BE LIKE THAT GET THAT FINE ASS OVER HERE!
440
Outerbri
WHAT IN FUCK ARE WE DOING ON *STATEN ISLAND*?
ARE YOU SURE THAT THING IS WORKING?
IT'S *WORKING*. WE'RE GETTING *CLOSER* TO HIM.
BELIEVE

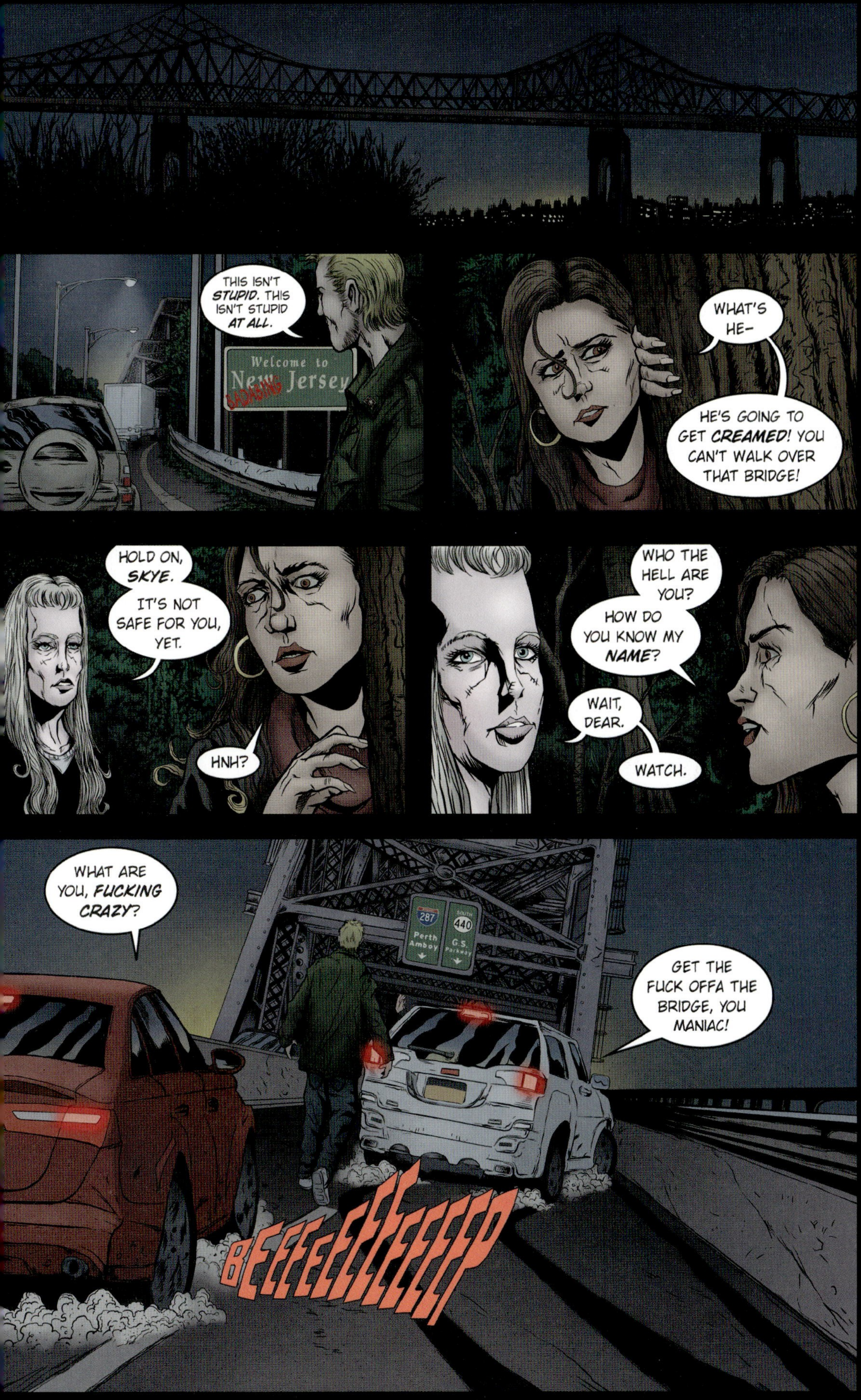
THIS ISN'T STUPID. THIS ISN'T STUPID AT ALL.
Welcome to New Jersey
BADABING
WHAT'S HE-
HE'S GOING TO GET CREAMED! YOU CAN'T WALK OVER THAT BRIDGE!
HOLD ON, SKYE.
IT'S NOT SAFE FOR YOU, YET.
HNH?
WHO THE HELL ARE YOU?
HOW DO YOU KNOW MY NAME?
WAIT, DEAR.
WATCH.
WHAT ARE YOU, FUCKING CRAZY?
287
Perth Amboy
440
G.S. Parkway
GET THE FUCK OFFA THE BRIDGE, YOU MANIAC!
BEEEEEEEEEEEEP

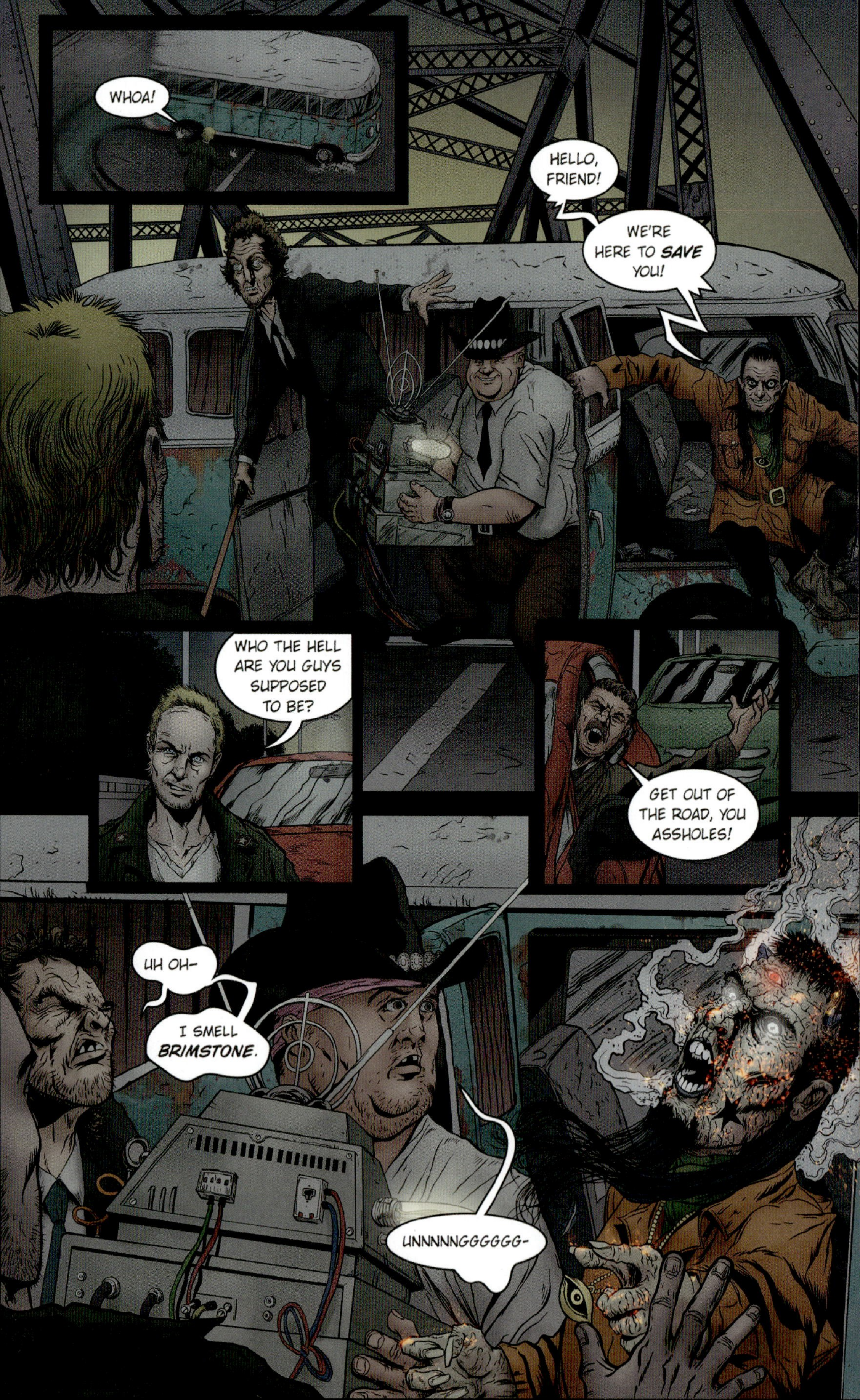
WHOA!
HELLO, FRIEND!
WE'RE HERE TO SAVE YOU!
WHO THE HELL ARE YOU GUYS SUPPOSED TO BE?
GET OUT OF THE ROAD, YOU ASSHOLES!
UH OH-
I SMELL BRIMSTONE.
UNNNNNGGGGG-

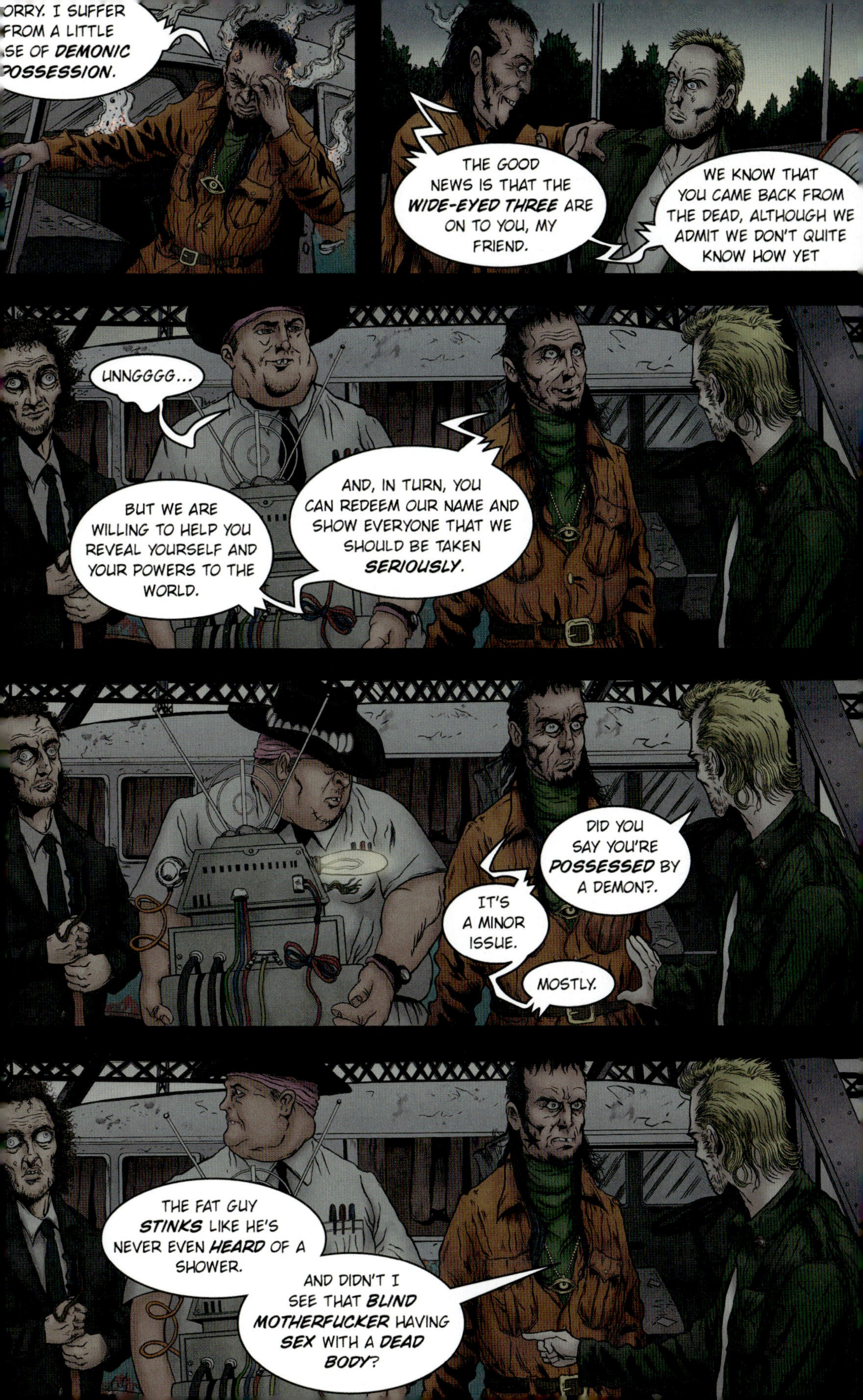
ORRY. I SUFFER FROM A LITTLE SE OF DEMONIC POSSESSION.
THE GOOD NEWS IS THAT THE WIDE-EYED THREE ARE ON TO YOU, MY FRIEND.
WE KNOW THAT YOU CAME BACK FROM THE DEAD, ALTHOUGH WE ADMIT WE DON'T QUITE KNOW HOW YET
UNNGGGG...
BUT WE ARE WILLING TO HELP YOU REVEAL YOURSELF AND YOUR POWERS TO THE WORLD.
AND, IN TURN, YOU CAN REDEEM OUR NAME AND SHOW EVERYONE THAT WE SHOULD BE TAKEN SERIOUSLY.
DID YOU SAY YOU'RE POSSESSED BY A DEMON?.
IT'S A MINOR ISSUE.
MOSTLY.
THE FAT GUY STINKS LIKE HE'S NEVER EVEN HEARD OF A SHOWER.
AND DIDN'T I SEE THAT BLIND MOTHERFUCKER HAVING SEX WITH A DEAD BODY?

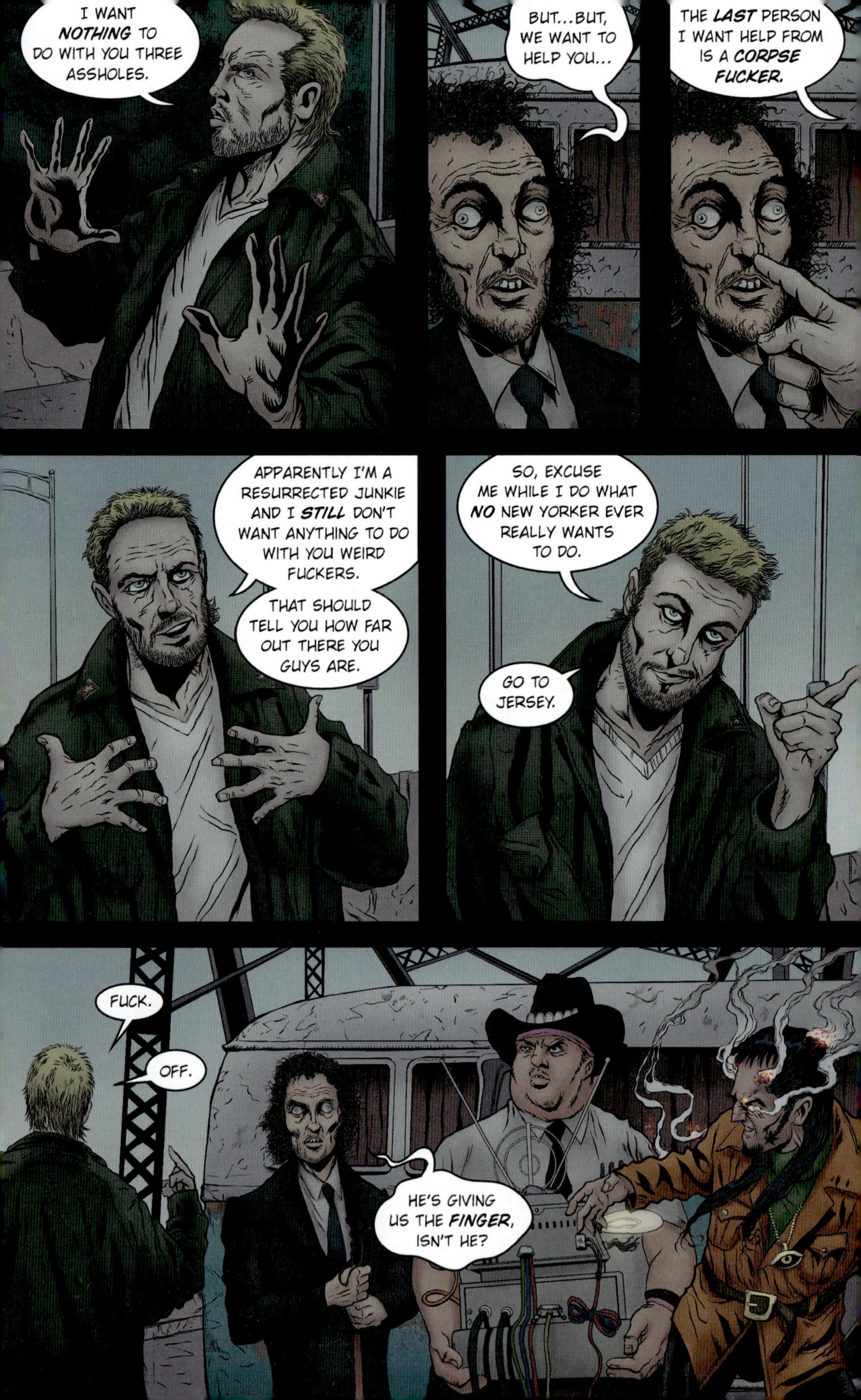
I WANT NOTHING TO DO WITH YOU THREE ASSHOLES.
BUT...BUT, WE WANT TO HELP YOU...
THE LAST PERSON I WANT HELP FROM IS A CORPSE FUCKER.
APPARENTLY I'M A RESURRECTED JUNKIE AND I STILL DON'T WANT ANYTHING TO DO WITH YOU WEIRD FUCKERS.
THAT SHOULD TELL YOU HOW FAR OUT THERE YOU GUYS ARE.
SO, EXCUSE ME WHILE I DO WHAT NO NEW YORKER EVER REALLY WANTS TO DO.
GO TO JERSEY.
FUCK.
OFF.
HE'S GIVING US THE FINGER, ISN'T HE?

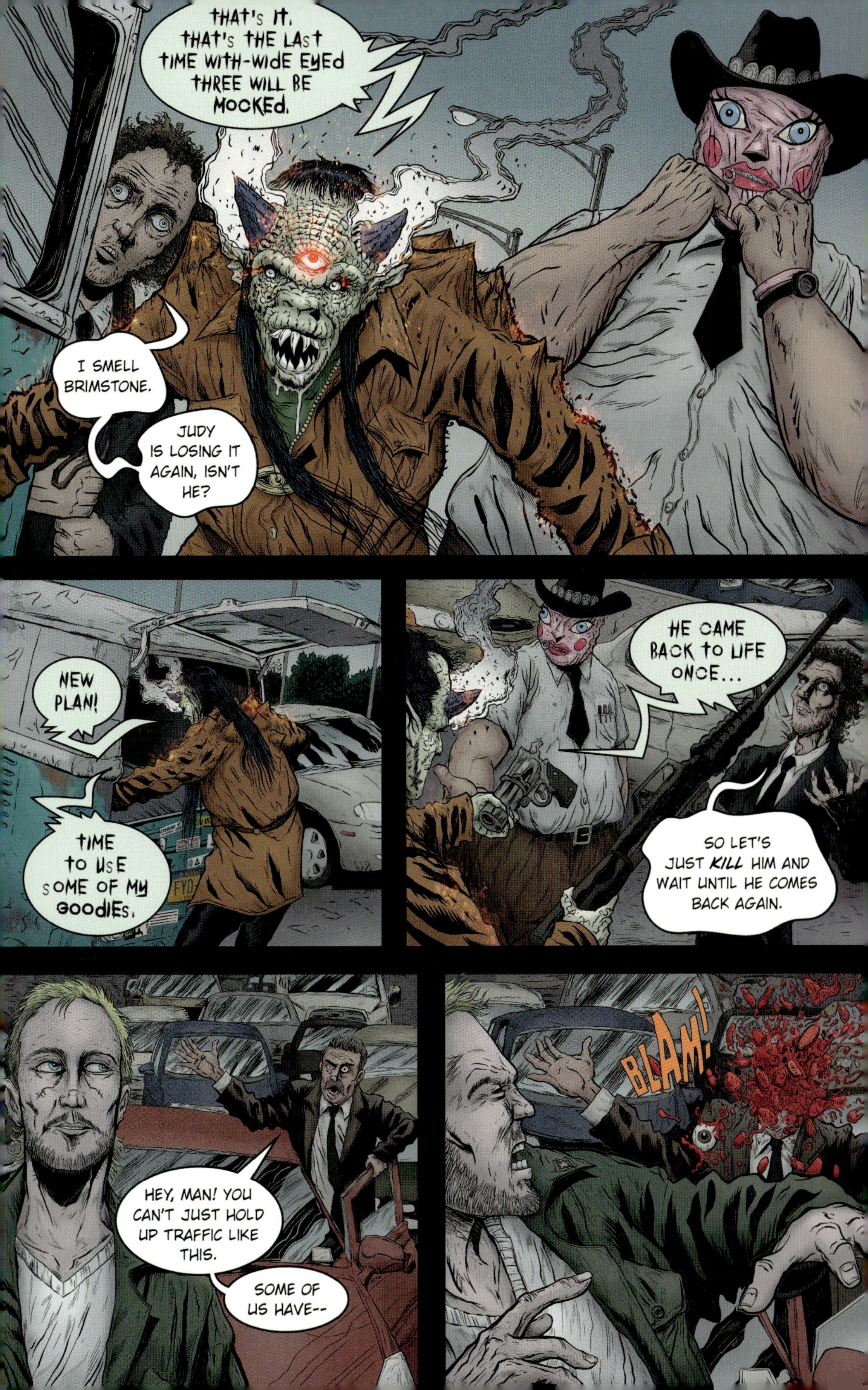
THAT'S IT. THAT'S THE LAST TIME WITH-WIDE EYED THREE WILL BE MOCKED.
I SMELL BRIMSTONE.
JUDY IS LOSING IT AGAIN, ISN'T HE?
NEW PLAN!
TIME TO USE SOME OF MY GOODIES.
HE CAME BACK TO LIFE ONCE...
SO LET'S JUST KILL HIM AND WAIT UNTIL HE COMES BACK AGAIN.
HEY, MAN! YOU CAN'T JUST HOLD UP TRAFFIC LIKE THIS.
SOME OF US HAVE--
BLAM!

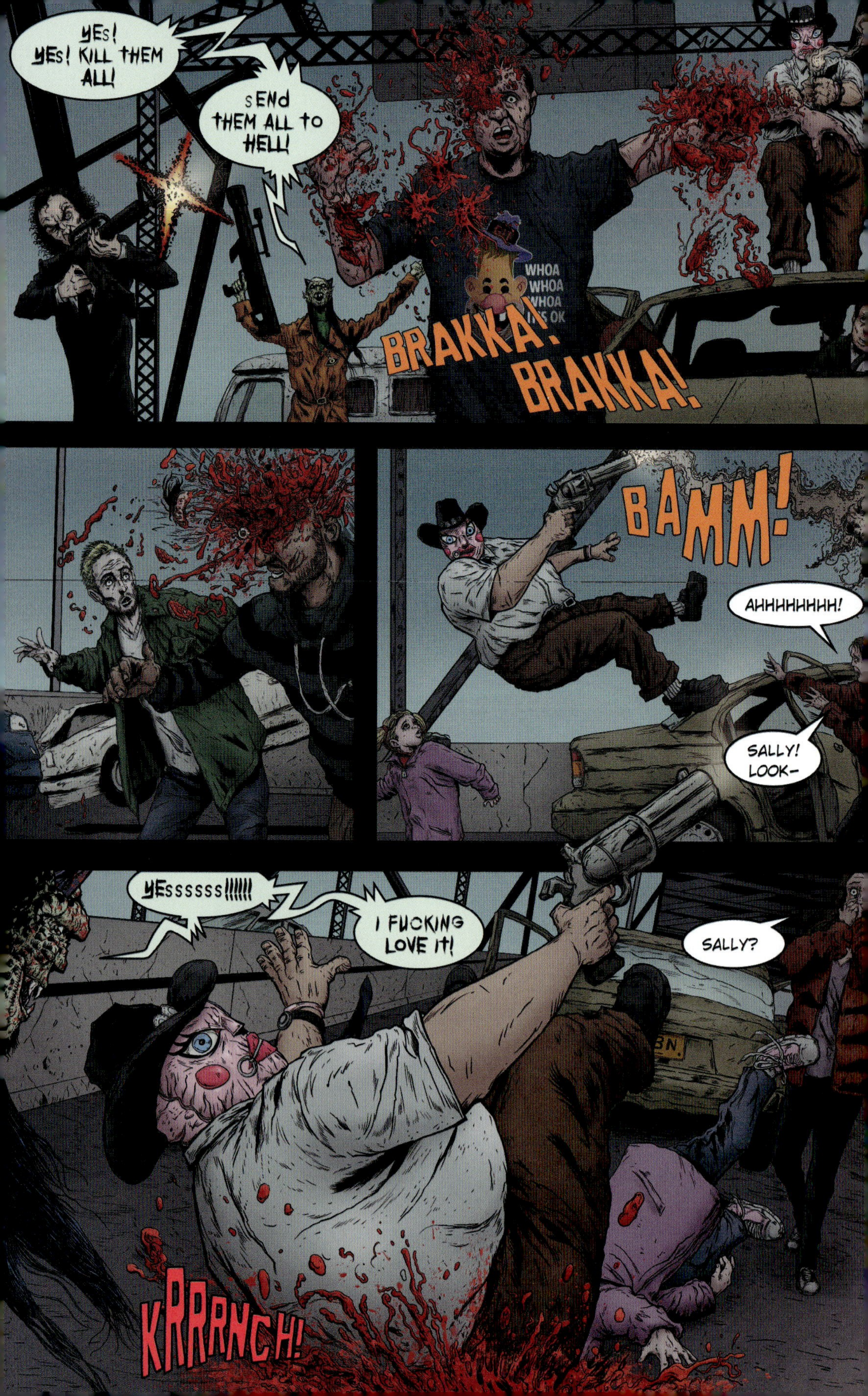
YES! YES! KILL THEM ALL!
SEND THEM ALL TO HELL!
WHOA WHOA WHOA IT'S OK
BRAKKA! BRAKKA!
BAMM!
AHHHHHHHH!
SALLY! LOOK-
YESSSSSS!!!!!!
I FUCKING LOVE IT!
SALLY?
KRRRNCH!

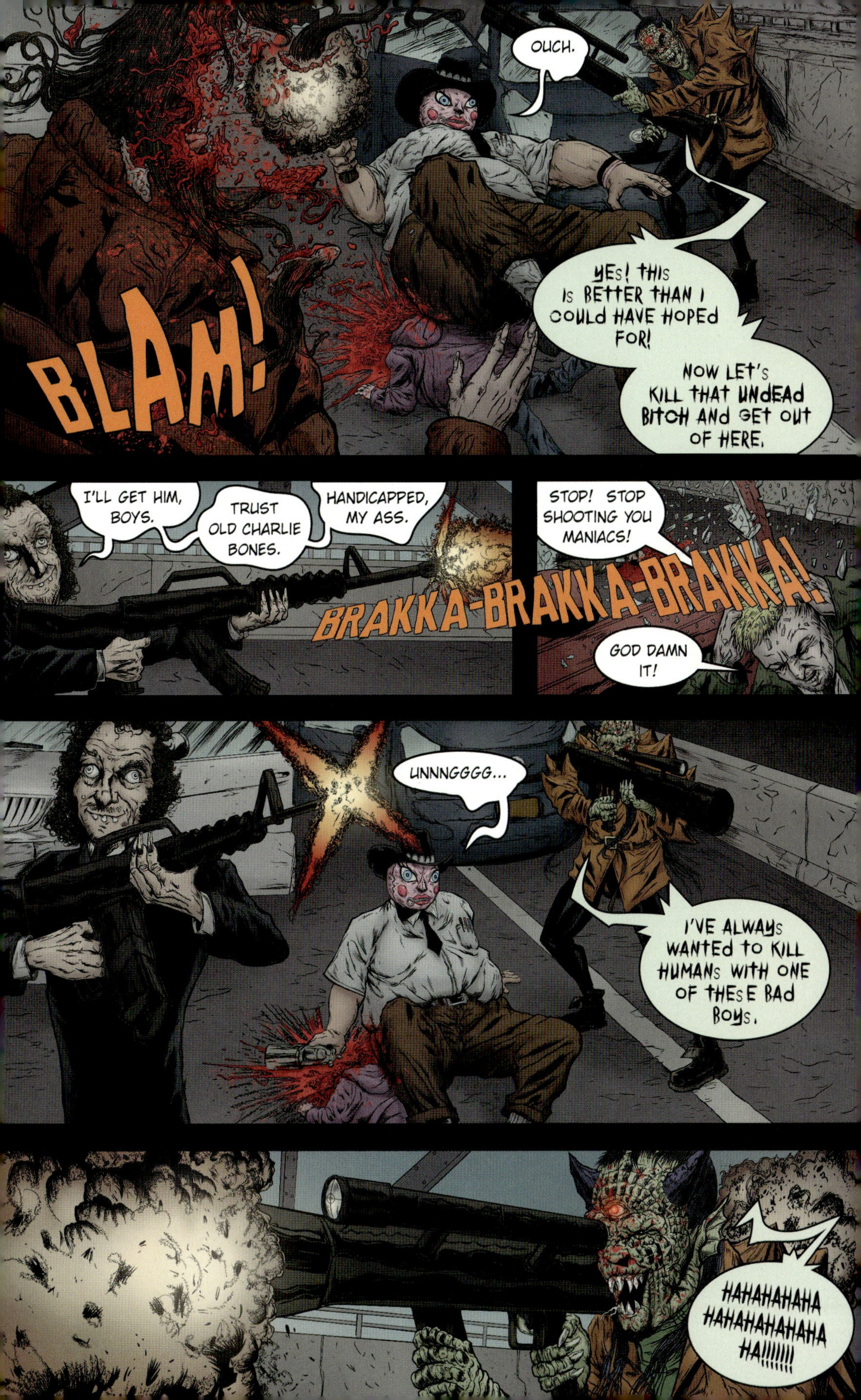
OUCH.
YES! THIS IS BETTER THAN I COULD HAVE HOPED FOR!
NOW LET'S KILL THAT UNDEAD BITCH AND GET OUT OF HERE.
BLAM!
I'LL GET HIM, BOYS.
TRUST OLD CHARLIE BONES.
HANDICAPPED, MY ASS.
STOP! STOP SHOOTING YOU MANIACS!
BRAKKA-BRAKKA-BRAKKA!
GOD DAMN IT!
UNNNGGGG...
I'VE ALWAYS WANTED TO KILL HUMANS WITH ONE OF THESE BAD BOYS.
HAHAHAHAHA HAHAHAHAHAHA HA!!!!!!!

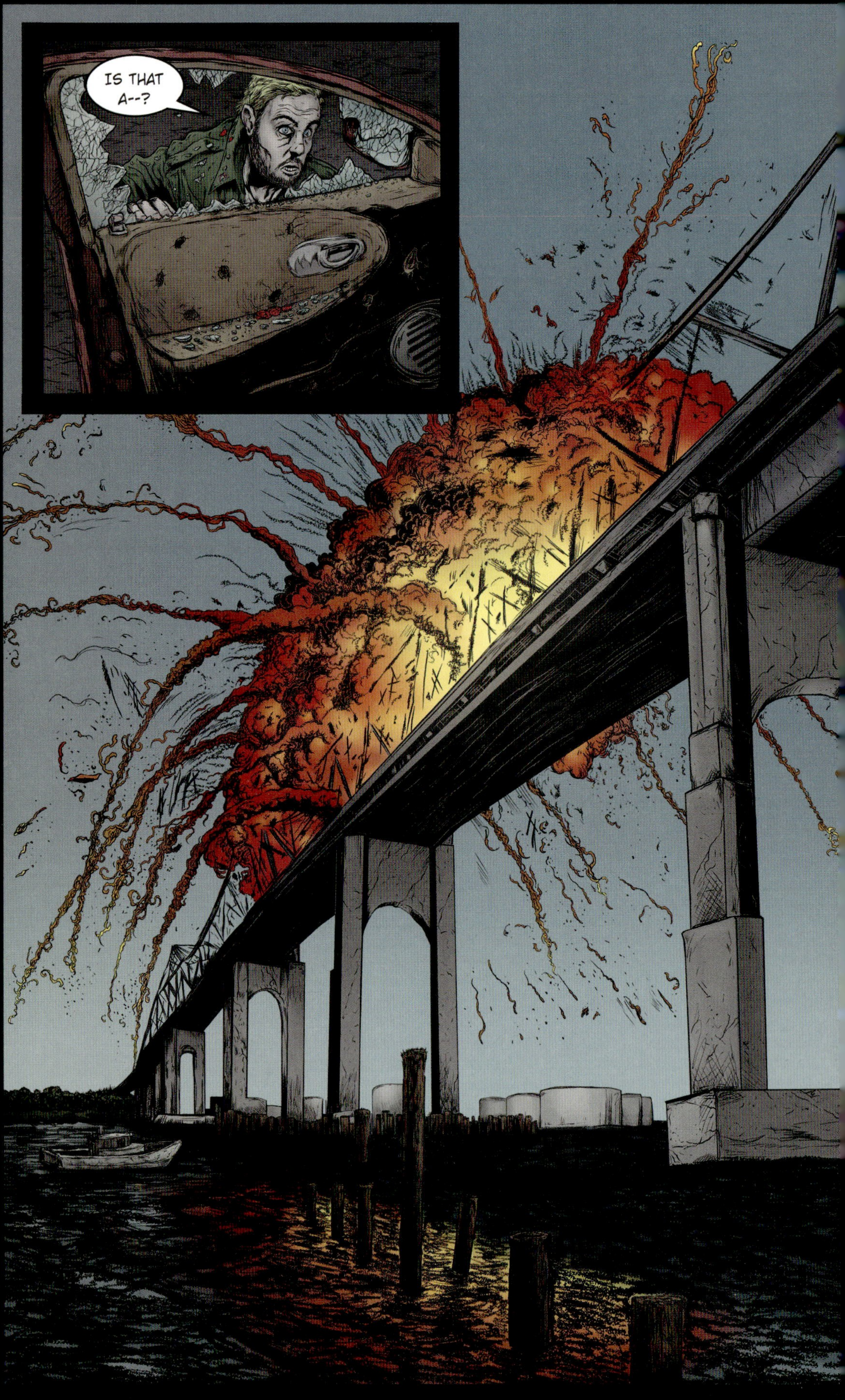
IS THAT A--?

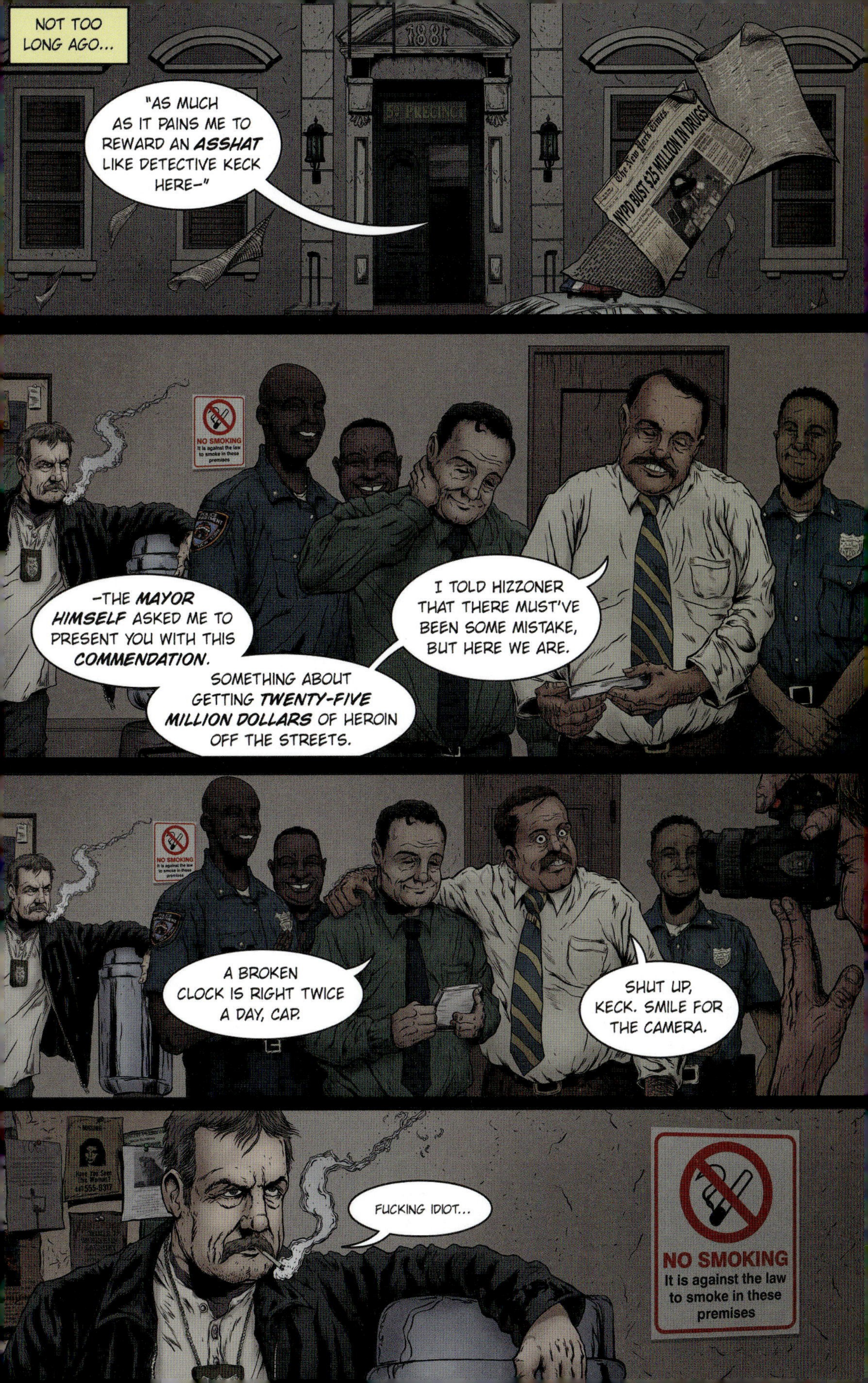
NOT TOO LONG AGO...
1881
"AS MUCH AS IT PAINS ME TO REWARD AN ***ASSHAT*** LIKE DETECTIVE KECK HERE–"
NYPD BUST $25 MILLION IN DRUGS
NO SMOKING
–THE ***MAYOR HIMSELF*** ASKED ME TO PRESENT YOU WITH THIS ***COMMENDATION***.
SOMETHING ABOUT GETTING ***TWENTY-FIVE MILLION DOLLARS*** OF HEROIN OFF THE STREETS.
I TOLD HIZZONER THAT THERE MUST'VE BEEN SOME MISTAKE, BUT HERE WE ARE.
NO SMOKING
A BROKEN CLOCK IS RIGHT TWICE A DAY, CAP.
SHUT UP, KECK. SMILE FOR THE CAMERA.
FUCKING IDIOT...
NO SMOKING
It is against the law to smoke in these premises

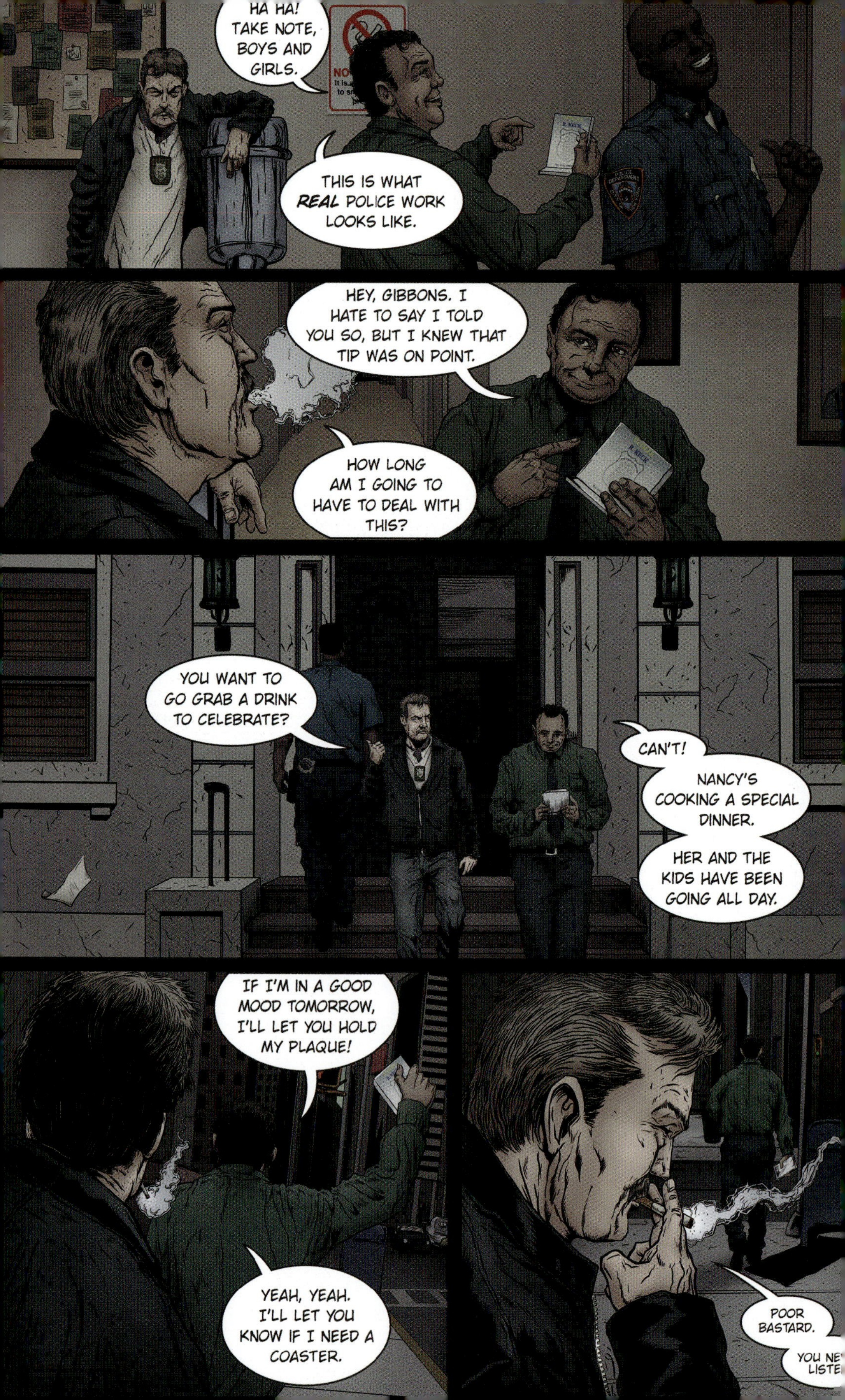
HA HA! TAKE NOTE, BOYS AND GIRLS.
THIS IS WHAT *REAL* POLICE WORK LOOKS LIKE.
HEY, GIBBONS. I HATE TO SAY I TOLD YOU SO, BUT I KNEW THAT TIP WAS ON POINT.
HOW LONG AM I GOING TO HAVE TO DEAL WITH THIS?
YOU WANT TO GO GRAB A DRINK TO CELEBRATE?
CAN'T!
NANCY'S COOKING A SPECIAL DINNER.
HER AND THE KIDS HAVE BEEN GOING ALL DAY.
IF I'M IN A GOOD MOOD TOMORROW, I'LL LET YOU HOLD MY PLAQUE!
YEAH, YEAH. I'LL LET YOU KNOW IF I NEED A COASTER.
POOR BASTARD.
YOU NE
LISTE

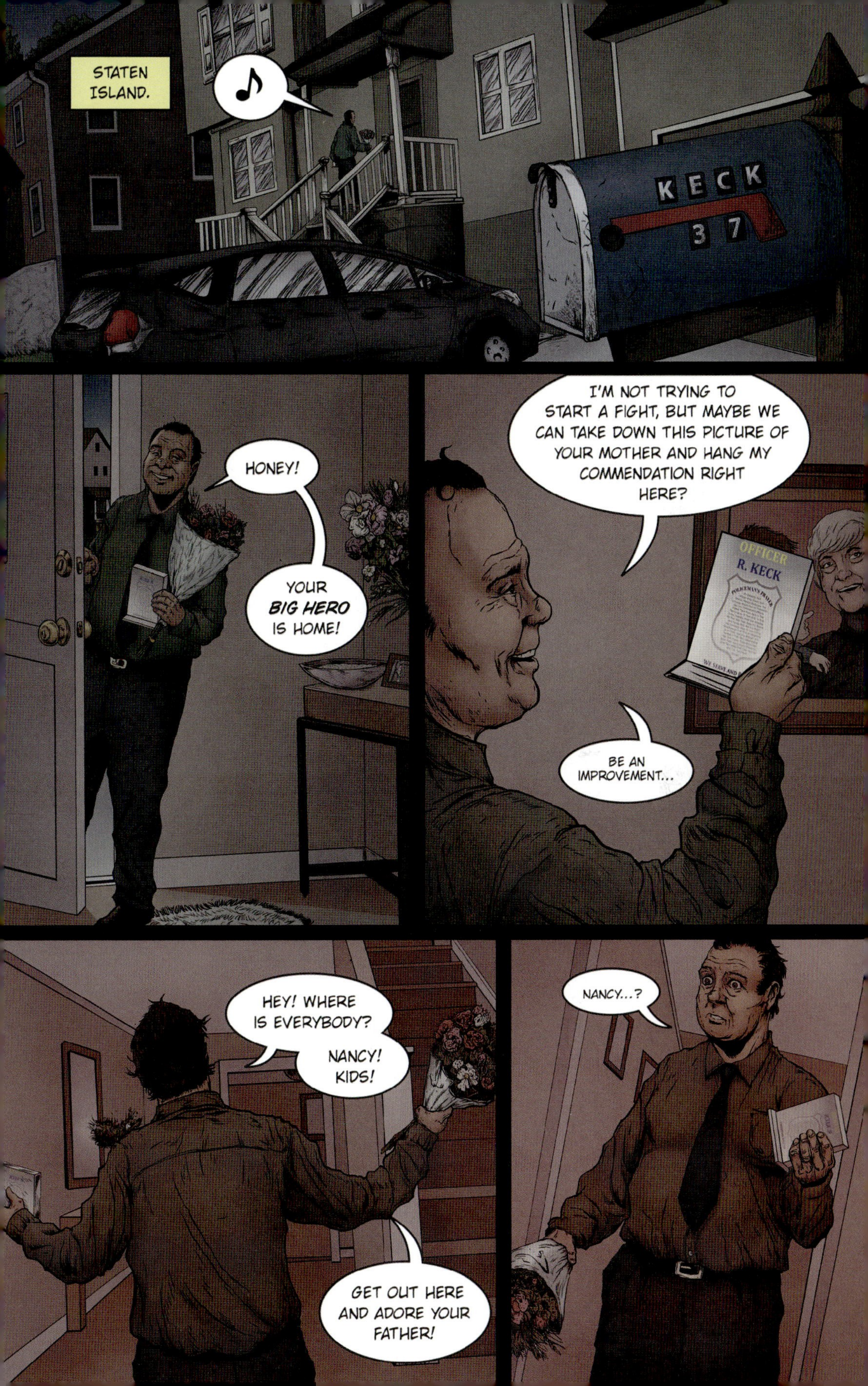

STATEN ISLAND.
♪
KECK
37
HONEY!
YOUR *BIG HERO* IS HOME!
I'M NOT TRYING TO START A FIGHT, BUT MAYBE WE CAN TAKE DOWN THIS PICTURE OF YOUR MOTHER AND HANG MY COMMENDATION RIGHT HERE?
OFFICER
R. KECK
BE AN IMPROVEMENT...
HEY! WHERE IS EVERYBODY?
NANCY! KIDS!
GET OUT HERE AND ADORE YOUR FATHER!
NANCY...?

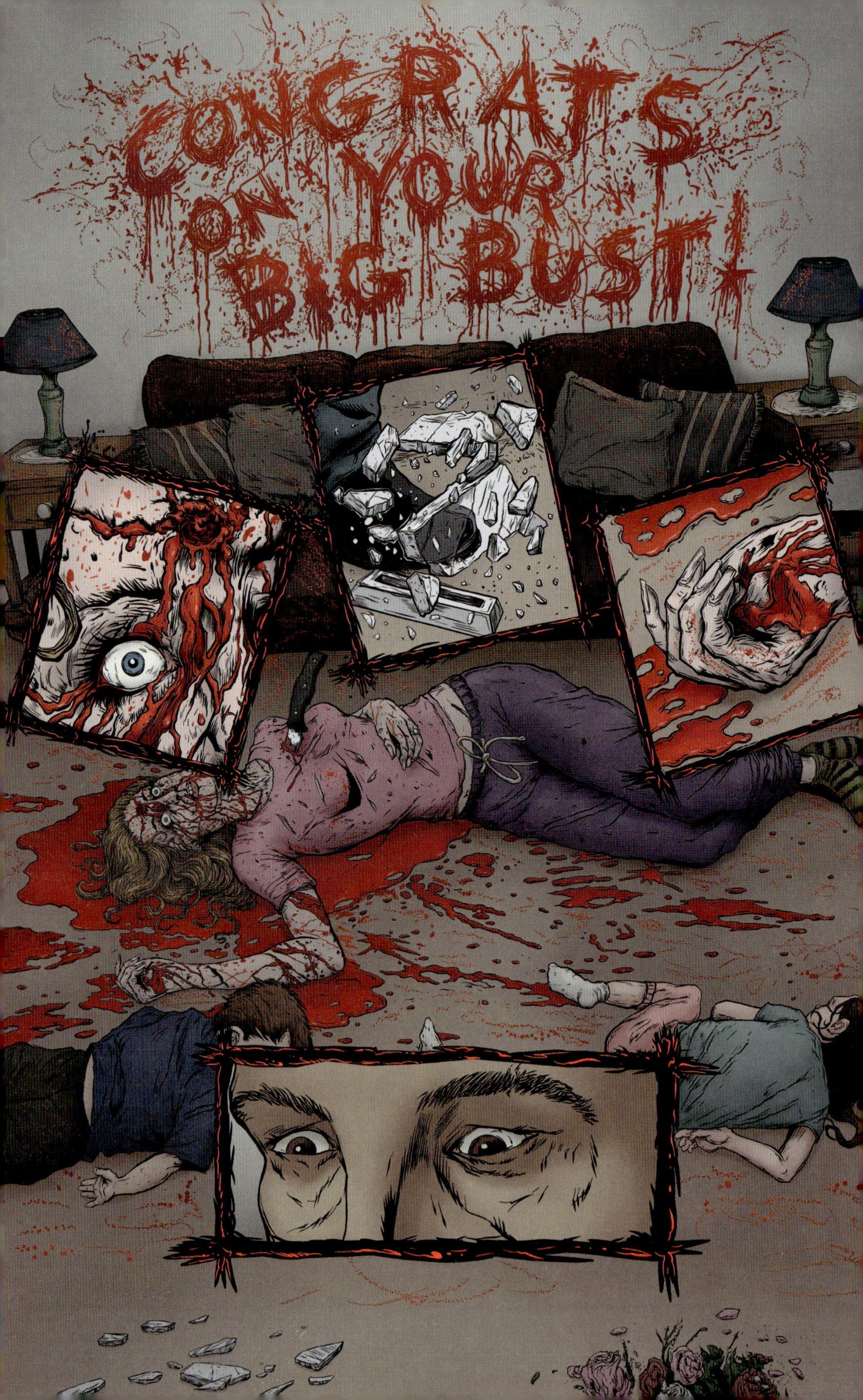
CONGRATS ON YOUR BIG BUST!

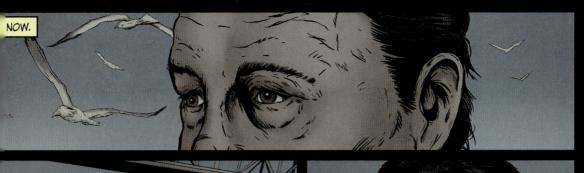
NOW.

BRAKKA!
BRAKKA!

FUCK.

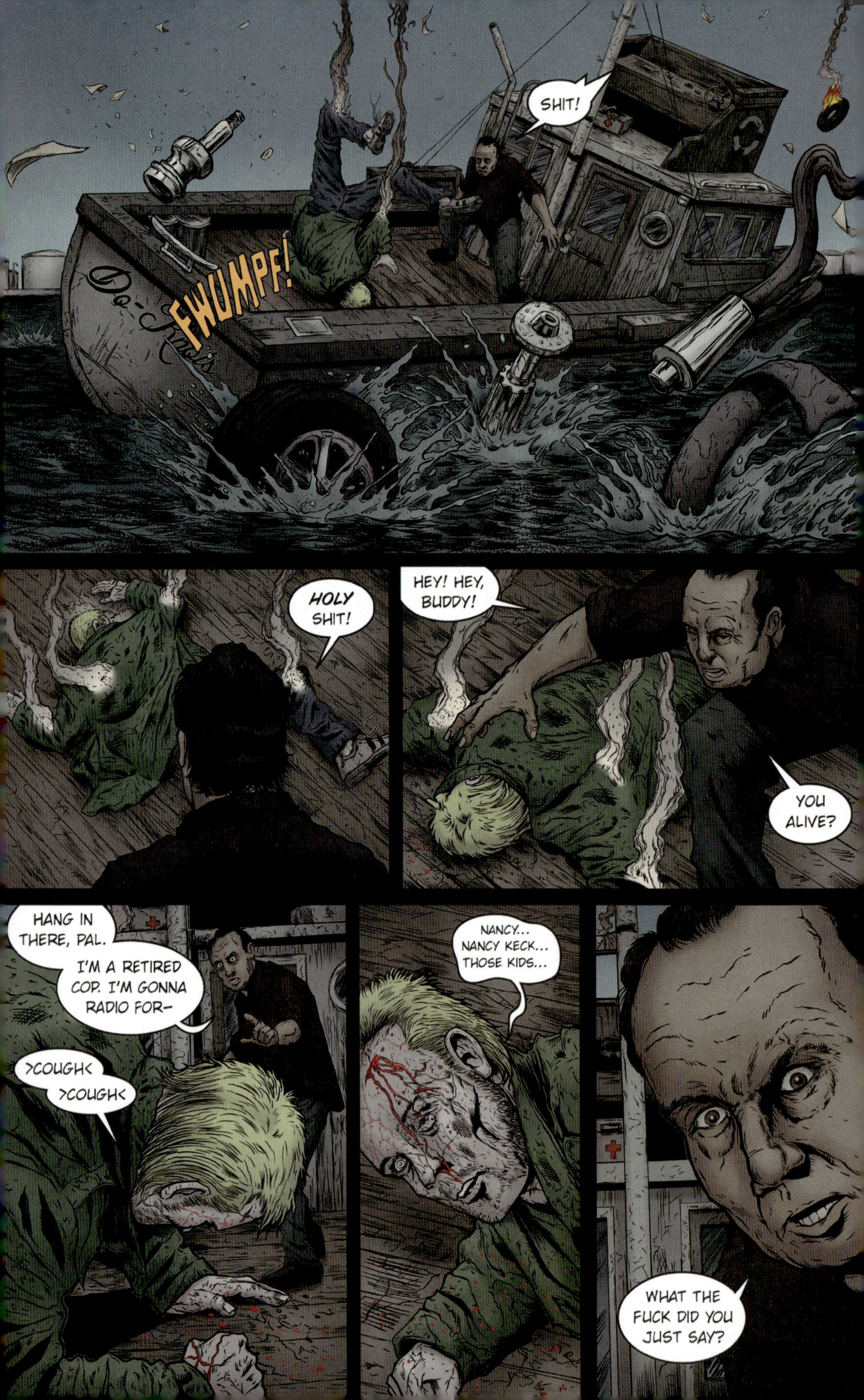
SHIT!
FWUMPF!
HOLY SHIT!
HEY! HEY, BUDDY!
YOU ALIVE?
HANG IN THERE, PAL.
I'M A RETIRED COP. I'M GONNA RADIO FOR–
>COUGH<
>COUGH<
NANCY... NANCY KECK... THOSE KIDS...
WHAT THE FUCK DID YOU JUST SAY?

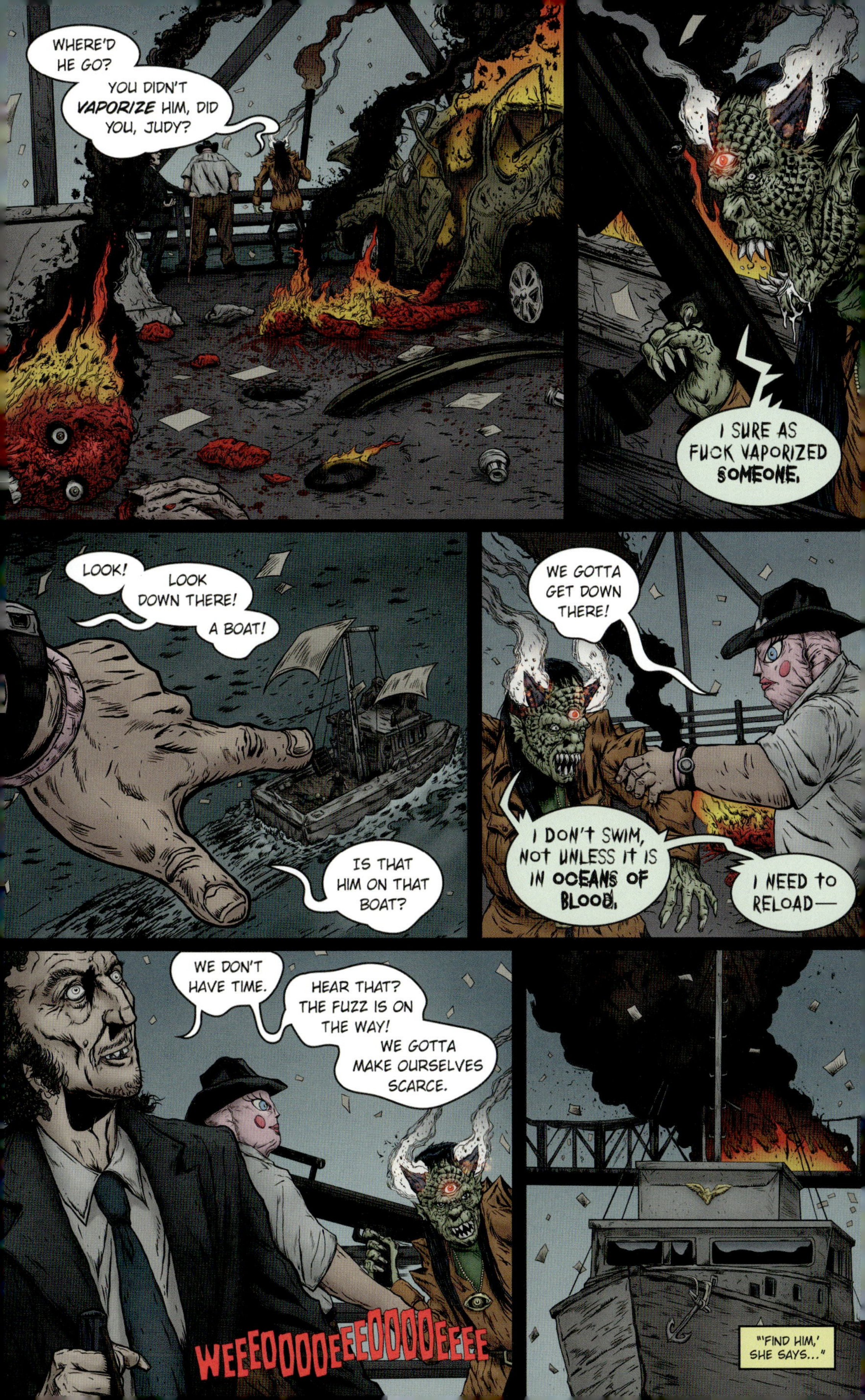
WHERE'D HE GO?
YOU DIDN'T *VAPORIZE* HIM, DID YOU, JUDY?
I SURE AS FUCK VAPORIZED **SOMEONE.**
LOOK!
LOOK DOWN THERE!
A BOAT!
IS THAT HIM ON THAT BOAT?
WE GOTTA GET DOWN THERE!
I DON'T SWIM, NOT UNLESS IT IS IN **OCEANS OF BLOOD.**
I NEED TO RELOAD—
WE DON'T HAVE TIME.
HEAR THAT? THE FUZZ IS ON THE WAY!
WE GOTTA MAKE OURSELVES SCARCE.
WEEEOOOOEEEOOOOEEEE
"'FIND HIM,' SHE SAYS..."

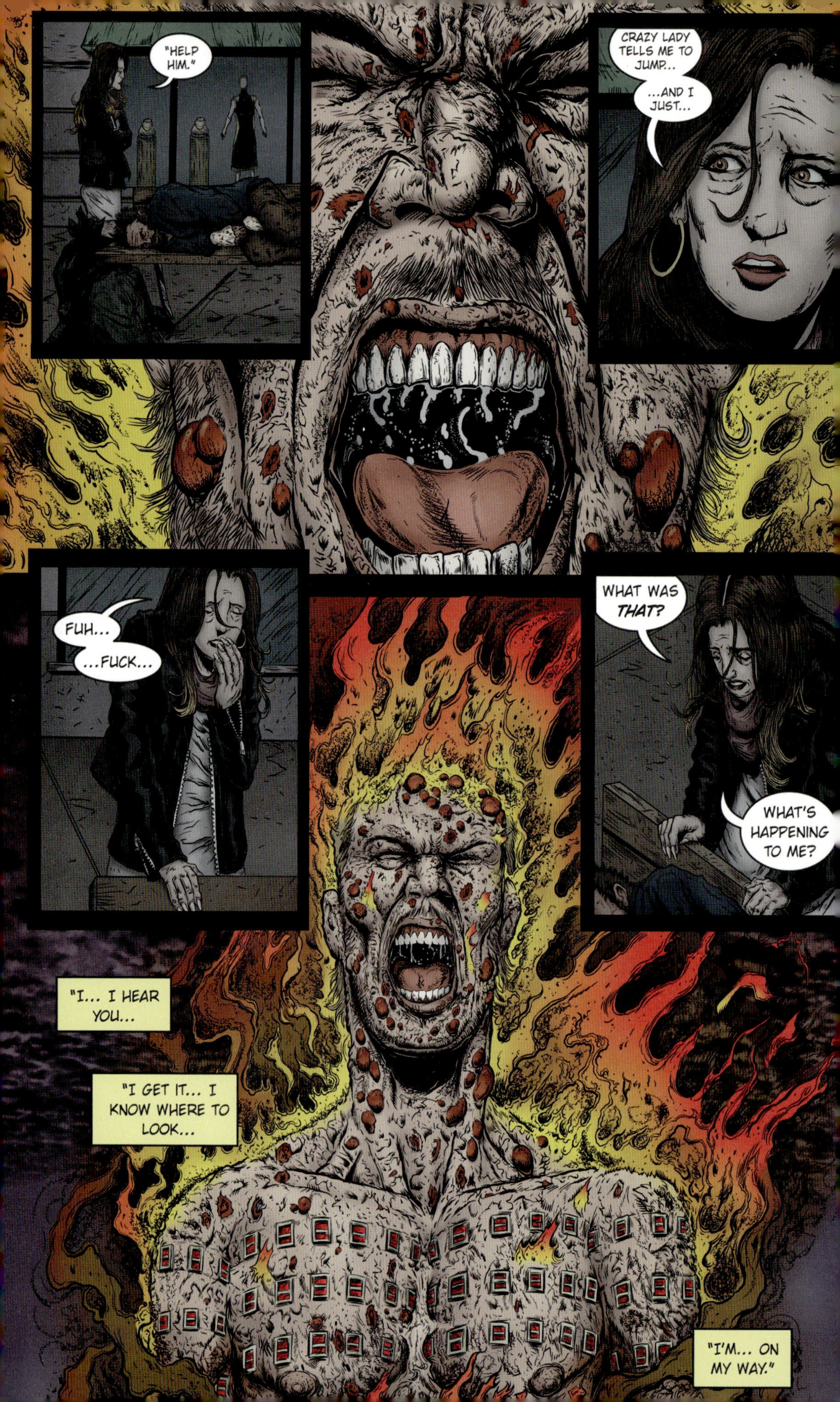
"HELP HIM."
CRAZY LADY TELLS ME TO JUMP...
...AND I JUST...
FUH...
...FUCK...
WHAT WAS THAT?
WHAT'S HAPPENING TO ME?
"I... I HEAR YOU...
"I GET IT... I KNOW WHERE TO LOOK...
"I'M... ON MY WAY."

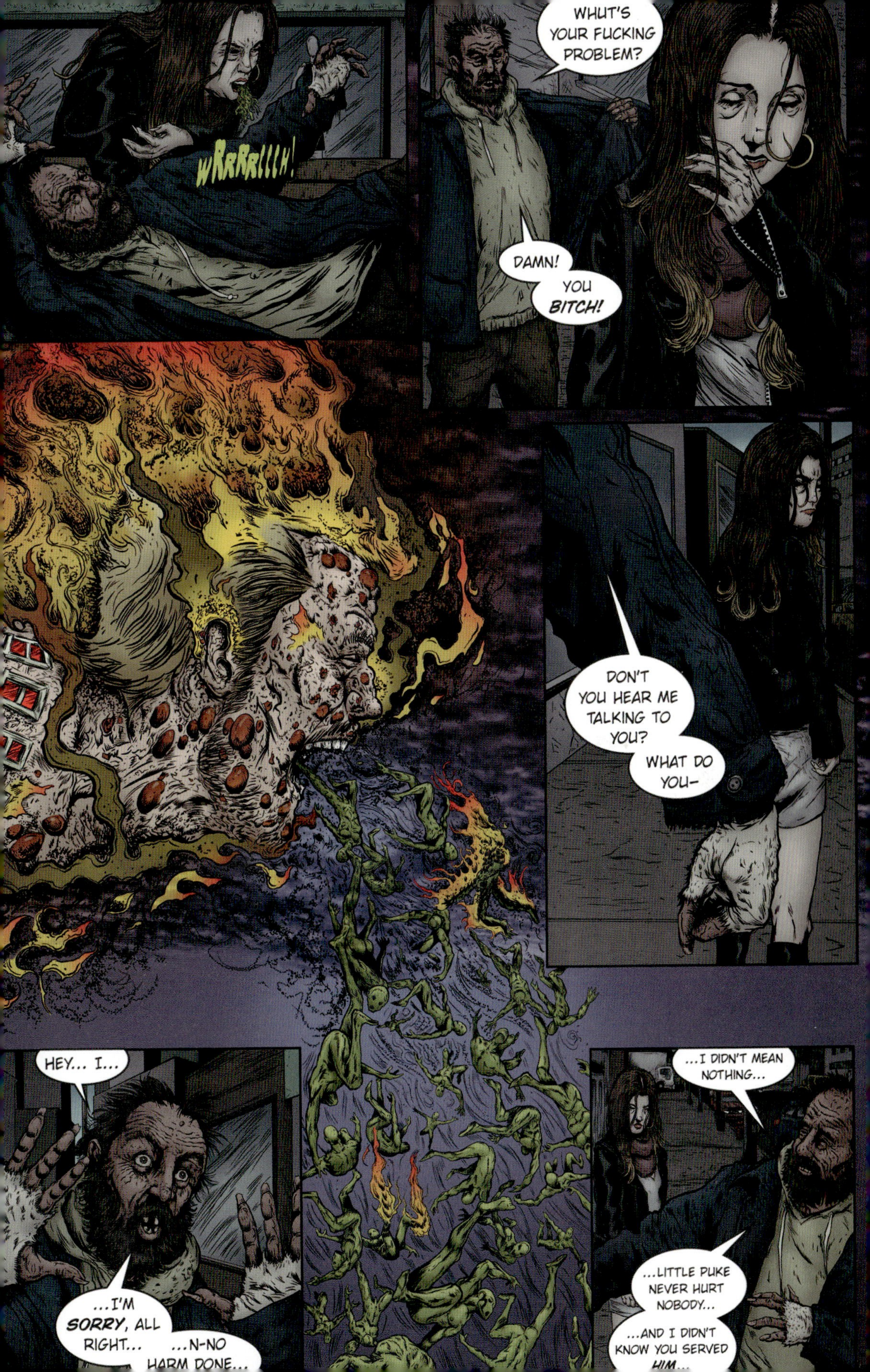
wRRRRLLLH!
WHUT'S YOUR FUCKING PROBLEM?
DAMN! YOU BITCH!
DON'T YOU HEAR ME TALKING TO YOU?
WHAT DO YOU–
HEY... I...
...I'M SORRY, ALL RIGHT...
...N-NO HARM DONE...
...I DIDN'T MEAN NOTHING...
...LITTLE PUKE NEVER HURT NOBODY...
...AND I DIDN'T KNOW YOU SERVED HIM...

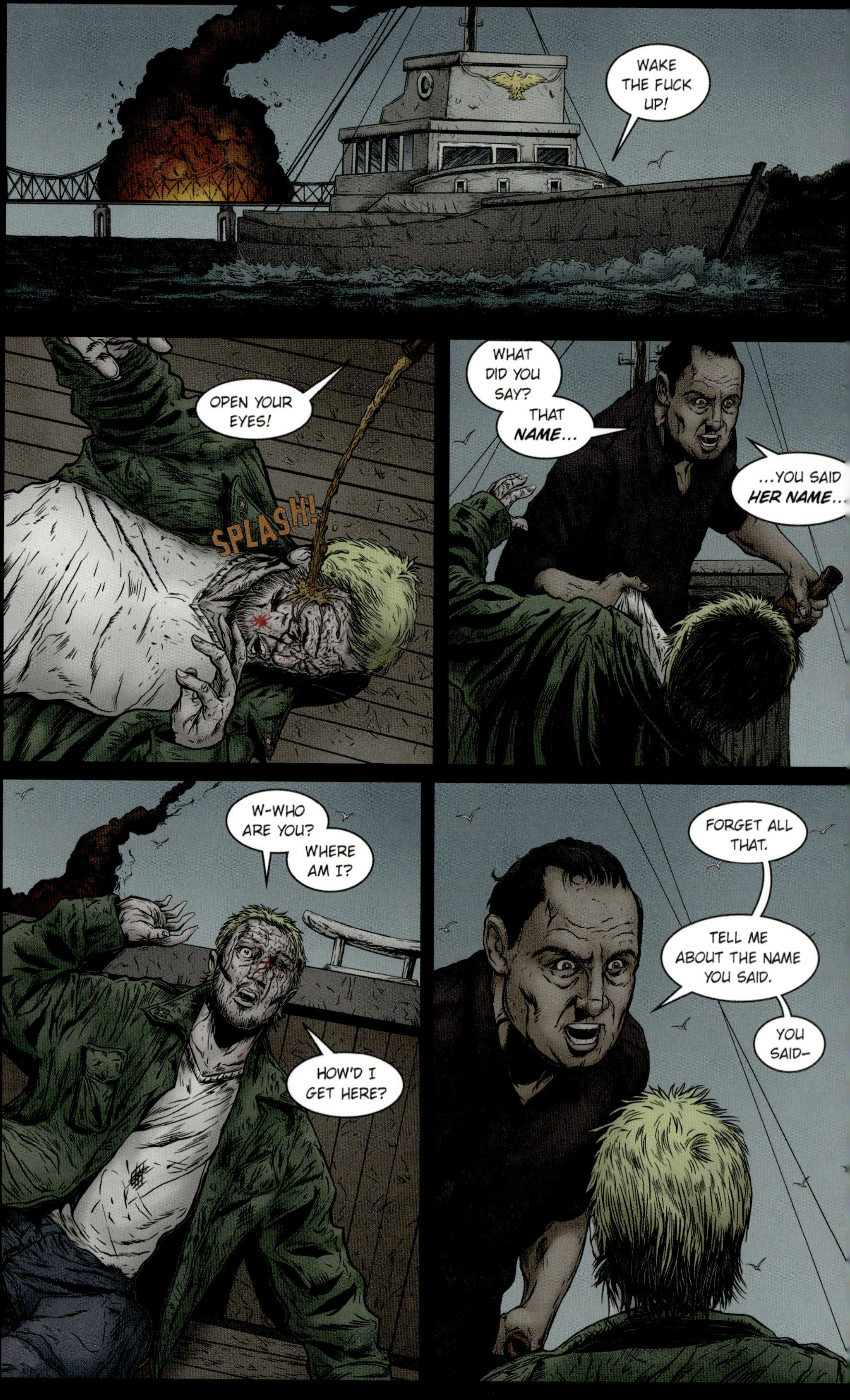
WAKE THE FUCK UP!
OPEN YOUR EYES!
SPLASH!
WHAT DID YOU SAY?
THAT NAME...
...YOU SAID HER NAME...
W-WHO ARE YOU?
WHERE AM I?
HOW'D I GET HERE?
FORGET ALL THAT.
TELL ME ABOUT THE NAME YOU SAID.
YOU SAID-

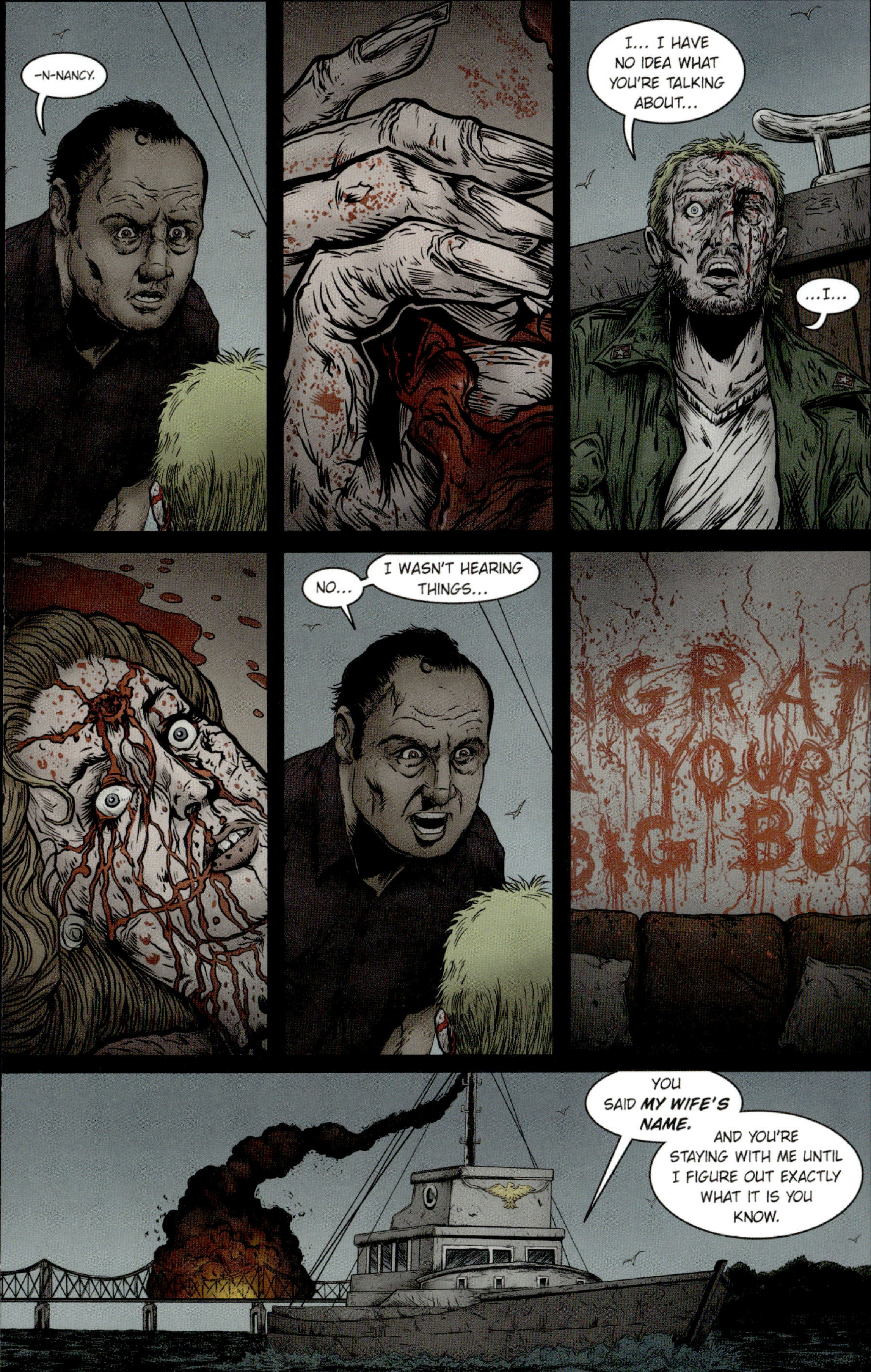
-N-NANCY.
I... I HAVE NO IDEA WHAT YOU'RE TALKING ABOUT...
...I...
NO...
I WASN'T HEARING THINGS...
YOUR
YOU SAID **MY WIFE'S NAME.**
AND YOU'RE STAYING WITH ME UNTIL I FIGURE OUT EXACTLY WHAT IT IS YOU KNOW.

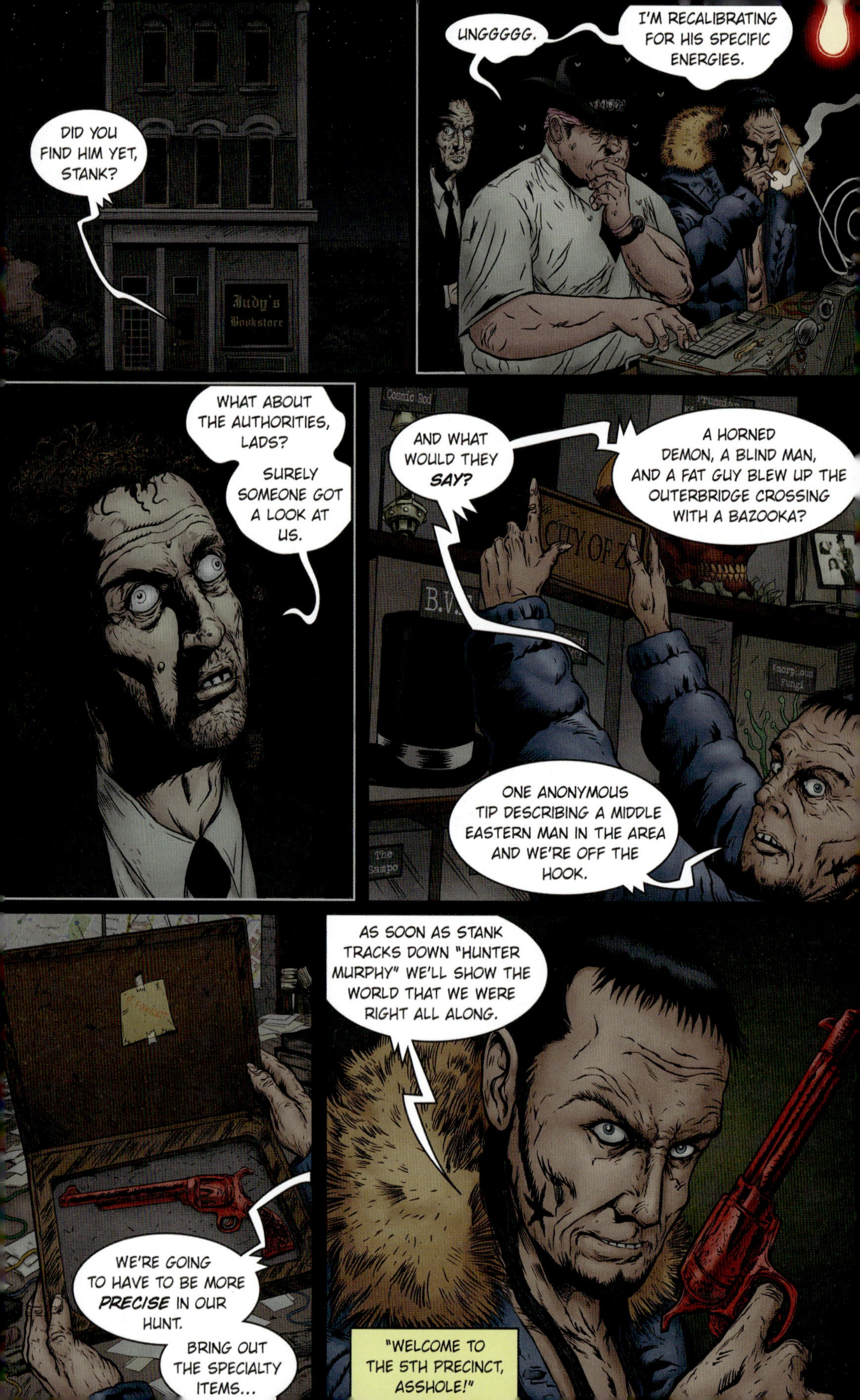
Judy's Bookstore
DID YOU FIND HIM YET, STANK?
UNGGGGG.
I'M RECALIBRATING FOR HIS SPECIFIC ENERGIES.
WHAT ABOUT THE AUTHORITIES, LADS?
SURELY SOMEONE GOT A LOOK AT US.
Cosmic Rod
AND WHAT WOULD THEY *SAY?*
A HORNED DEMON, A BLIND MAN, AND A FAT GUY BLEW UP THE OUTERBRIDGE CROSSING WITH A BAZOOKA?
CITY OF Z
ONE ANONYMOUS TIP DESCRIBING A MIDDLE EASTERN MAN IN THE AREA AND WE'RE OFF THE HOOK.
WE'RE GOING TO HAVE TO BE MORE *PRECISE* IN OUR HUNT.
BRING OUT THE SPECIALTY ITEMS...
AS SOON AS STANK TRACKS DOWN "HUNTER MURPHY" WE'LL SHOW THE WORLD THAT WE WERE RIGHT ALL ALONG.
"WELCOME TO THE 5TH PRECINCT, ASSHOLE!"

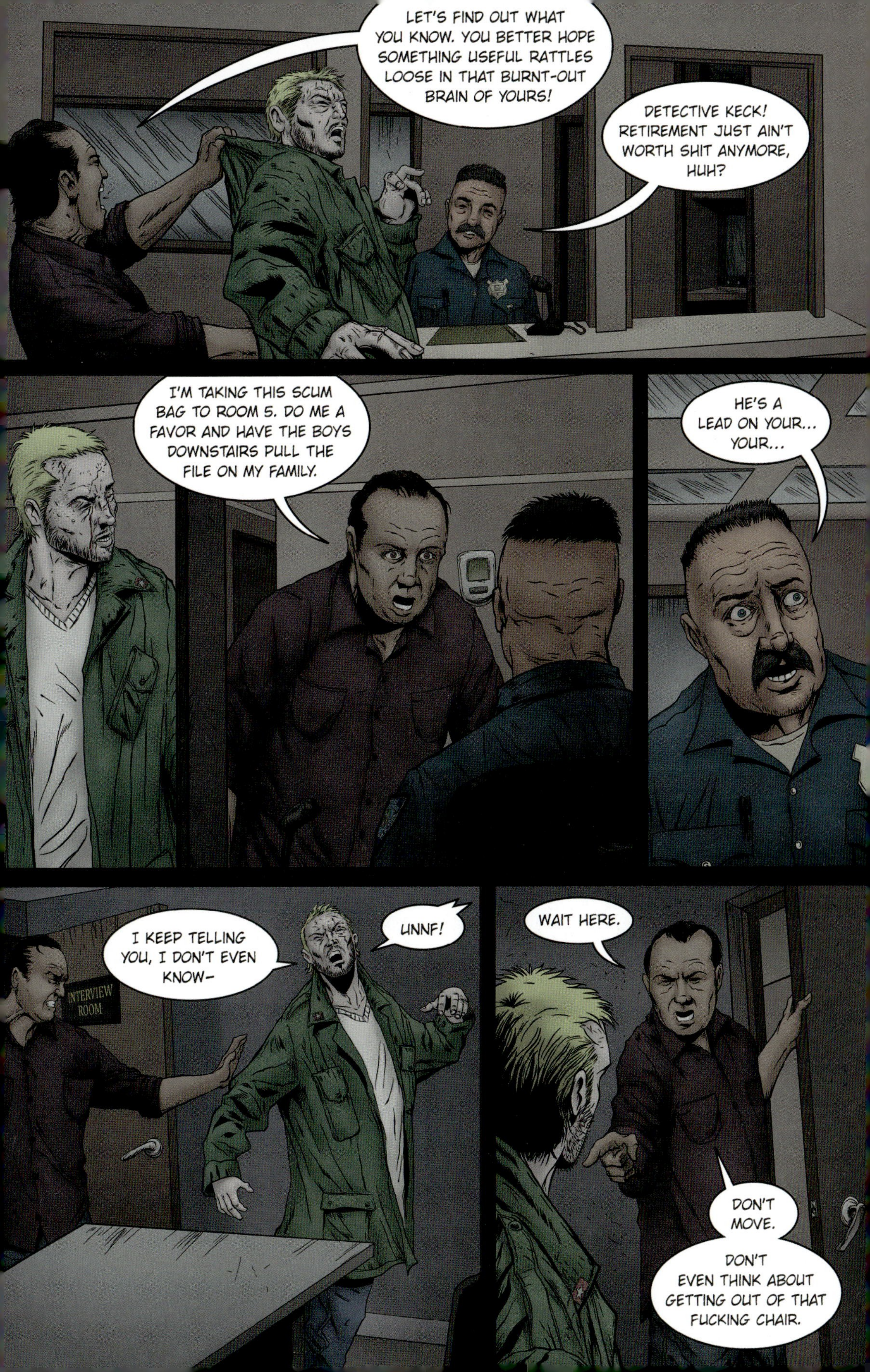
LET'S FIND OUT WHAT YOU KNOW. YOU BETTER HOPE SOMETHING USEFUL RATTLES LOOSE IN THAT BURNT-OUT BRAIN OF YOURS!
DETECTIVE KECK! RETIREMENT JUST AIN'T WORTH SHIT ANYMORE, HUH?
I'M TAKING THIS SCUM BAG TO ROOM 5. DO ME A FAVOR AND HAVE THE BOYS DOWNSTAIRS PULL THE FILE ON MY FAMILY.
HE'S A LEAD ON YOUR... YOUR...
I KEEP TELLING YOU, I DON'T EVEN KNOW-
UNNF!
INTERVIEW ROOM
WAIT HERE.
DON'T MOVE.
DON'T EVEN THINK ABOUT GETTING OUT OF THAT FUCKING CHAIR.

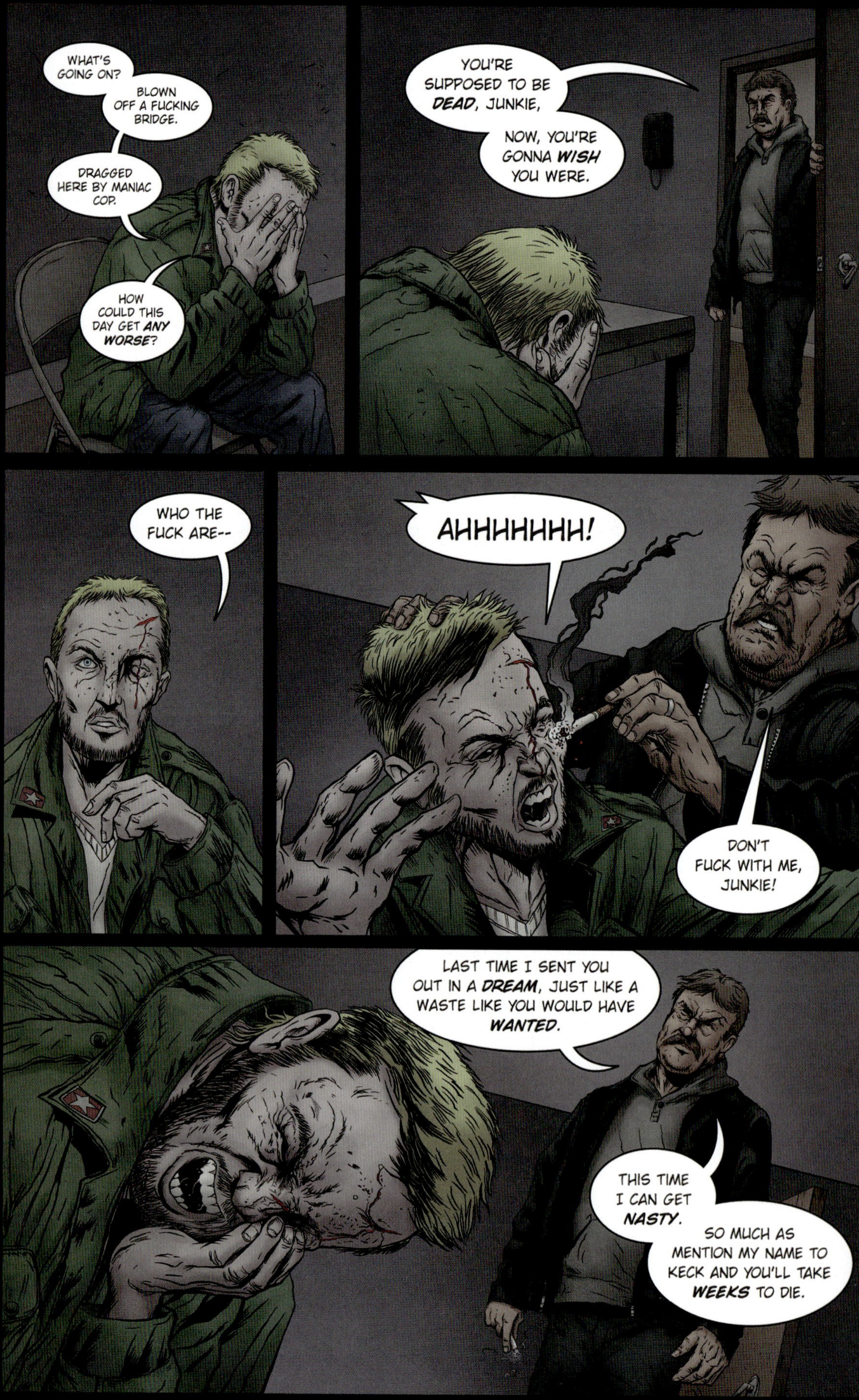
WHAT'S GOING ON?
BLOWN OFF A FUCKING BRIDGE.
DRAGGED HERE BY MANIAC COP.
HOW COULD THIS DAY GET ANY WORSE?
YOU'RE SUPPOSED TO BE DEAD, JUNKIE,
NOW, YOU'RE GONNA WISH YOU WERE.
WHO THE FUCK ARE--
AHHHHHHH!
DON'T FUCK WITH ME, JUNKIE!
LAST TIME I SENT YOU OUT IN A DREAM, JUST LIKE A WASTE LIKE YOU WOULD HAVE WANTED.
THIS TIME I CAN GET NASTY.
SO MUCH AS MENTION MY NAME TO KECK AND YOU'LL TAKE WEEKS TO DIE.

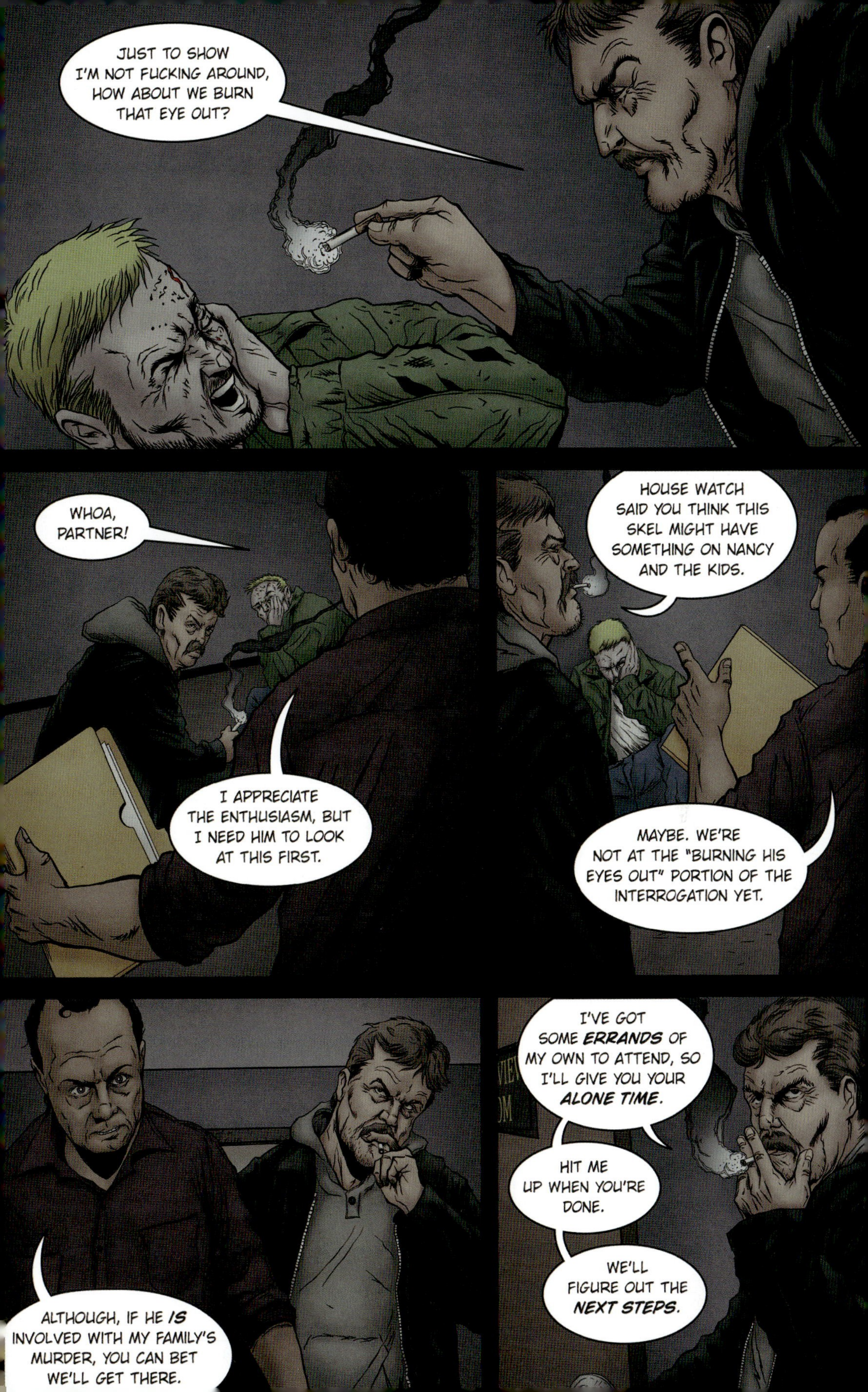
JUST TO SHOW I'M NOT FUCKING AROUND, HOW ABOUT WE BURN THAT EYE OUT?
WHOA, PARTNER!
I APPRECIATE THE ENTHUSIASM, BUT I NEED HIM TO LOOK AT THIS FIRST.
HOUSE WATCH SAID YOU THINK THIS SKEL MIGHT HAVE SOMETHING ON NANCY AND THE KIDS.
MAYBE. WE'RE NOT AT THE "BURNING HIS EYES OUT" PORTION OF THE INTERROGATION YET.
ALTHOUGH, IF HE *IS* INVOLVED WITH MY FAMILY'S MURDER, YOU CAN BET WE'LL GET THERE.
I'VE GOT SOME **ERRANDS** OF MY OWN TO ATTEND, SO I'LL GIVE YOU YOUR **ALONE TIME.**
HIT ME UP WHEN YOU'RE DONE.
WE'LL FIGURE OUT THE **NEXT STEPS.**

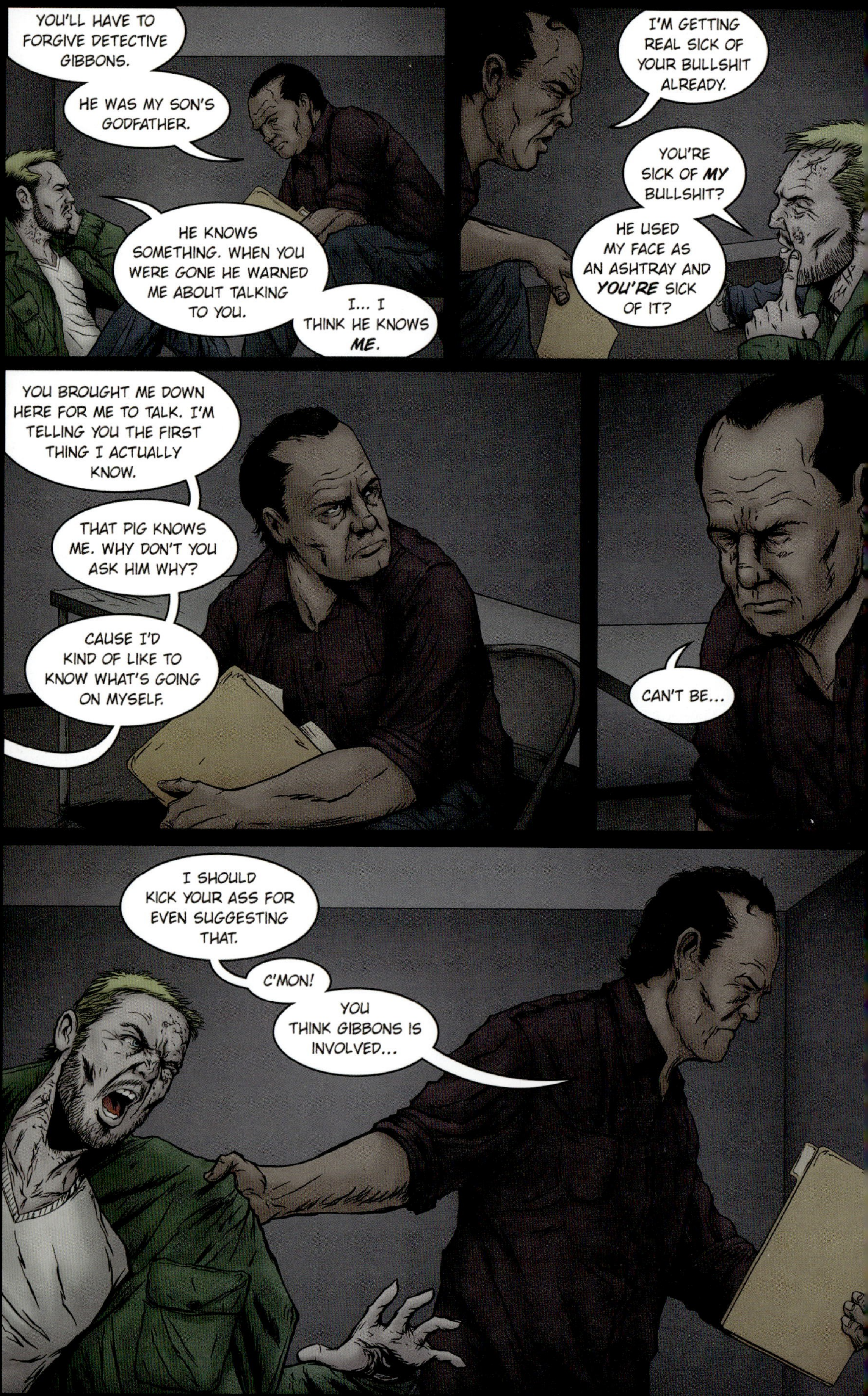
YOU'LL HAVE TO FORGIVE DETECTIVE GIBBONS.
HE WAS MY SON'S GODFATHER.
HE KNOWS SOMETHING. WHEN YOU WERE GONE HE WARNED ME ABOUT TALKING TO YOU.
I... I THINK HE KNOWS ME.
I'M GETTING REAL SICK OF YOUR BULLSHIT ALREADY.
YOU'RE SICK OF MY BULLSHIT?
HE USED MY FACE AS AN ASHTRAY AND YOU'RE SICK OF IT?
YOU BROUGHT ME DOWN HERE FOR ME TO TALK. I'M TELLING YOU THE FIRST THING I ACTUALLY KNOW.
THAT PIG KNOWS ME. WHY DON'T YOU ASK HIM WHY?
CAUSE I'D KIND OF LIKE TO KNOW WHAT'S GOING ON MYSELF.
CAN'T BE...
I SHOULD KICK YOUR ASS FOR EVEN SUGGESTING THAT.
C'MON!
YOU THINK GIBBONS IS INVOLVED...

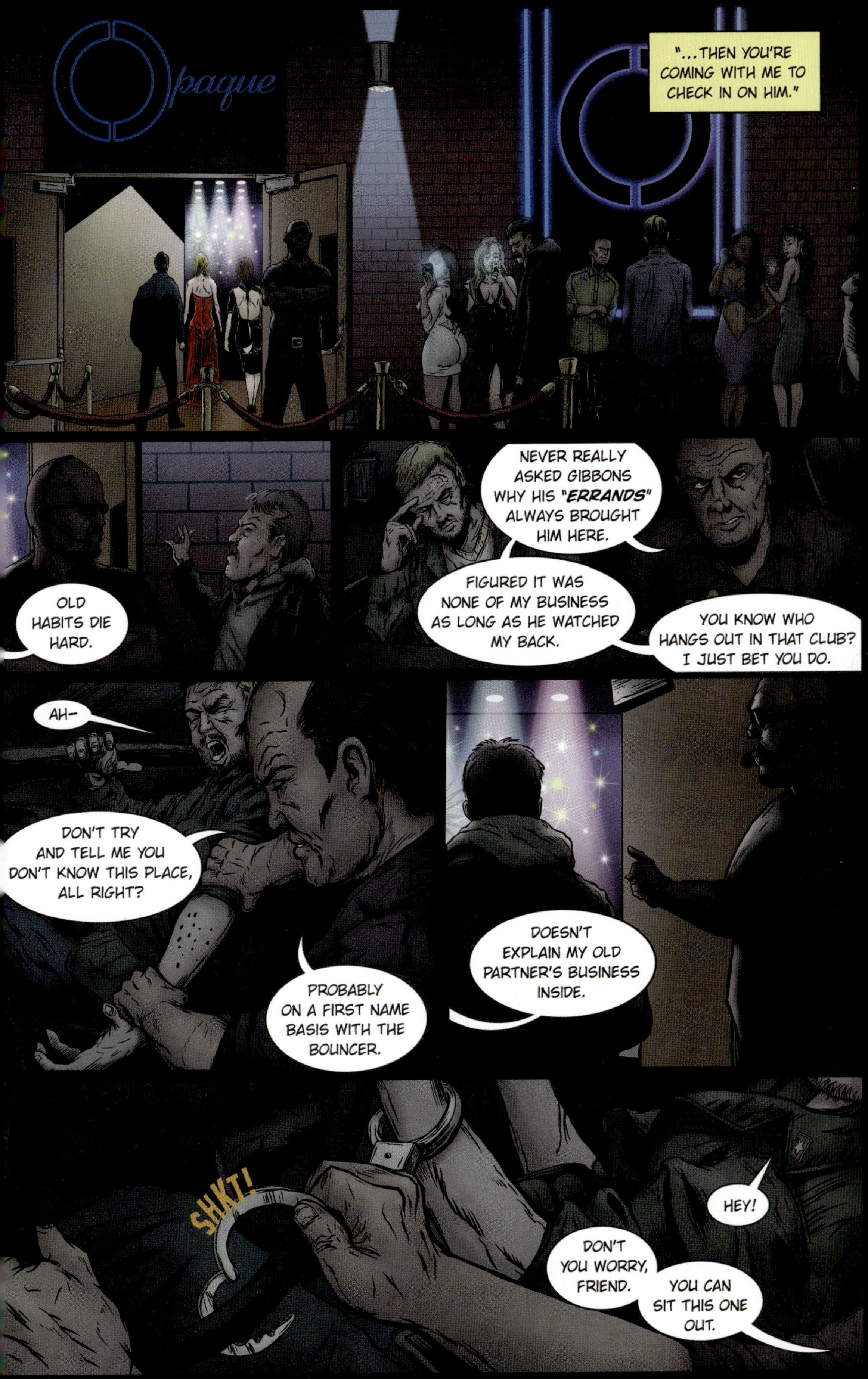

Opaque
"...THEN YOU'RE COMING WITH ME TO CHECK IN ON HIM."
OLD HABITS DIE HARD.
NEVER REALLY ASKED GIBBONS WHY HIS "ERRANDS" ALWAYS BROUGHT HIM HERE.
FIGURED IT WAS NONE OF MY BUSINESS AS LONG AS HE WATCHED MY BACK.
YOU KNOW WHO HANGS OUT IN THAT CLUB? I JUST BET YOU DO.
AH-
DON'T TRY AND TELL ME YOU DON'T KNOW THIS PLACE, ALL RIGHT?
PROBABLY ON A FIRST NAME BASIS WITH THE BOUNCER.
DOESN'T EXPLAIN MY OLD PARTNER'S BUSINESS INSIDE.
SHKT!
HEY!
DON'T YOU WORRY, FRIEND.
YOU CAN SIT THIS ONE OUT.

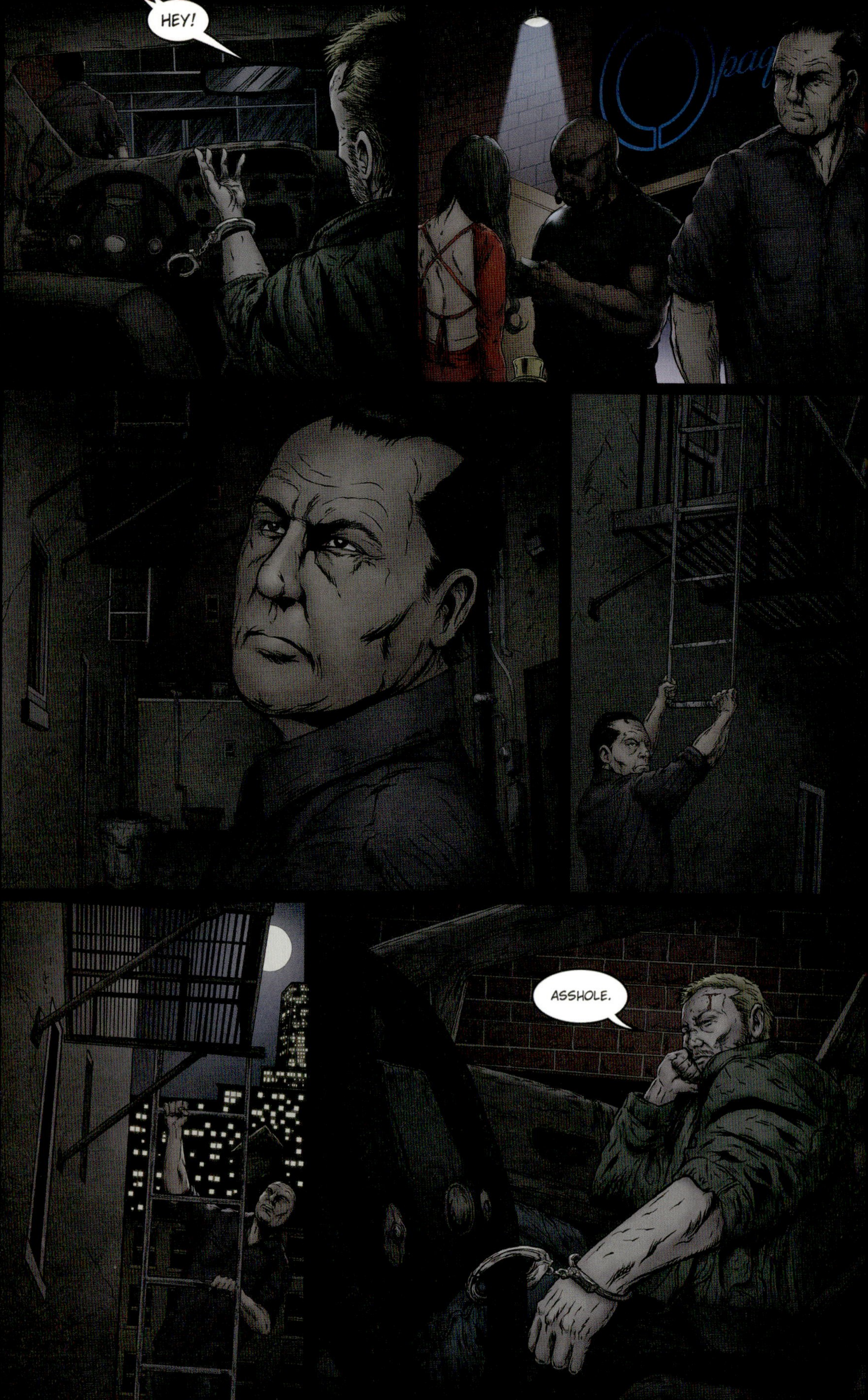
HEY!
paq
ASSHOLE.

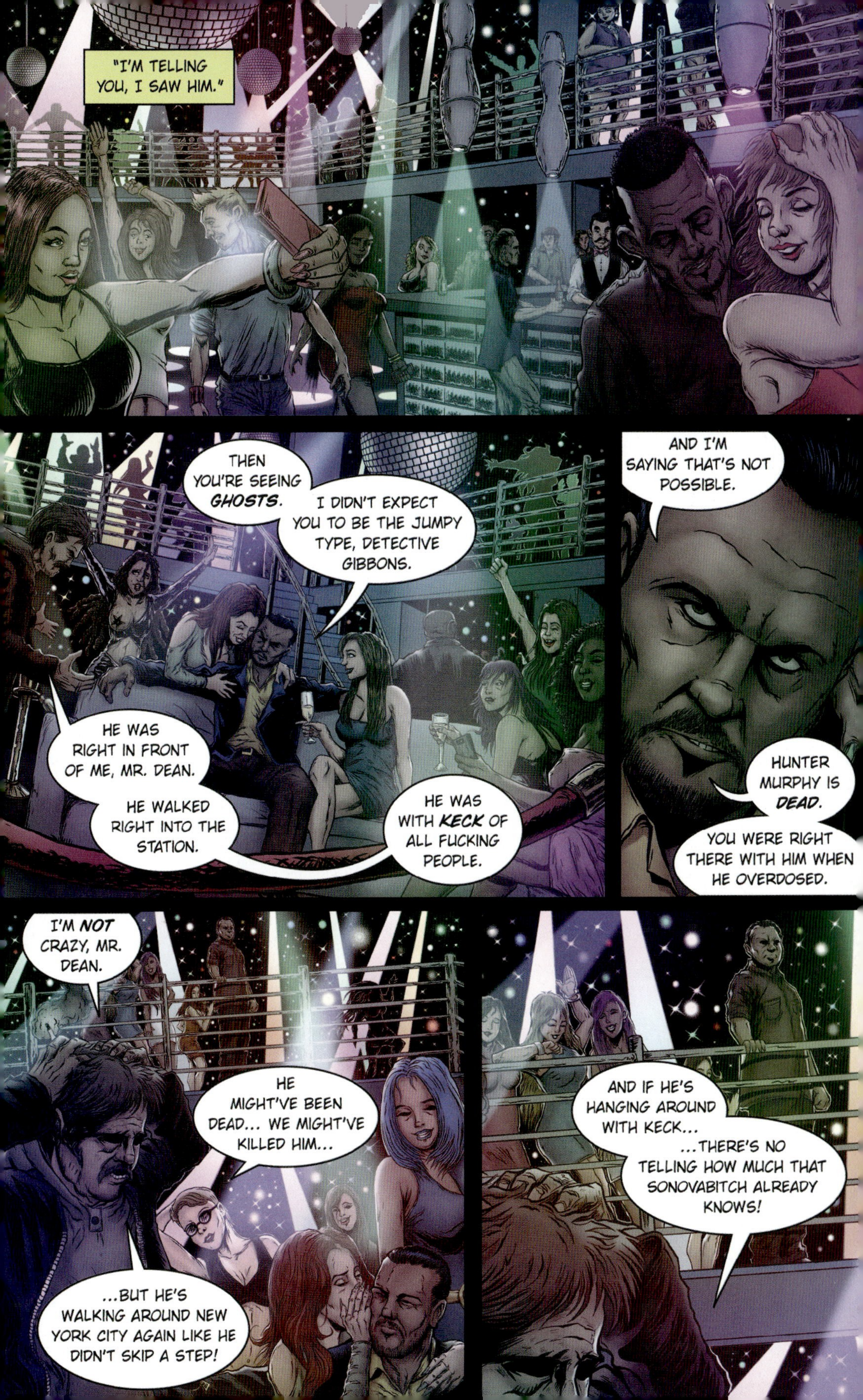
"I'M TELLING YOU, I SAW HIM."
THEN YOU'RE SEEING **GHOSTS**.
I DIDN'T EXPECT YOU TO BE THE JUMPY TYPE, DETECTIVE GIBBONS.
HE WAS RIGHT IN FRONT OF ME, MR. DEAN.
HE WALKED RIGHT INTO THE STATION.
HE WAS WITH **KECK** OF ALL FUCKING PEOPLE.
AND I'M SAYING THAT'S NOT POSSIBLE.
HUNTER MURPHY IS **DEAD**.
YOU WERE RIGHT THERE WITH HIM WHEN HE OVERDOSED.
I'M **NOT** CRAZY, MR. DEAN.
HE MIGHT'VE BEEN DEAD... WE MIGHT'VE KILLED HIM...
...BUT HE'S WALKING AROUND NEW YORK CITY AGAIN LIKE HE DIDN'T SKIP A STEP!
AND IF HE'S HANGING AROUND WITH KECK...
...THERE'S NO TELLING HOW MUCH THAT SONOVABITCH ALREADY KNOWS!

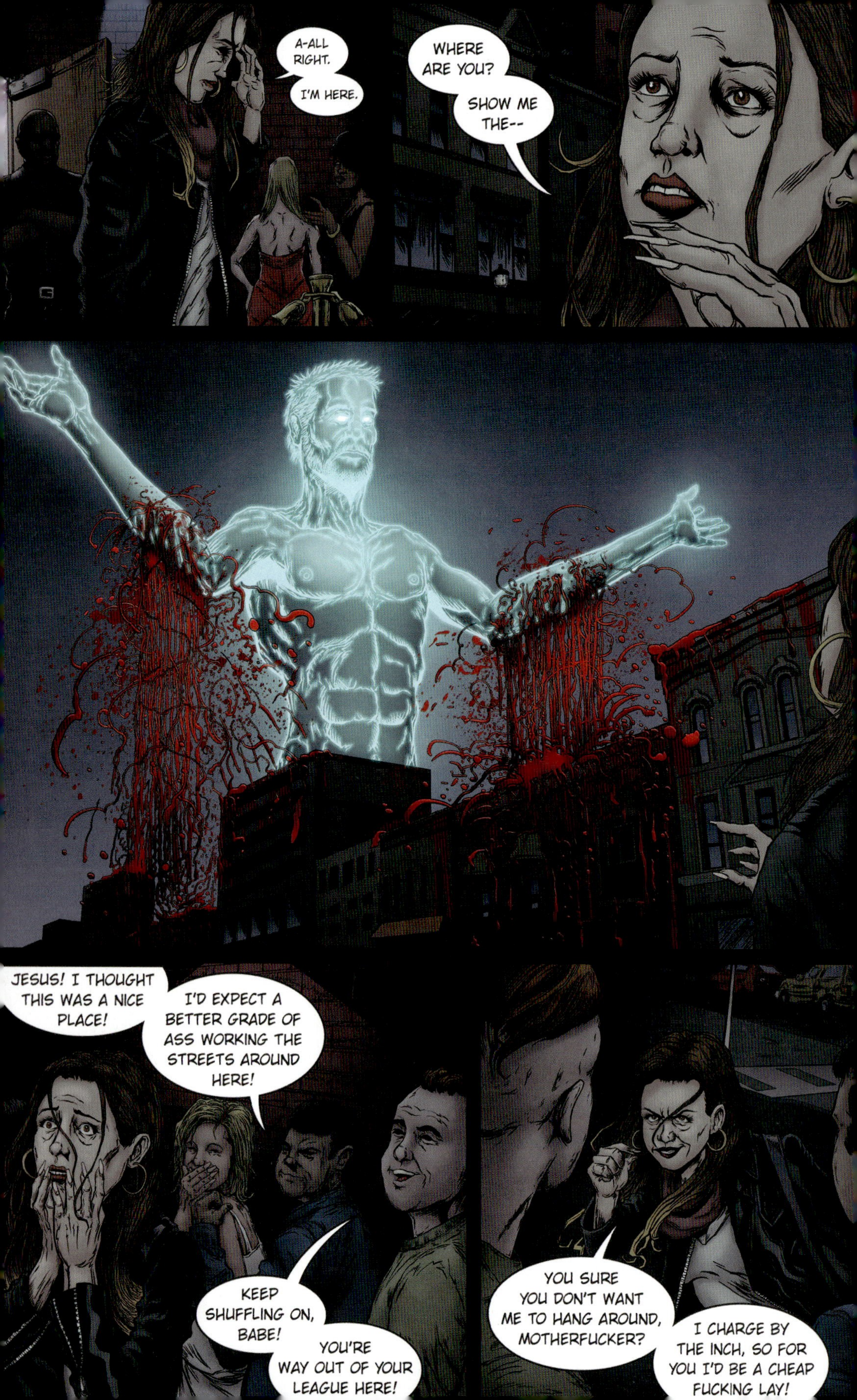
A-ALL RIGHT.
I'M HERE.
WHERE ARE YOU?
SHOW ME THE--
JESUS! I THOUGHT THIS WAS A NICE PLACE!
I'D EXPECT A BETTER GRADE OF ASS WORKING THE STREETS AROUND HERE!
KEEP SHUFFLING ON, BABE!
YOU'RE WAY OUT OF YOUR LEAGUE HERE!
YOU SURE YOU DON'T WANT ME TO HANG AROUND, MOTHERFUCKER?
I CHARGE BY THE INCH, SO FOR YOU I'D BE A CHEAP FUCKING LAY!

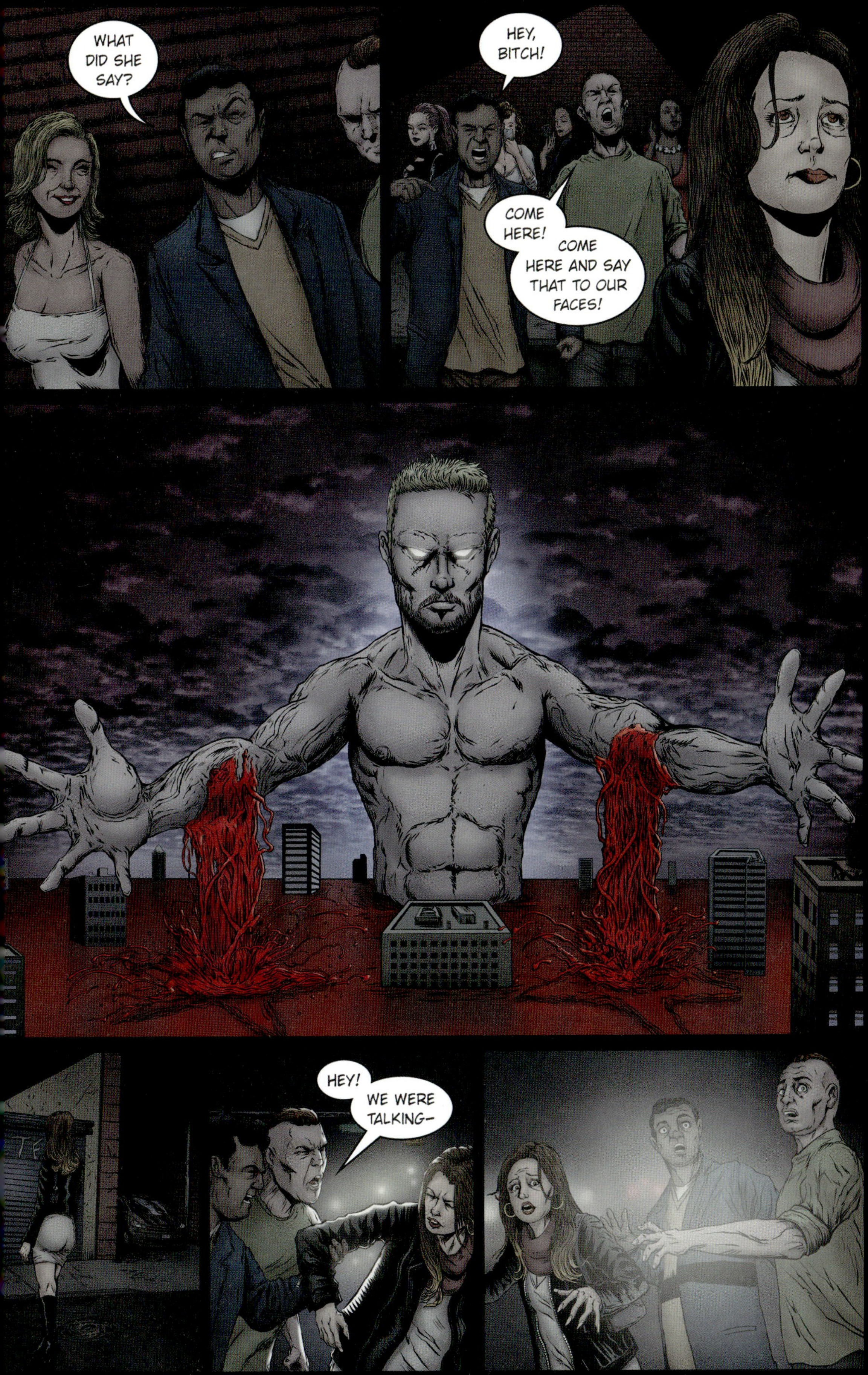
WHAT DID SHE SAY?
HEY, BITCH!
COME HERE!
COME HERE AND SAY THAT TO OUR FACES!
HEY! WE WERE TALKING-

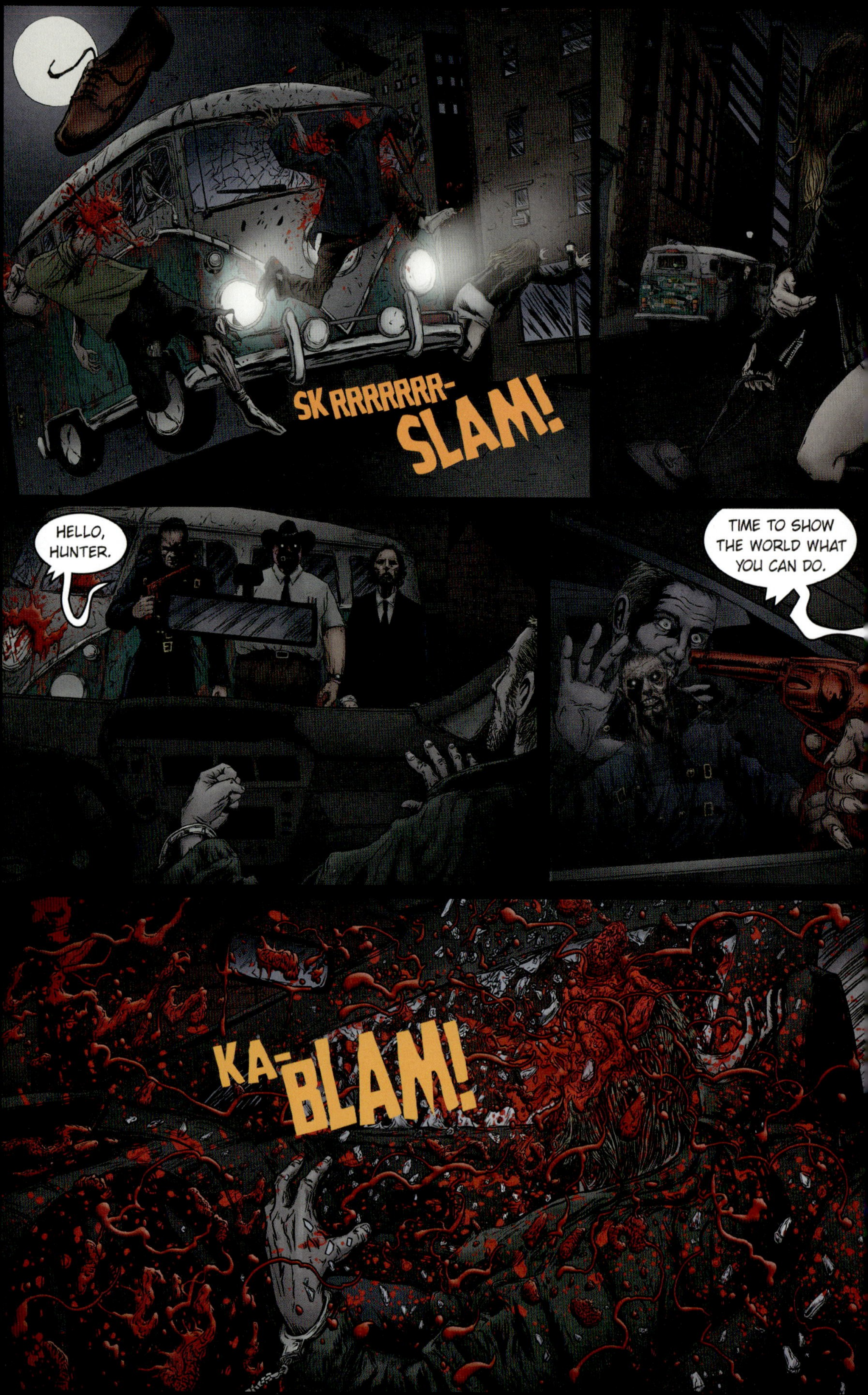
SK RRRRRRR-
SLAM!
HELLO, HUNTER.
TIME TO SHOW THE WORLD WHAT YOU CAN DO.
KA-BLAM!

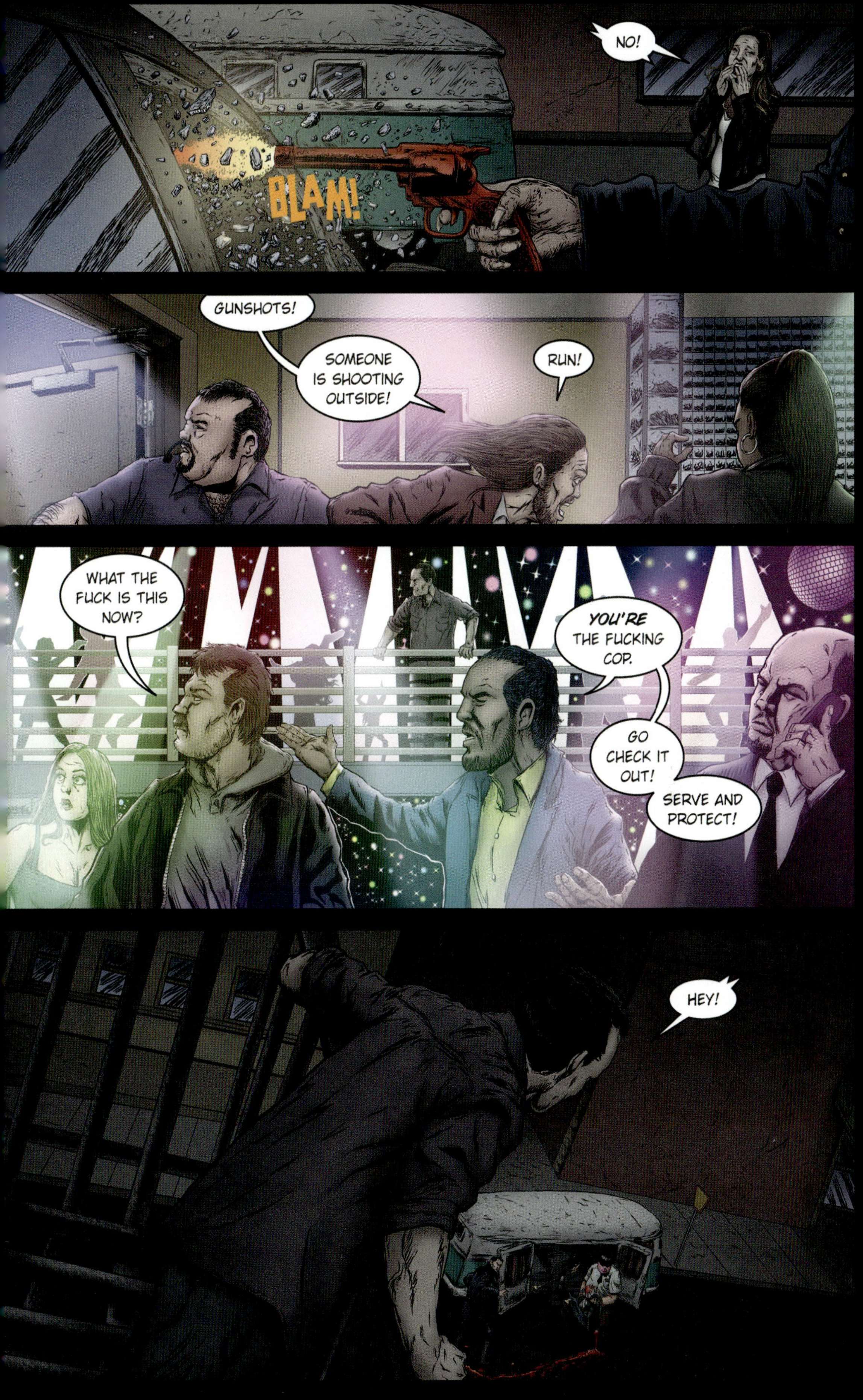
NO!
BLAM!
GUNSHOTS!
SOMEONE IS SHOOTING OUTSIDE!
RUN!
WHAT THE FUCK IS THIS NOW?
YOU'RE THE FUCKING COP.
GO CHECK IT OUT!
SERVE AND PROTECT!
HEY!

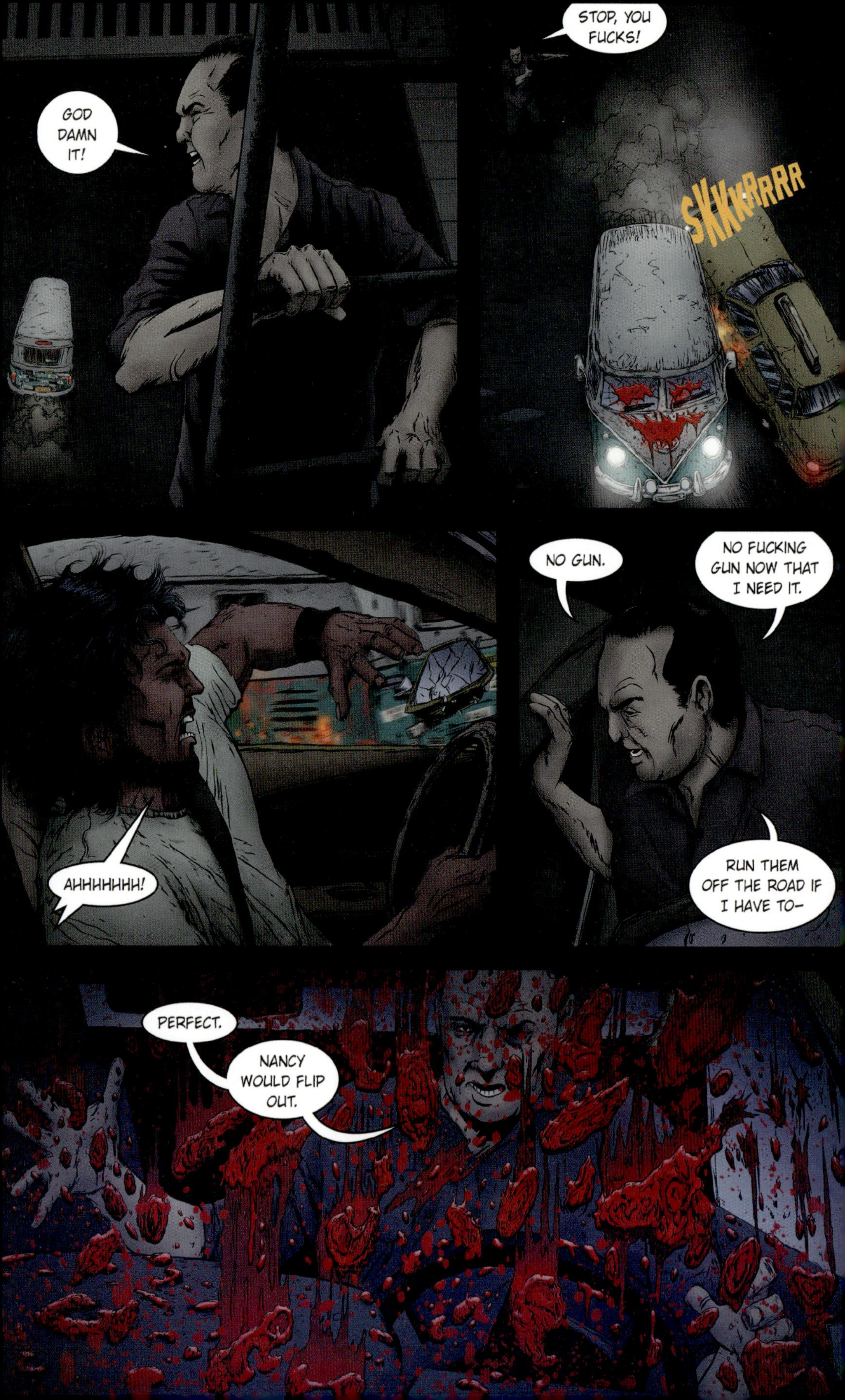
GOD DAMN IT!
STOP, YOU FUCKS!
SKKRRRR
NO GUN.
NO FUCKING GUN NOW THAT I NEED IT.
AHHHHHHH!
RUN THEM OFF THE ROAD IF I HAVE TO-
PERFECT.
NANCY WOULD FLIP OUT.

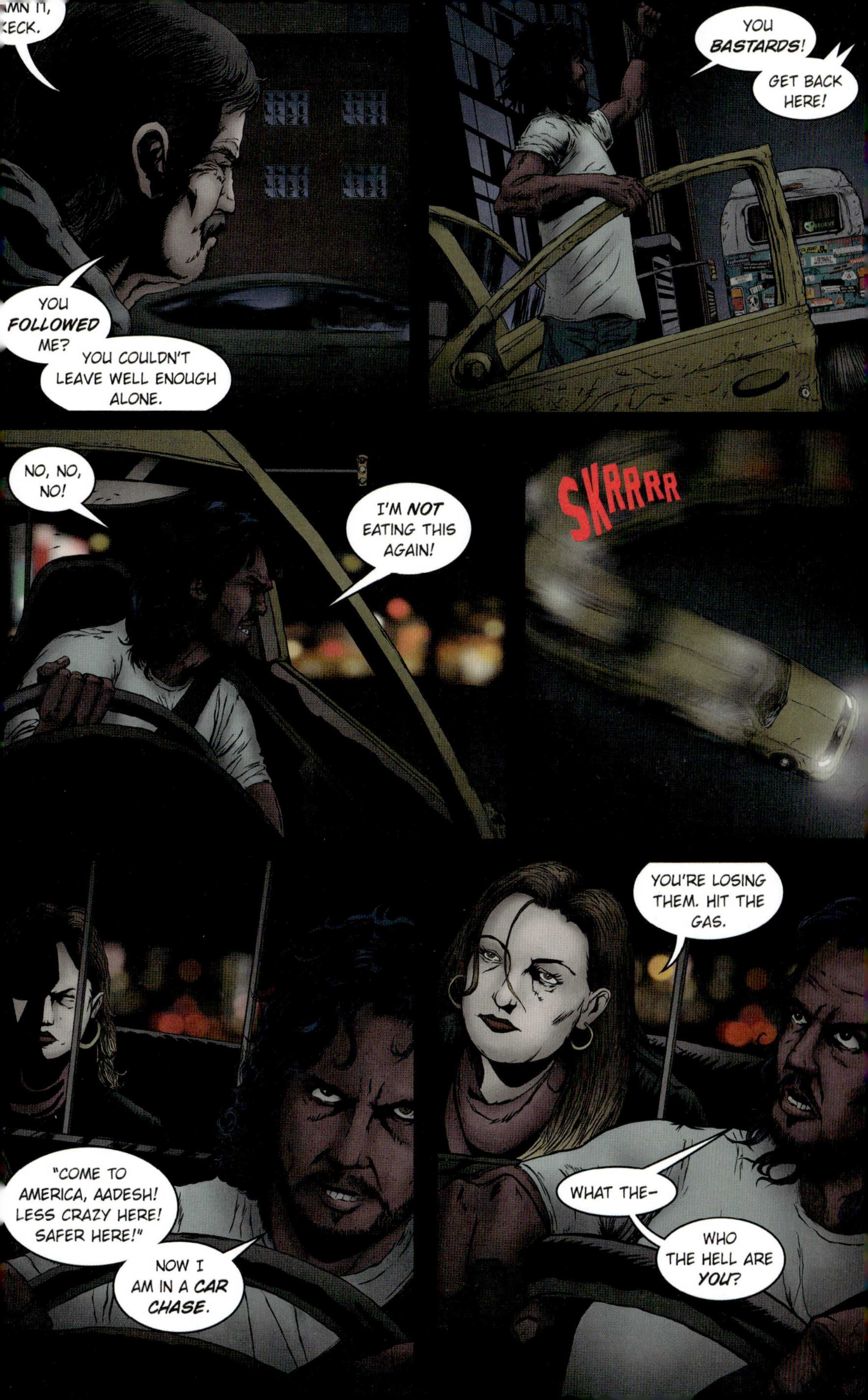

MN IT, ECK.
YOU FOLLOWED ME?
YOU COULDN'T LEAVE WELL ENOUGH ALONE.
YOU BASTARDS!
GET BACK HERE!
NO, NO, NO!
I'M NOT EATING THIS AGAIN!
SKRRRR
"COME TO AMERICA, AADESH! LESS CRAZY HERE! SAFER HERE!"
NOW I AM IN A CAR CHASE.
YOU'RE LOSING THEM. HIT THE GAS.
WHAT THE-
WHO THE HELL ARE YOU?

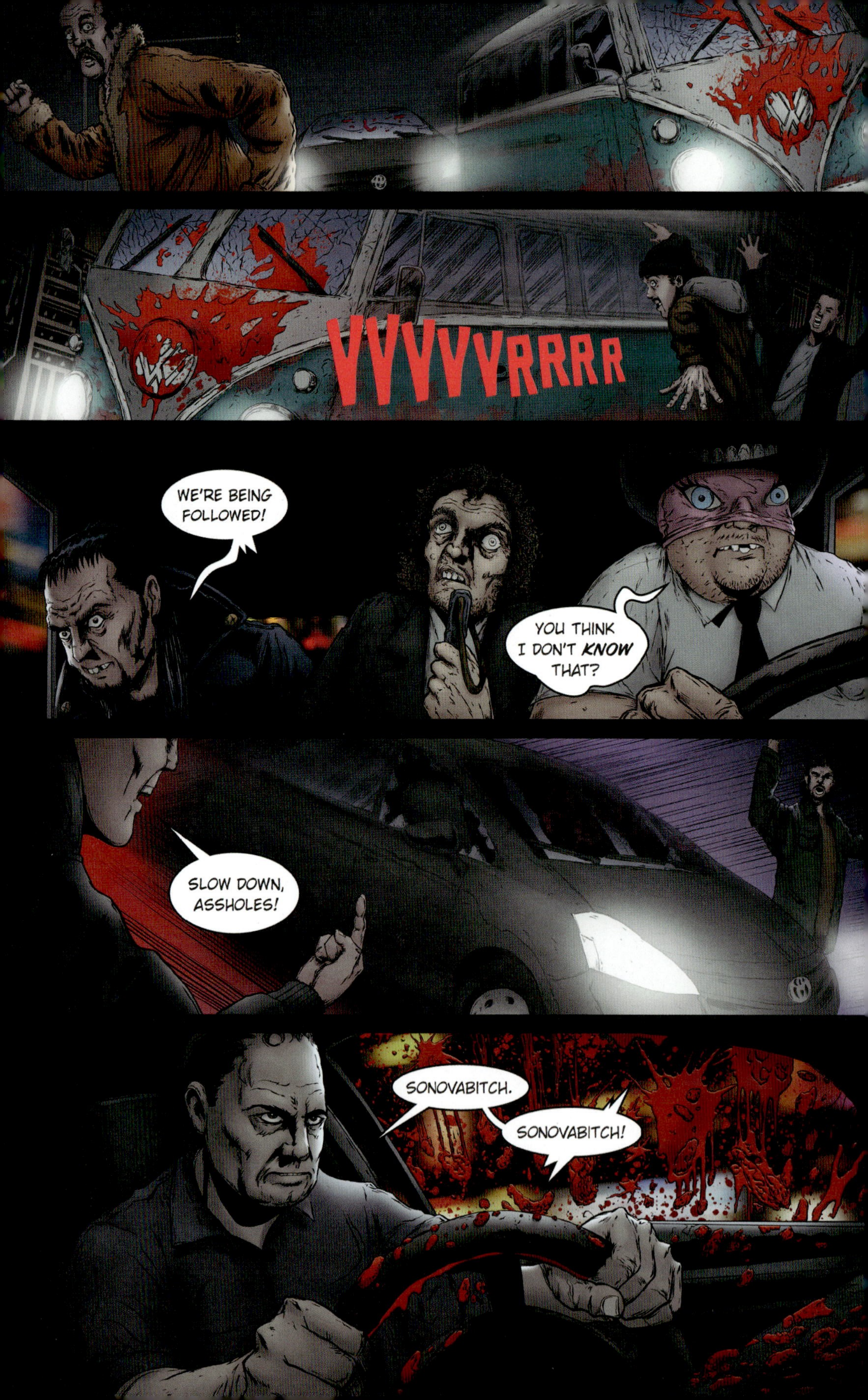
VVVVVRRRR
WE'RE BEING FOLLOWED!
YOU THINK I DON'T ***KNOW*** THAT?
SLOW DOWN, ASSHOLES!
SONOVABITCH.
SONOVABITCH!

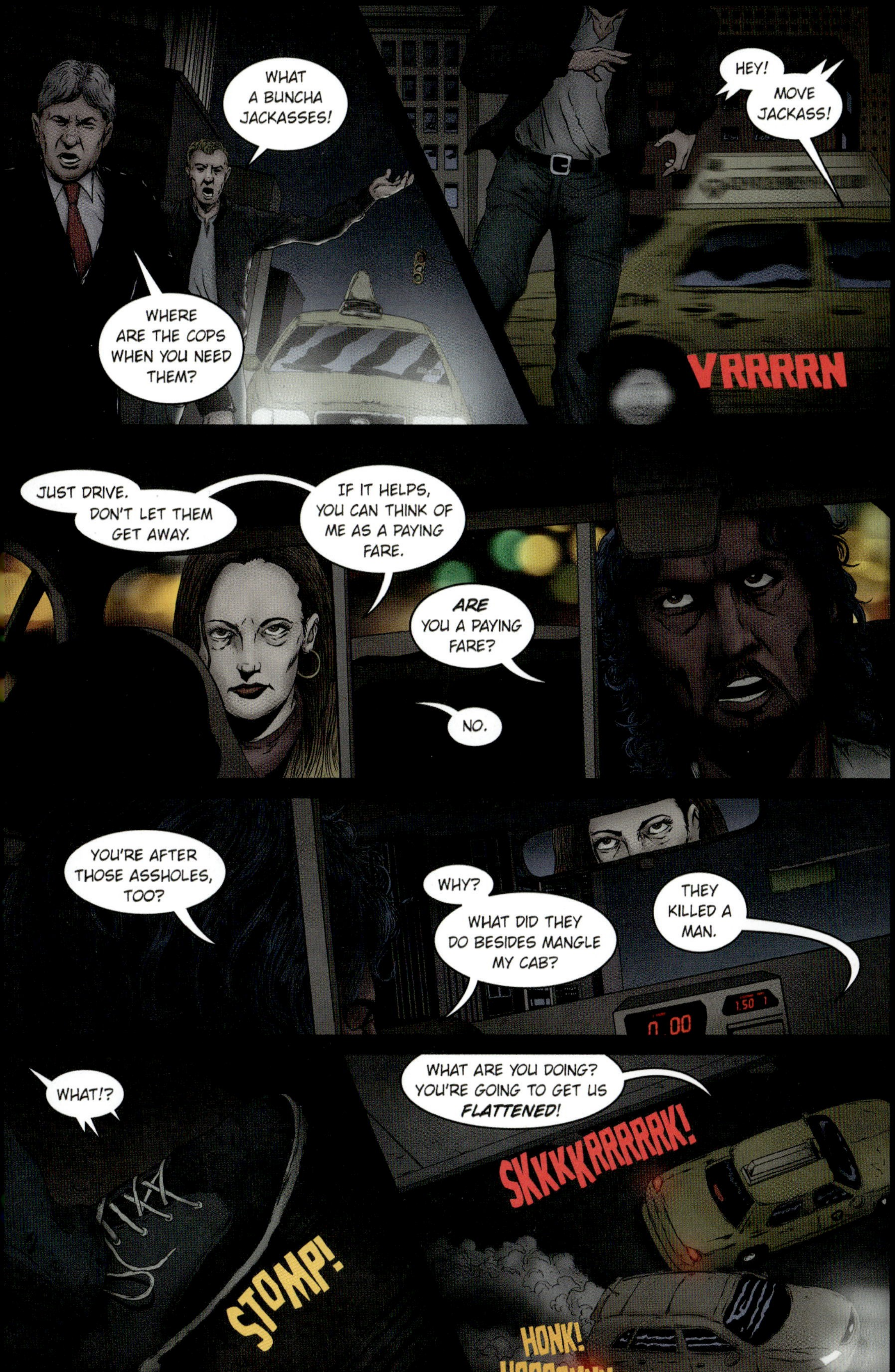
WHAT A BUNCHA JACKASSES!
WHERE ARE THE COPS WHEN YOU NEED THEM?
HEY!
MOVE JACKASS!
VRRRRN
JUST DRIVE. DON'T LET THEM GET AWAY.
IF IT HELPS, YOU CAN THINK OF ME AS A PAYING FARE.
ARE YOU A PAYING FARE?
NO.
YOU'RE AFTER THOSE ASSHOLES, TOO?
WHY?
WHAT DID THEY DO BESIDES MANGLE MY CAB?
THEY KILLED A MAN.
0.00
1.50
WHAT!?
WHAT ARE YOU DOING? YOU'RE GOING TO GET US *FLATTENED*!
SKKKRRRRRK!
STOMP!
HONK! HOOOONNNNNNNK!

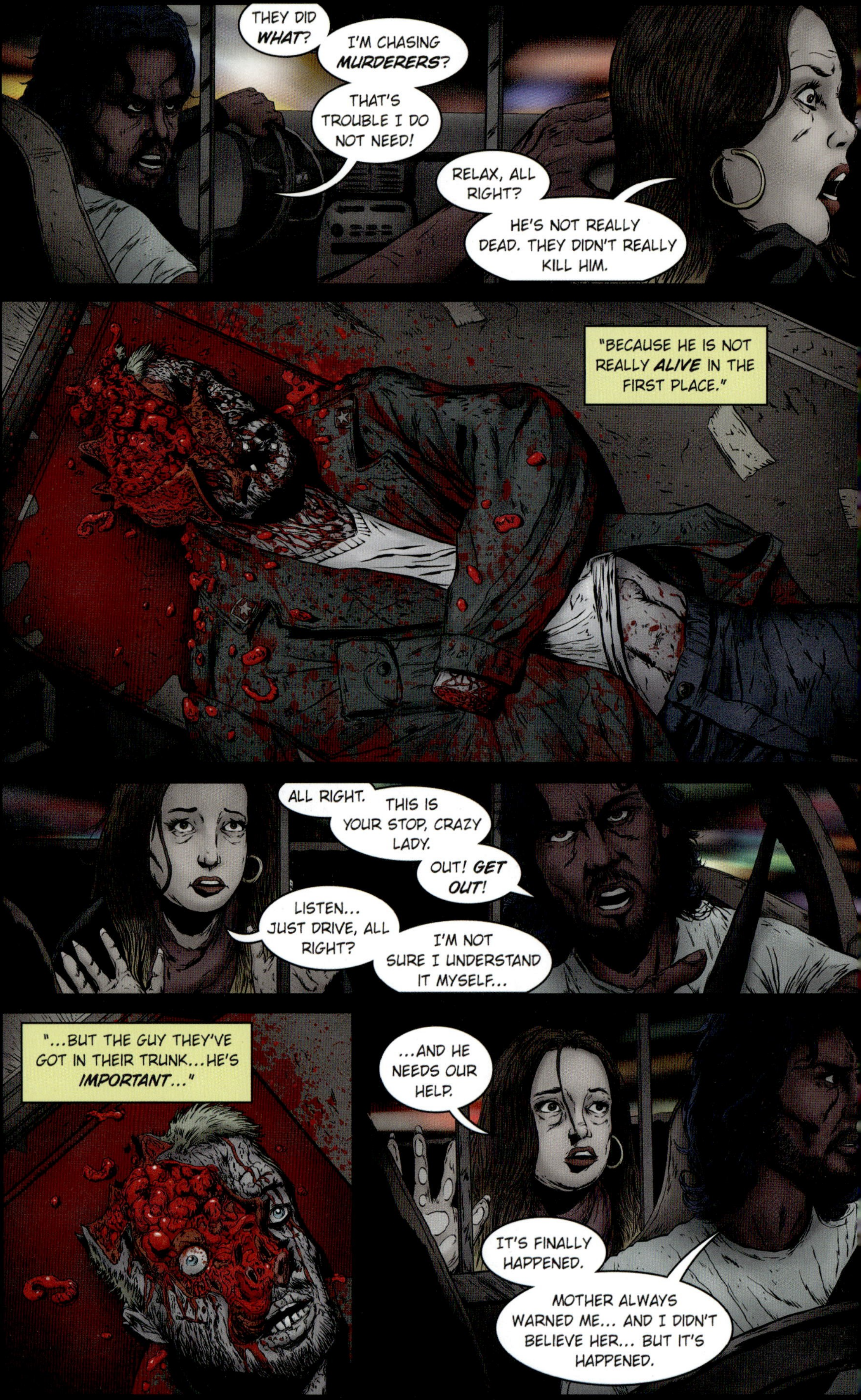
THEY DID WHAT?
I'M CHASING MURDERERS?
THAT'S TROUBLE I DO NOT NEED!
RELAX, ALL RIGHT?
HE'S NOT REALLY DEAD. THEY DIDN'T REALLY KILL HIM.
"BECAUSE HE IS NOT REALLY ALIVE IN THE FIRST PLACE."
ALL RIGHT.
THIS IS YOUR STOP, CRAZY LADY.
OUT! GET OUT!
LISTEN... JUST DRIVE, ALL RIGHT?
I'M NOT SURE I UNDERSTAND IT MYSELF...
"...BUT THE GUY THEY'VE GOT IN THEIR TRUNK...HE'S IMPORTANT..."
...AND HE NEEDS OUR HELP.
IT'S FINALLY HAPPENED.
MOTHER ALWAYS WARNED ME... AND I DIDN'T BELIEVE HER... BUT IT'S HAPPENED.

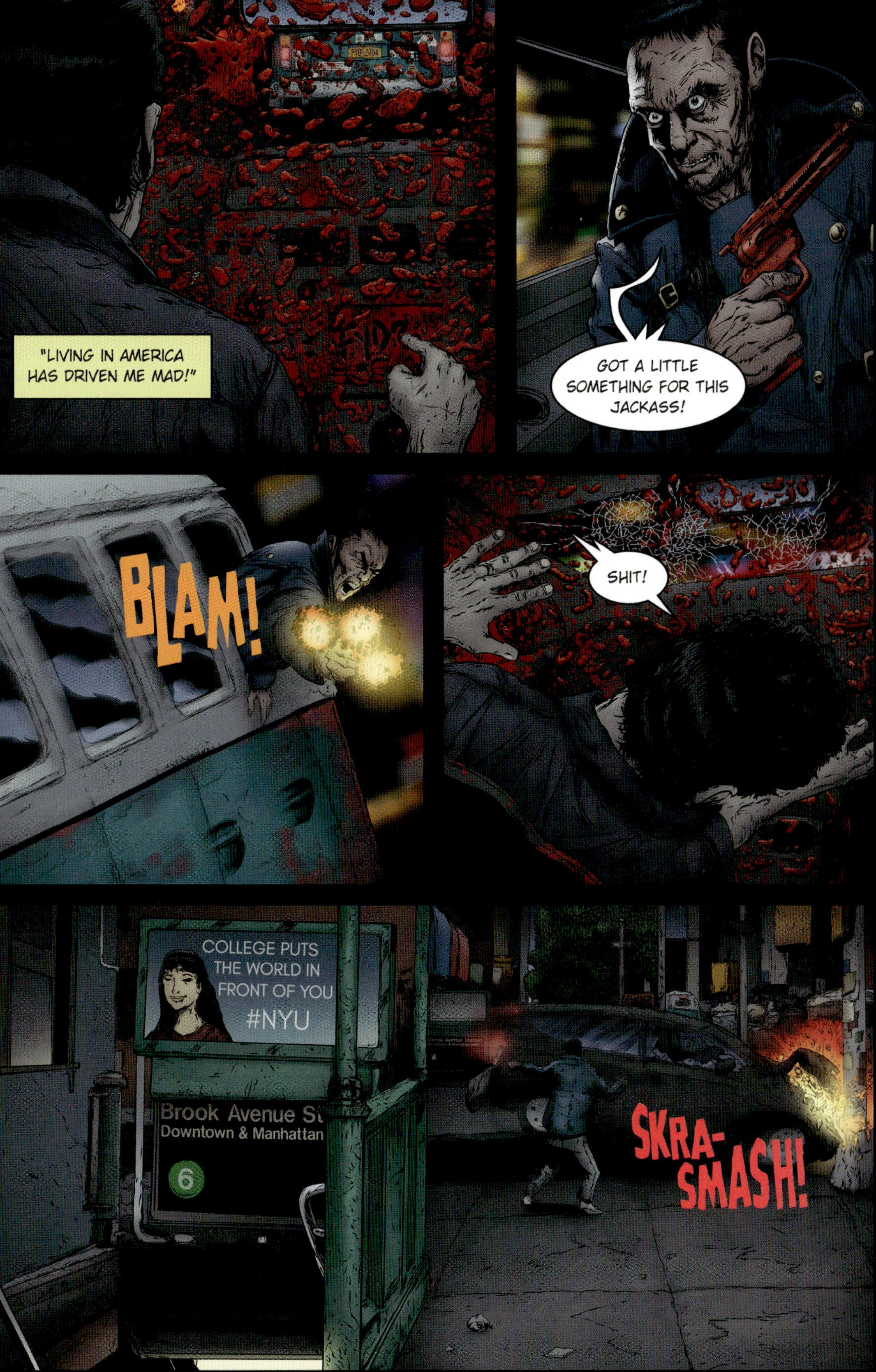
"LIVING IN AMERICA HAS DRIVEN ME MAD!"
GOT A LITTLE SOMETHING FOR THIS JACKASS!
BLAM!
SHIT!
COLLEGE PUTS THE WORLD IN FRONT OF YOU
#NYU
Brook Avenue St
Downtown & Manhattan
6
SKRA-SMASH!

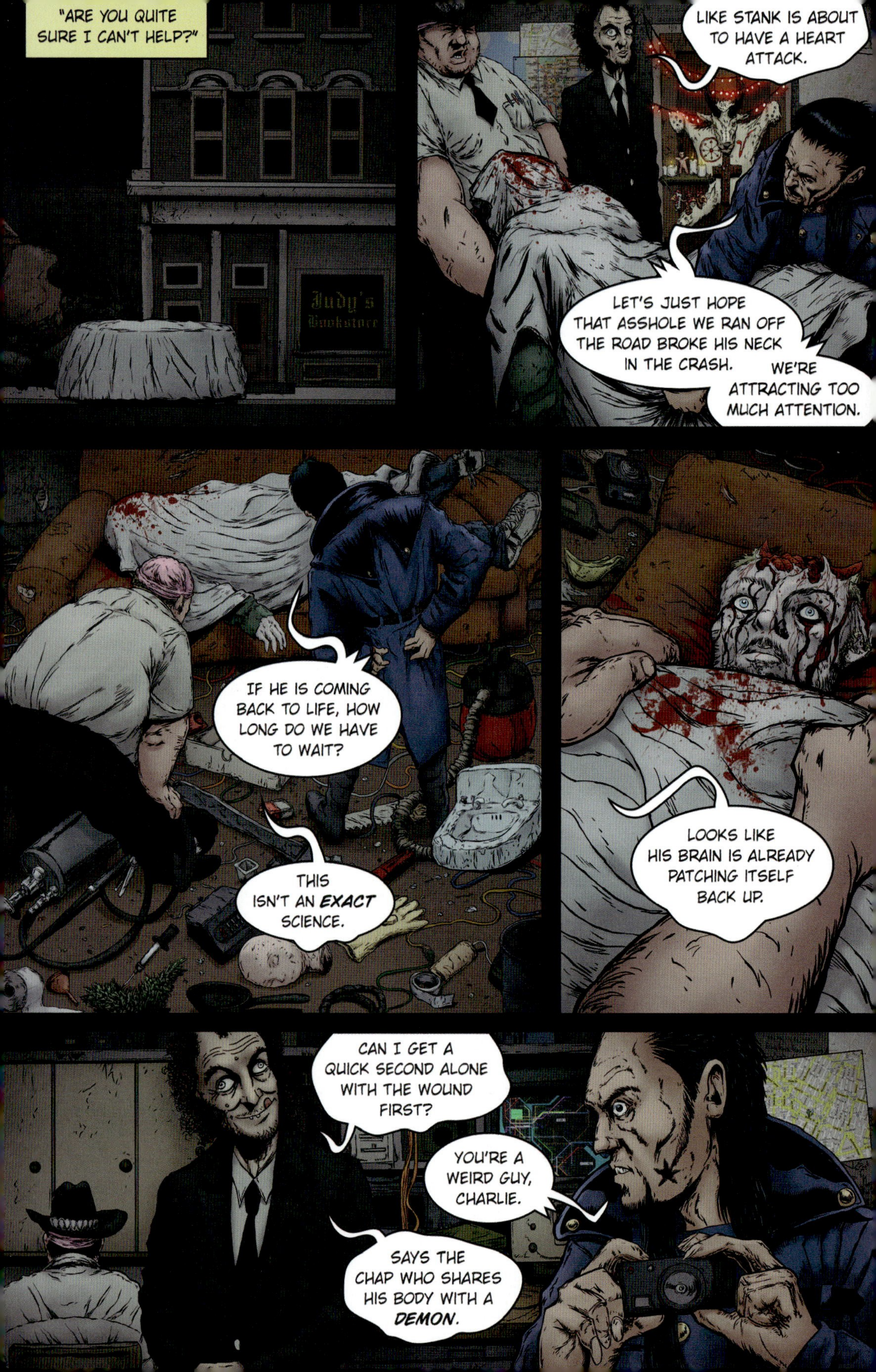
"ARE YOU QUITE SURE I CAN'T HELP?"
Judy's Bookstore
LIKE STANK IS ABOUT TO HAVE A HEART ATTACK.
LET'S JUST HOPE THAT ASSHOLE WE RAN OFF THE ROAD BROKE HIS NECK IN THE CRASH.
WE'RE ATTRACTING TOO MUCH ATTENTION.
IF HE IS COMING BACK TO LIFE, HOW LONG DO WE HAVE TO WAIT?
THIS ISN'T AN EXACT SCIENCE.
LOOKS LIKE HIS BRAIN IS ALREADY PATCHING ITSELF BACK UP.
CAN I GET A QUICK SECOND ALONE WITH THE WOUND FIRST?
YOU'RE A WEIRD GUY, CHARLIE.
SAYS THE CHAP WHO SHARES HIS BODY WITH A DEMON.

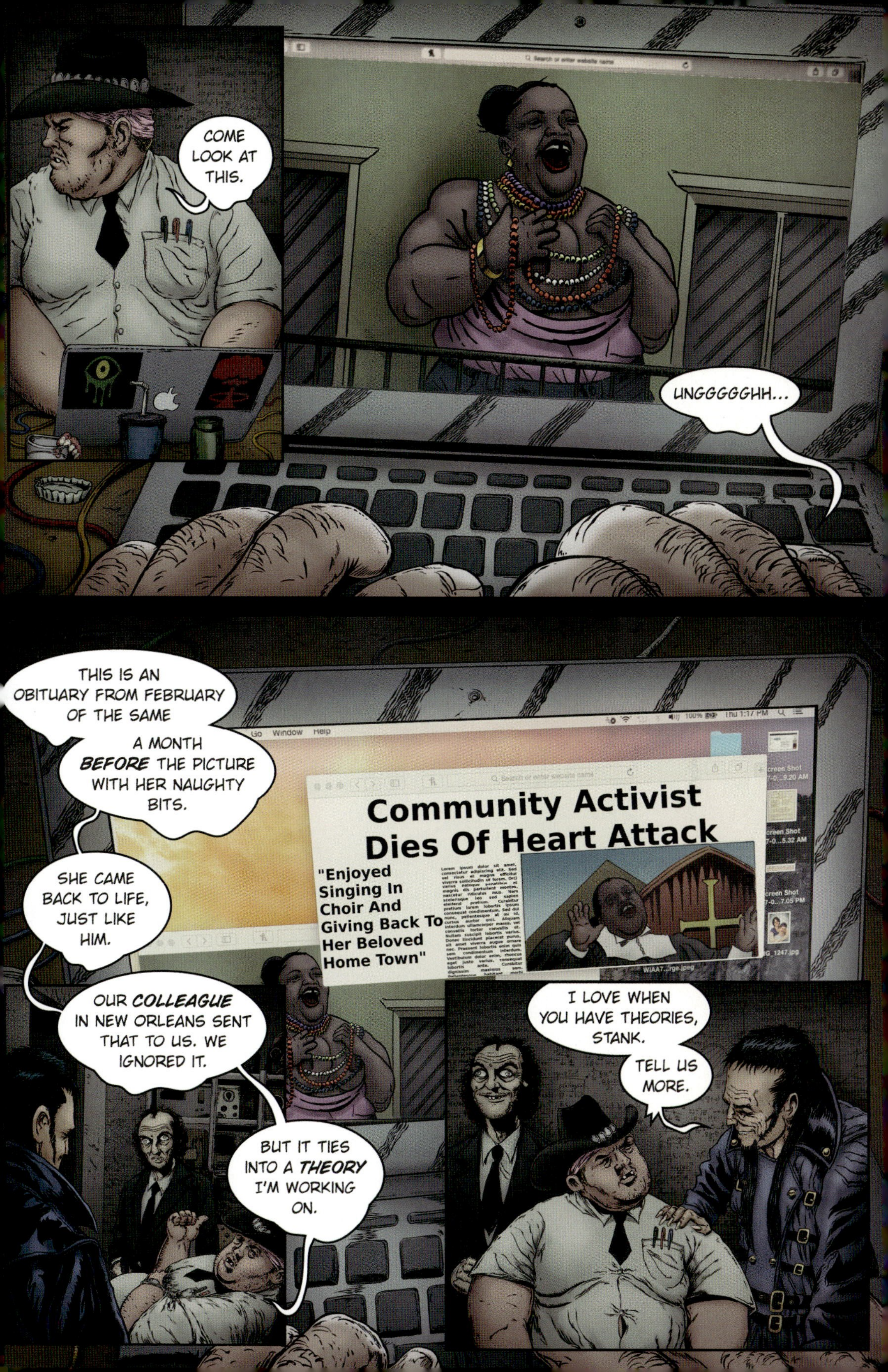
COME LOOK AT THIS.
UNGGGGGHH...
THIS IS AN OBITUARY FROM FEBRUARY OF THE SAME
A MONTH ***BEFORE*** THE PICTURE WITH HER NAUGHTY BITS.
Community Activist Dies Of Heart Attack
"Enjoyed Singing In Choir And Giving Back To Her Beloved Home Town"
SHE CAME BACK TO LIFE, JUST LIKE HIM.
OUR ***COLLEAGUE*** IN NEW ORLEANS SENT THAT TO US. WE IGNORED IT.
BUT IT TIES INTO A ***THEORY*** I'M WORKING ON.
I LOVE WHEN YOU HAVE THEORIES, STANK.
TELL US MORE.

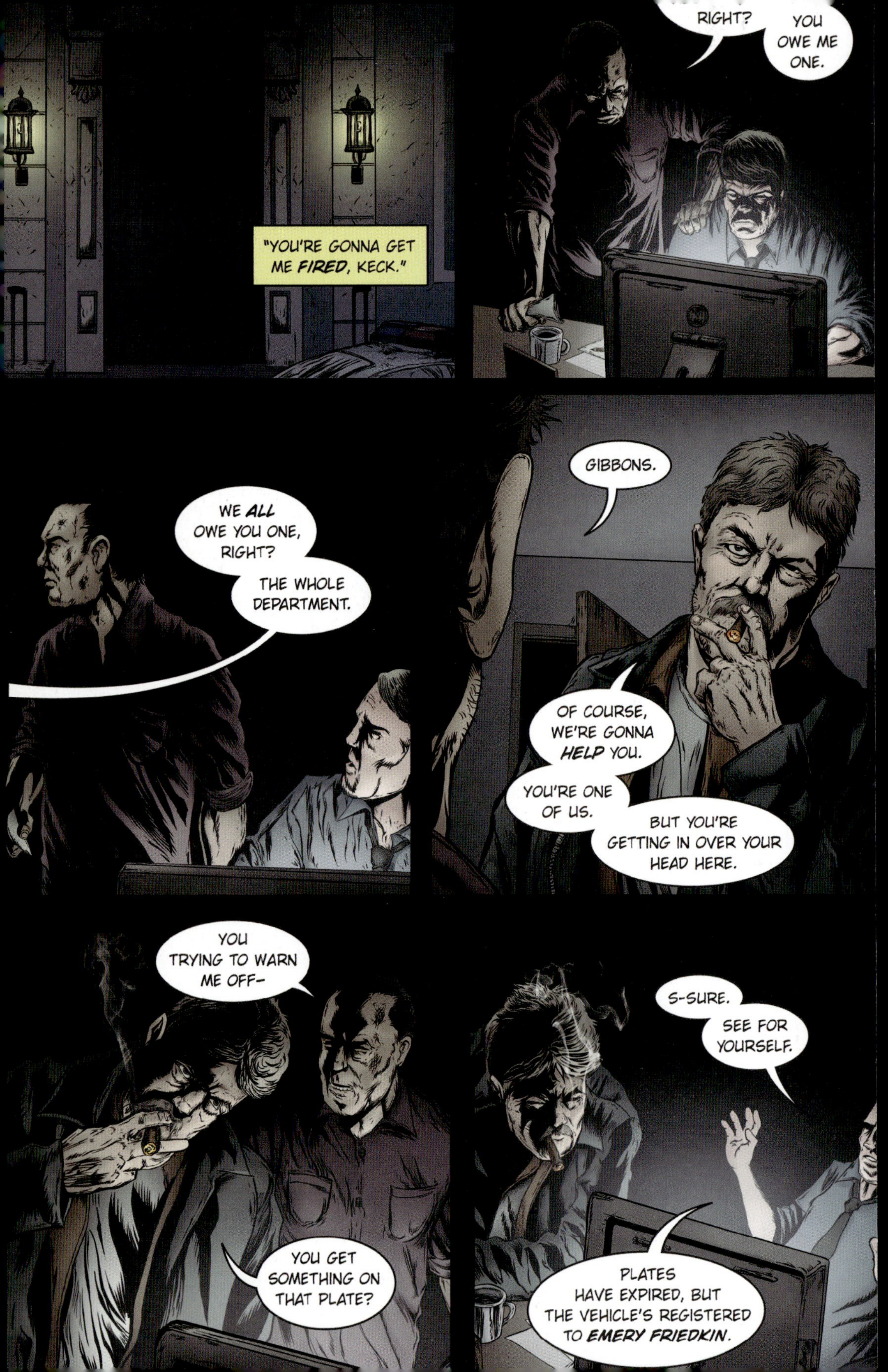
"YOU'RE GONNA GET ME *FIRED*, KECK."
RIGHT?
YOU OWE ME ONE.
WE *ALL* OWE YOU ONE, RIGHT?
THE WHOLE DEPARTMENT.
GIBBONS.
OF COURSE, WE'RE GONNA *HELP* YOU.
YOU'RE ONE OF US.
BUT YOU'RE GETTING IN OVER YOUR HEAD HERE.
YOU TRYING TO WARN ME OFF-
YOU GET SOMETHING ON THAT PLATE?
S-SURE.
SEE FOR YOURSELF.
PLATES HAVE EXPIRED, BUT THE VEHICLE'S REGISTERED TO *EMERY FRIEDKIN*.

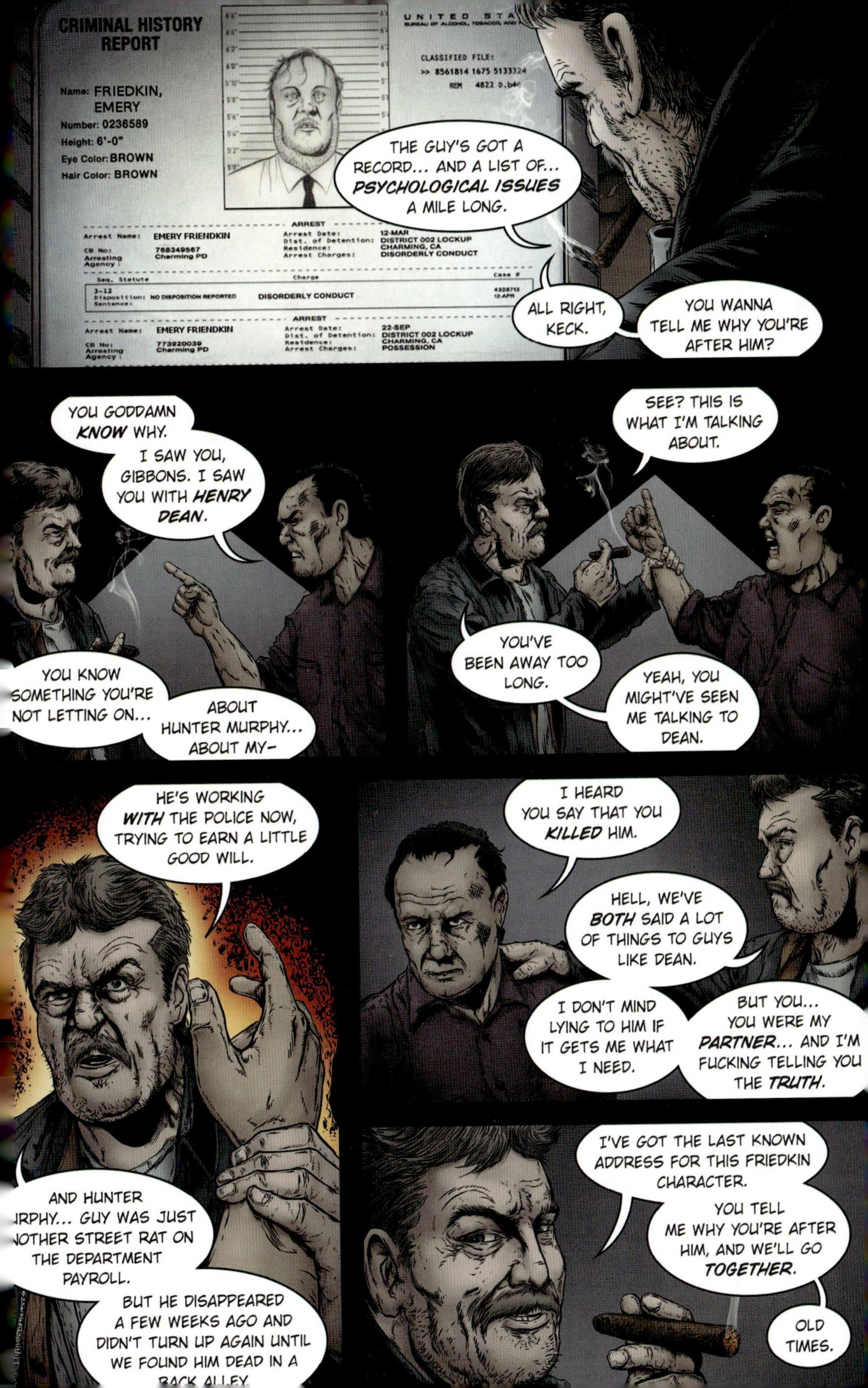
CRIMINAL HISTORY REPORT
Name: FRIEDKIN, EMERY
Number: 0236589
Height: 6'-0"
Eye Color: BROWN
Hair Color: BROWN
UNITED STA
CLASSIFIED FILE:
>> 8561814 1675 5133324
ARREST
Arrest Name: EMERY FRIENDKIN
Arresting Agency: Charming PD
Arrest Date: 12-MAR
Dist. of Detention: DISTRICT 002 LOCKUP
Residence: CHARMING, CA
Arrest Charges: DISORDERLY CONDUCT
Disposition: NO DISPOSITION REPORTED
DISORDERLY CONDUCT
ARREST
Arrest Name: EMERY FRIENDKIN
Arresting Agency: Charming PD
Arrest Date: 22-SEP
Dist. of Detention: DISTRICT 002 LOCKUP
Residence: CHARMING, CA
Arrest Charges: POSSESSION
THE GUY'S GOT A RECORD... AND A LIST OF... PSYCHOLOGICAL ISSUES A MILE LONG.
ALL RIGHT, KECK.
YOU WANNA TELL ME WHY YOU'RE AFTER HIM?
YOU GODDAMN KNOW WHY.
I SAW YOU, GIBBONS. I SAW YOU WITH HENRY DEAN.
YOU KNOW SOMETHING YOU'RE NOT LETTING ON...
ABOUT HUNTER MURPHY... ABOUT MY–
SEE? THIS IS WHAT I'M TALKING ABOUT.
YOU'VE BEEN AWAY TOO LONG.
YEAH, YOU MIGHT'VE SEEN ME TALKING TO DEAN.
HE'S WORKING WITH THE POLICE NOW, TRYING TO EARN A LITTLE GOOD WILL.
AND HUNTER RPHY... GUY WAS JUST NOTHER STREET RAT ON THE DEPARTMENT PAYROLL.
BUT HE DISAPPEARED A FEW WEEKS AGO AND DIDN'T TURN UP AGAIN UNTIL WE FOUND HIM DEAD IN A BACK ALLEY.
I HEARD YOU SAY THAT YOU KILLED HIM.
HELL, WE'VE BOTH SAID A LOT OF THINGS TO GUYS LIKE DEAN.
I DON'T MIND LYING TO HIM IF IT GETS ME WHAT I NEED.
BUT YOU... YOU WERE MY PARTNER... AND I'M FUCKING TELLING YOU THE TRUTH.
I'VE GOT THE LAST KNOWN ADDRESS FOR THIS FRIEDKIN CHARACTER.
YOU TELL ME WHY YOU'RE AFTER HIM, AND WE'LL GO TOGETHER.
OLD TIMES.

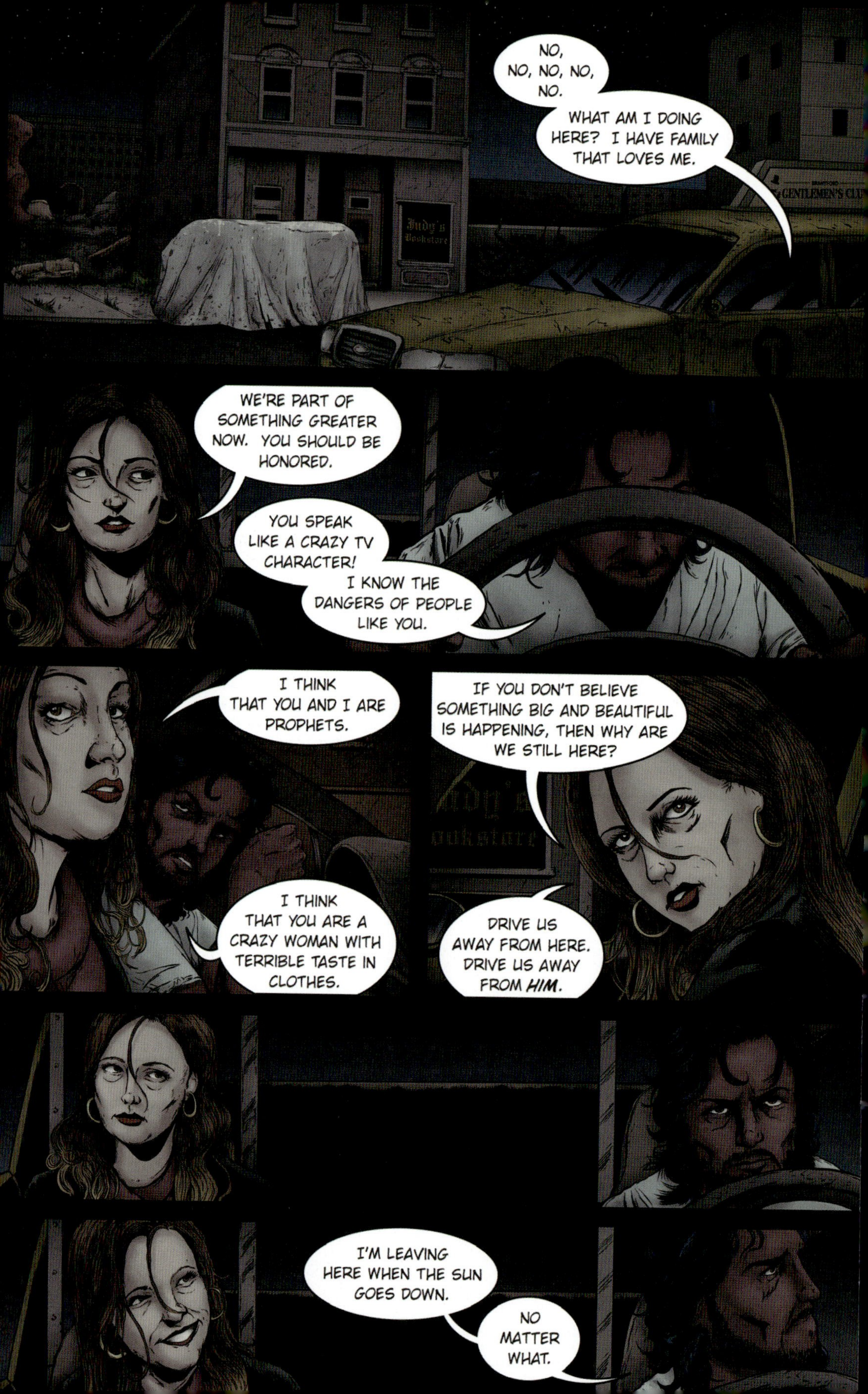
NO, NO, NO, NO, NO.
WHAT AM I DOING HERE? I HAVE FAMILY THAT LOVES ME.
Judy's Bookstore
GENTLEMEN'S CLU
WE'RE PART OF SOMETHING GREATER NOW. YOU SHOULD BE HONORED.
YOU SPEAK LIKE A CRAZY TV CHARACTER!
I KNOW THE DANGERS OF PEOPLE LIKE YOU.
I THINK THAT YOU AND I ARE PROPHETS.
I THINK THAT YOU ARE A CRAZY WOMAN WITH TERRIBLE TASTE IN CLOTHES.
IF YOU DON'T BELIEVE SOMETHING BIG AND BEAUTIFUL IS HAPPENING, THEN WHY ARE WE STILL HERE?
DRIVE US AWAY FROM HERE. DRIVE US AWAY FROM *HIM*.
I'M LEAVING HERE WHEN THE SUN GOES DOWN.
NO MATTER WHAT.

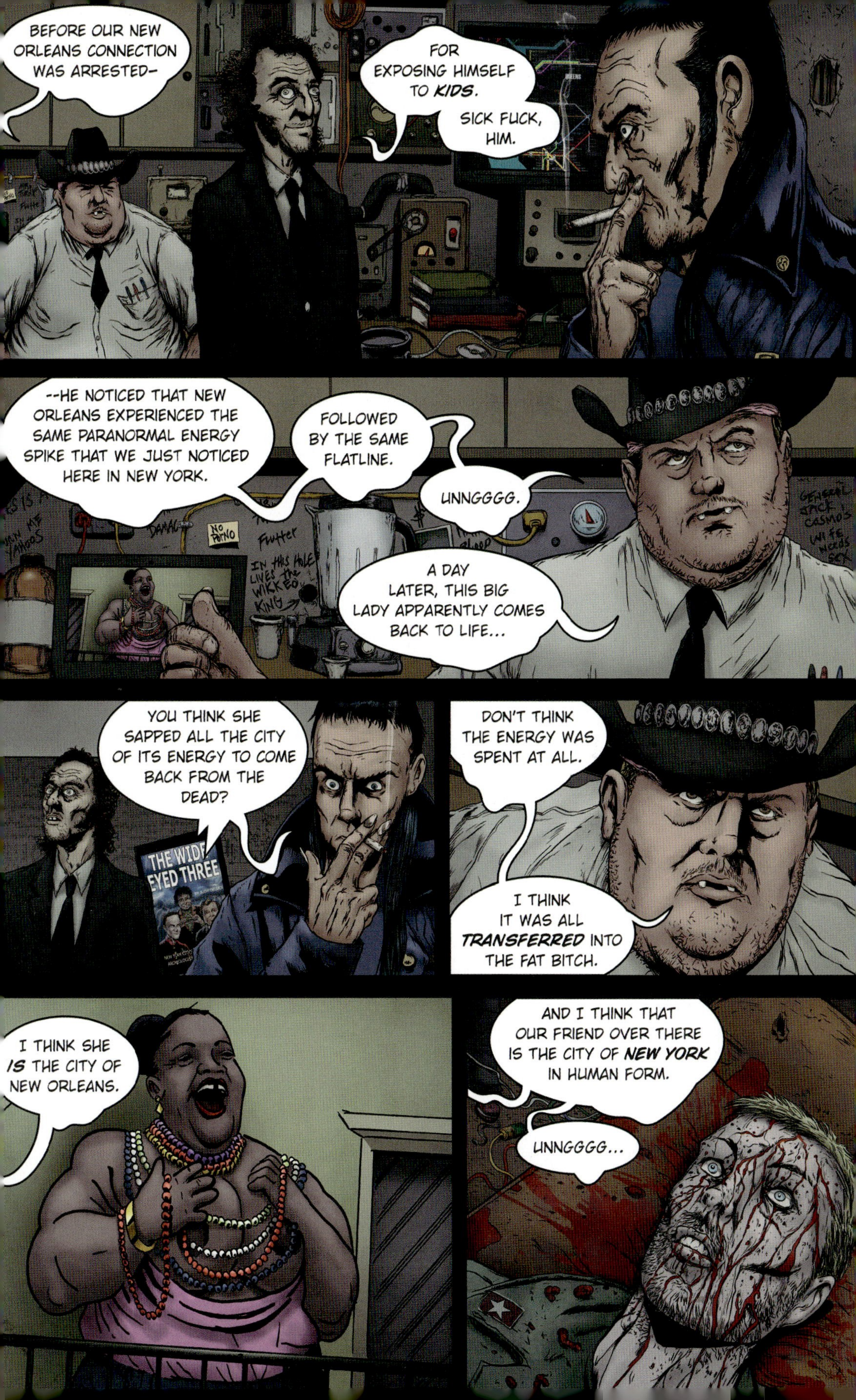
BEFORE OUR NEW ORLEANS CONNECTION WAS ARRESTED-
FOR EXPOSING HIMSELF TO **KIDS.**
SICK FUCK, HIM.
--HE NOTICED THAT NEW ORLEANS EXPERIENCED THE SAME PARANORMAL ENERGY SPIKE THAT WE JUST NOTICED HERE IN NEW YORK.
FOLLOWED BY THE SAME FLATLINE.
UNNGGGG.
A DAY LATER, THIS BIG LADY APPARENTLY COMES BACK TO LIFE...
YOU THINK SHE SAPPED ALL THE CITY OF ITS ENERGY TO COME BACK FROM THE DEAD?
THE WIDE EYED THREE
DON'T THINK THE ENERGY WAS SPENT AT ALL.
I THINK IT WAS ALL ***TRANSFERRED*** INTO THE FAT BITCH.
I THINK SHE ***IS*** THE CITY OF NEW ORLEANS.
AND I THINK THAT OUR FRIEND OVER THERE IS THE CITY OF ***NEW YORK*** IN HUMAN FORM.
UNNGGGG...

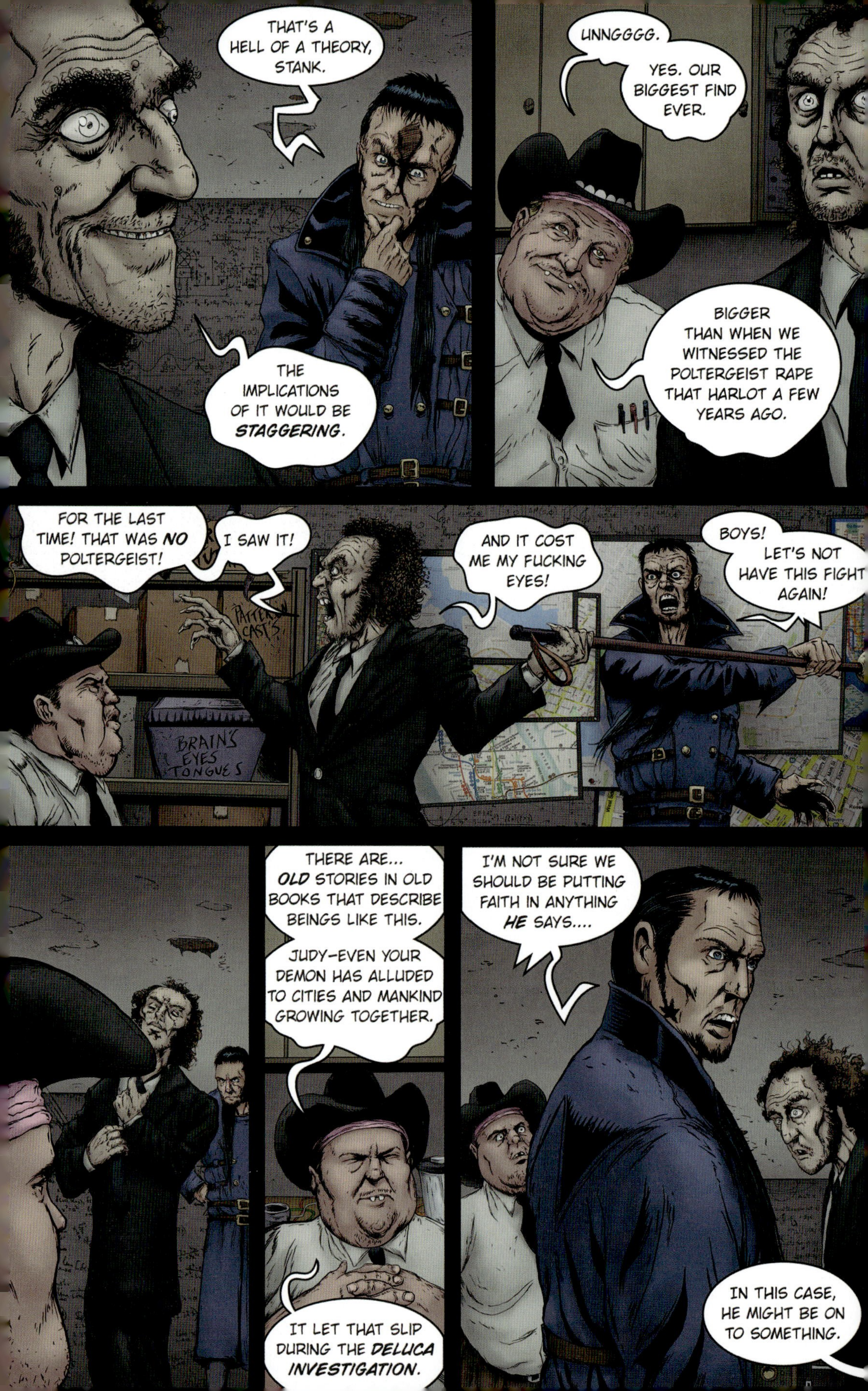
THAT'S A HELL OF A THEORY, STANK.
THE IMPLICATIONS OF IT WOULD BE **STAGGERING**.
UNNGGGG.
YES. OUR BIGGEST FIND EVER.
BIGGER THAN WHEN WE WITNESSED THE POLTERGEIST RAPE THAT HARLOT A FEW YEARS AGO.
FOR THE LAST TIME! THAT WAS **NO** POLTERGEIST!
I SAW IT!
AND IT COST ME MY FUCKING EYES!
BOYS! LET'S NOT HAVE THIS FIGHT AGAIN!
BRAINS EYES TONGUES
THERE ARE... **OLD** STORIES IN OLD BOOKS THAT DESCRIBE BEINGS LIKE THIS.
JUDY–EVEN YOUR DEMON HAS ALLUDED TO CITIES AND MANKIND GROWING TOGETHER.
IT LET THAT SLIP DURING THE **DELUCA INVESTIGATION**.
I'M NOT SURE WE SHOULD BE PUTTING FAITH IN ANYTHING **HE** SAYS....
IN THIS CASE, HE MIGHT BE ON TO SOMETHING.

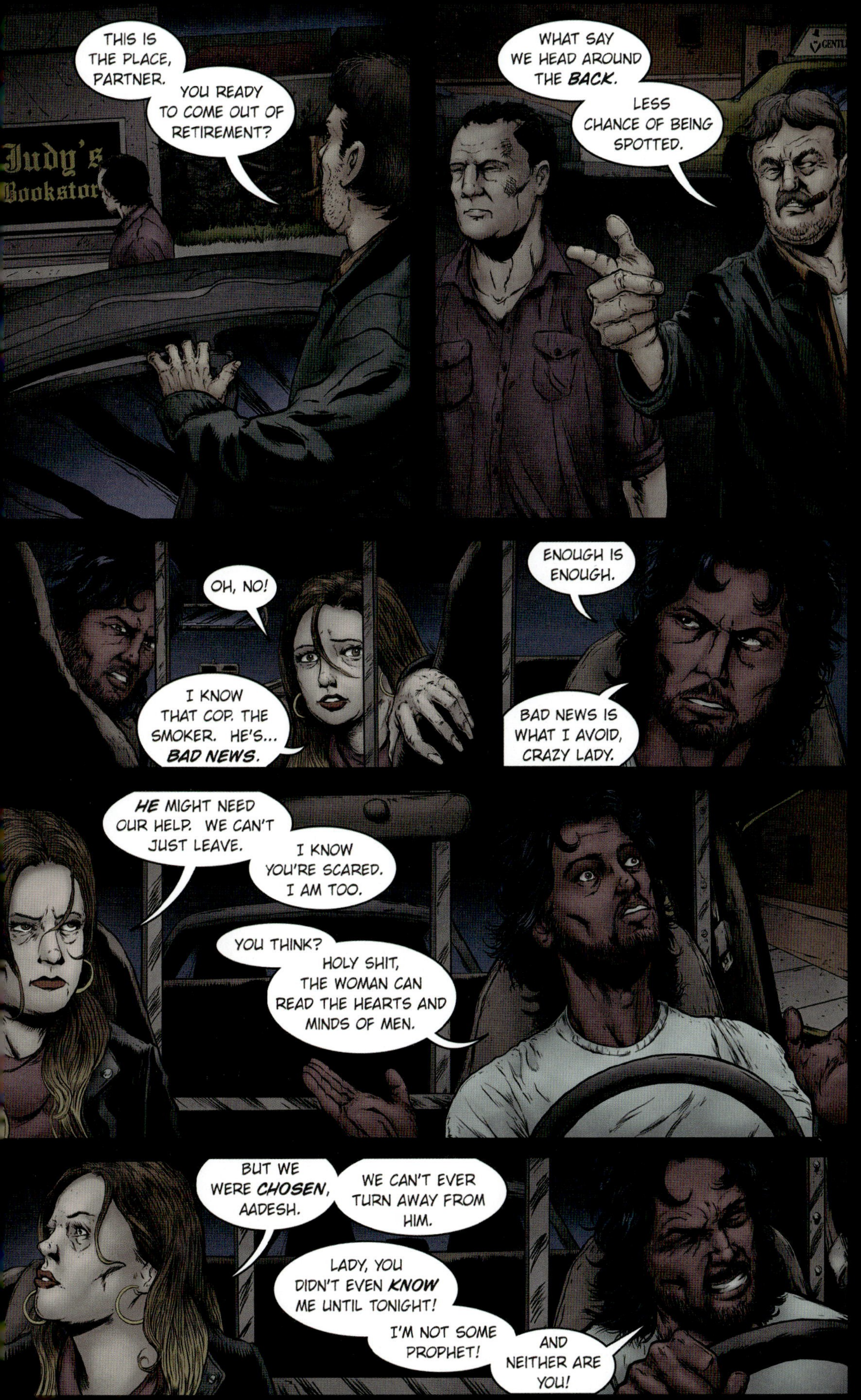
Judy's Bookstore
THIS IS THE PLACE, PARTNER.
YOU READY TO COME OUT OF RETIREMENT?
WHAT SAY WE HEAD AROUND THE BACK.
LESS CHANCE OF BEING SPOTTED.
OH, NO!
I KNOW THAT COP. THE SMOKER. HE'S... BAD NEWS.
ENOUGH IS ENOUGH.
BAD NEWS IS WHAT I AVOID, CRAZY LADY.
HE MIGHT NEED OUR HELP. WE CAN'T JUST LEAVE.
I KNOW YOU'RE SCARED. I AM TOO.
YOU THINK? HOLY SHIT, THE WOMAN CAN READ THE HEARTS AND MINDS OF MEN.
BUT WE WERE CHOSEN, AADESH.
WE CAN'T EVER TURN AWAY FROM HIM.
LADY, YOU DIDN'T EVEN KNOW ME UNTIL TONIGHT!
I'M NOT SOME PROPHET!
AND NEITHER ARE YOU!

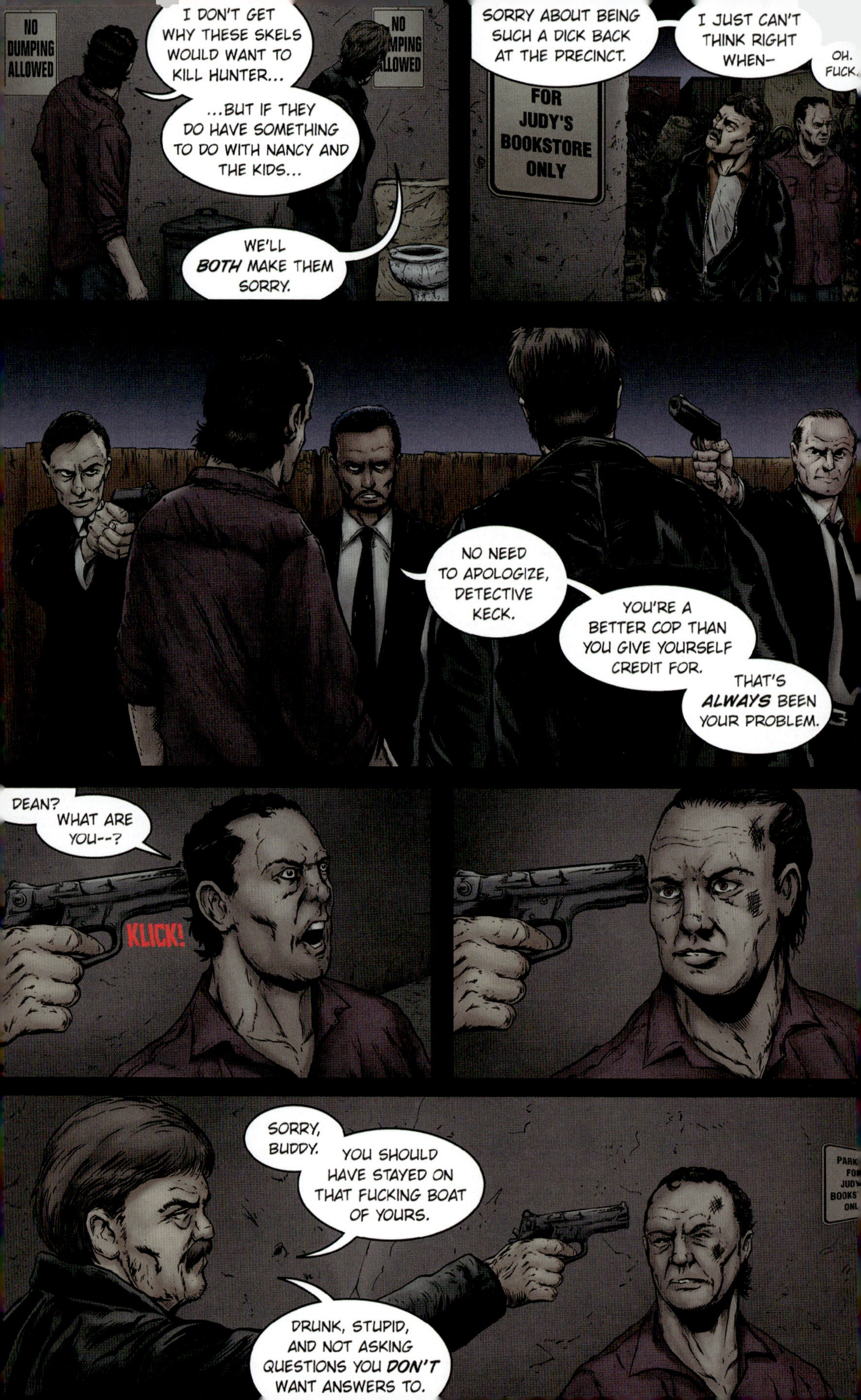
NO DUMPING ALLOWED
I DON'T GET WHY THESE SKELS WOULD WANT TO KILL HUNTER...
...BUT IF THEY DO HAVE SOMETHING TO DO WITH NANCY AND THE KIDS...
WE'LL BOTH MAKE THEM SORRY.
SORRY ABOUT BEING SUCH A DICK BACK AT THE PRECINCT.
I JUST CAN'T THINK RIGHT WHEN–
OH. FUCK.
FOR JUDY'S BOOKSTORE ONLY
NO NEED TO APOLOGIZE, DETECTIVE KECK.
YOU'RE A BETTER COP THAN YOU GIVE YOURSELF CREDIT FOR.
THAT'S ALWAYS BEEN YOUR PROBLEM.
DEAN? WHAT ARE YOU--?
KLICK!
SORRY, BUDDY.
YOU SHOULD HAVE STAYED ON THAT FUCKING BOAT OF YOURS.
DRUNK, STUPID, AND NOT ASKING QUESTIONS YOU DON'T WANT ANSWERS TO.

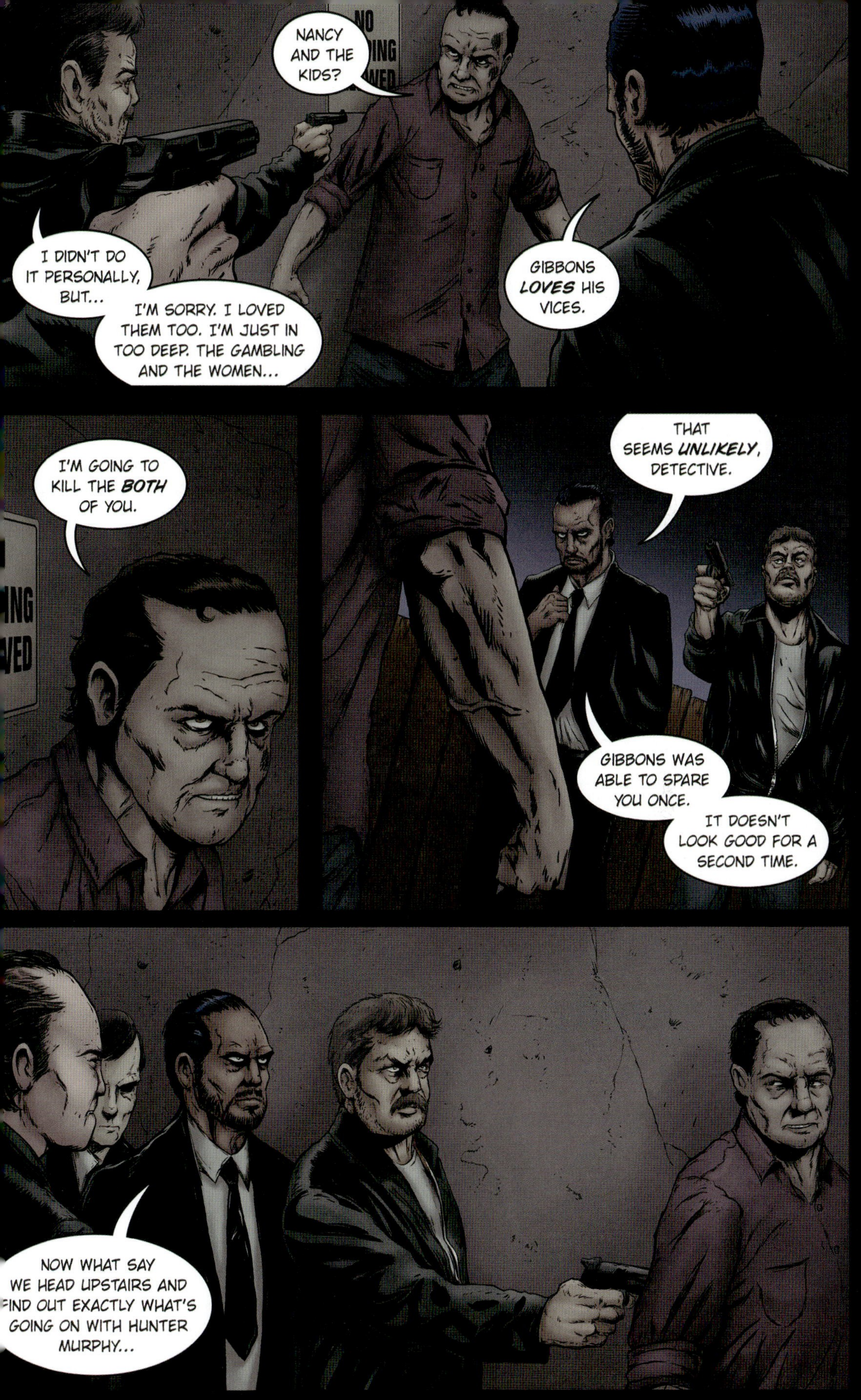

NANCY AND THE KIDS?
I DIDN'T DO IT PERSONALLY, BUT...
I'M SORRY. I LOVED THEM TOO. I'M JUST IN TOO DEEP. THE GAMBLING AND THE WOMEN...
GIBBONS LOVES HIS VICES.
I'M GOING TO KILL THE BOTH OF YOU.
THAT SEEMS UNLIKELY, DETECTIVE.
GIBBONS WAS ABLE TO SPARE YOU ONCE.
IT DOESN'T LOOK GOOD FOR A SECOND TIME.
NOW WHAT SAY WE HEAD UPSTAIRS AND FIND OUT EXACTLY WHAT'S GOING ON WITH HUNTER MURPHY...

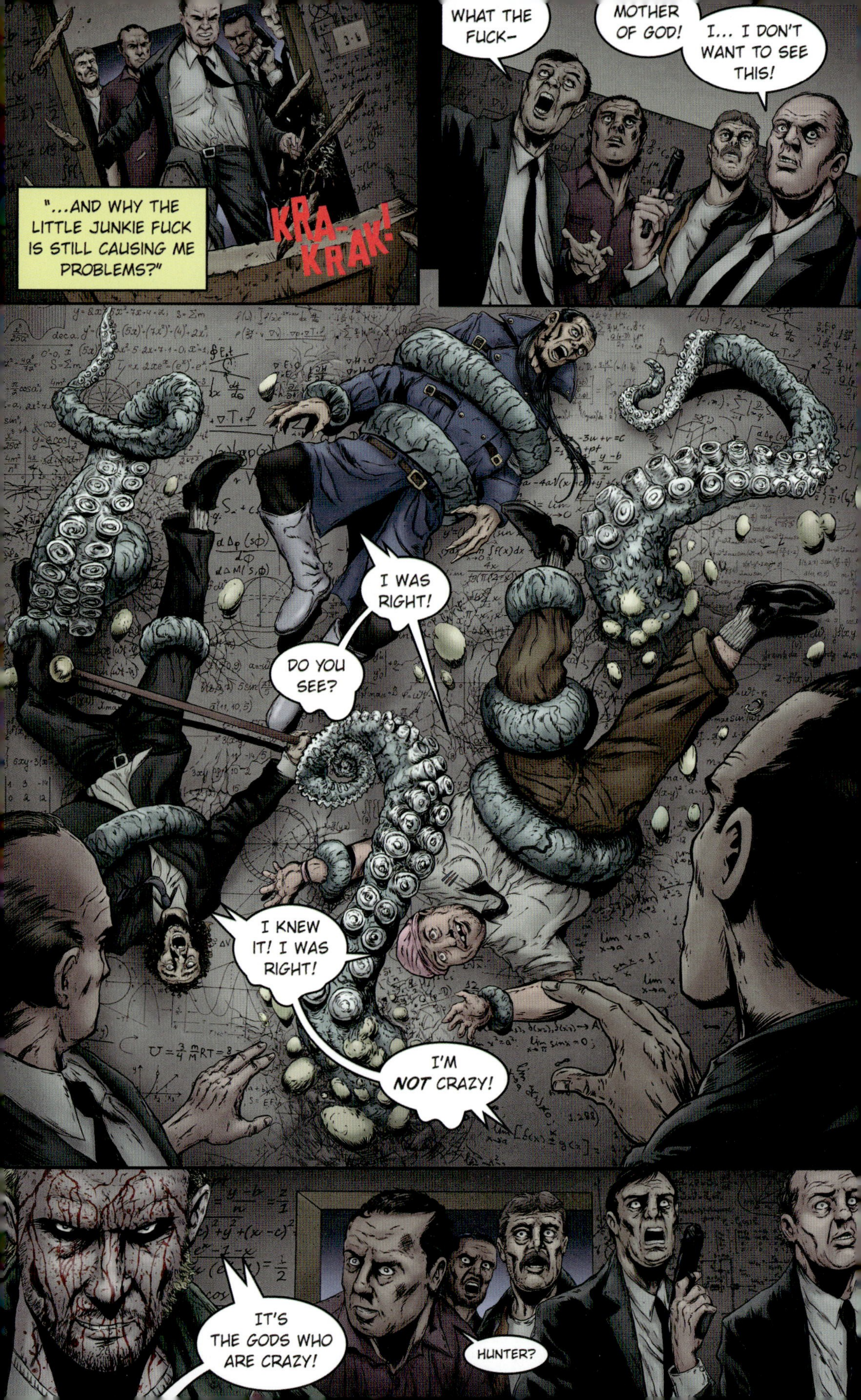
"...AND WHY THE LITTLE JUNKIE FUCK IS STILL CAUSING ME PROBLEMS?"
KRA-KRAK!
WHAT THE FUCK-
MOTHER OF GOD!
I... I DON'T WANT TO SEE THIS!
I WAS RIGHT!
DO YOU SEE?
I KNEW IT! I WAS RIGHT!
I'M NOT CRAZY!
IT'S THE GODS WHO ARE CRAZY!
HUNTER?

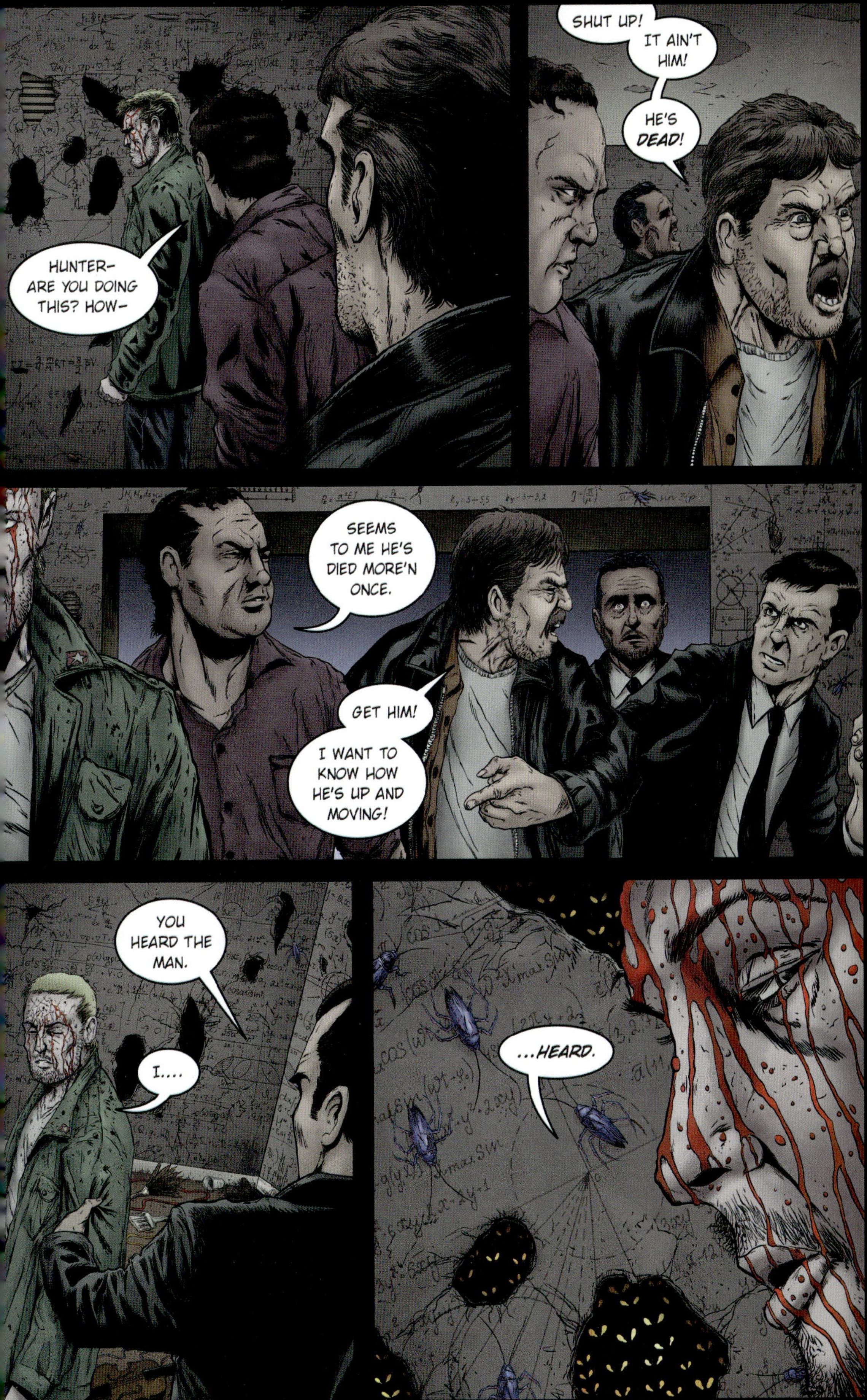
HUNTER- ARE YOU DOING THIS? HOW-
SHUT UP!
IT AIN'T HIM!
HE'S *DEAD!*
SEEMS TO ME HE'S DIED MORE'N ONCE.
GET HIM!
I WANT TO KNOW HOW HE'S UP AND MOVING!
YOU HEARD THE MAN.
I....
...*HEARD.*

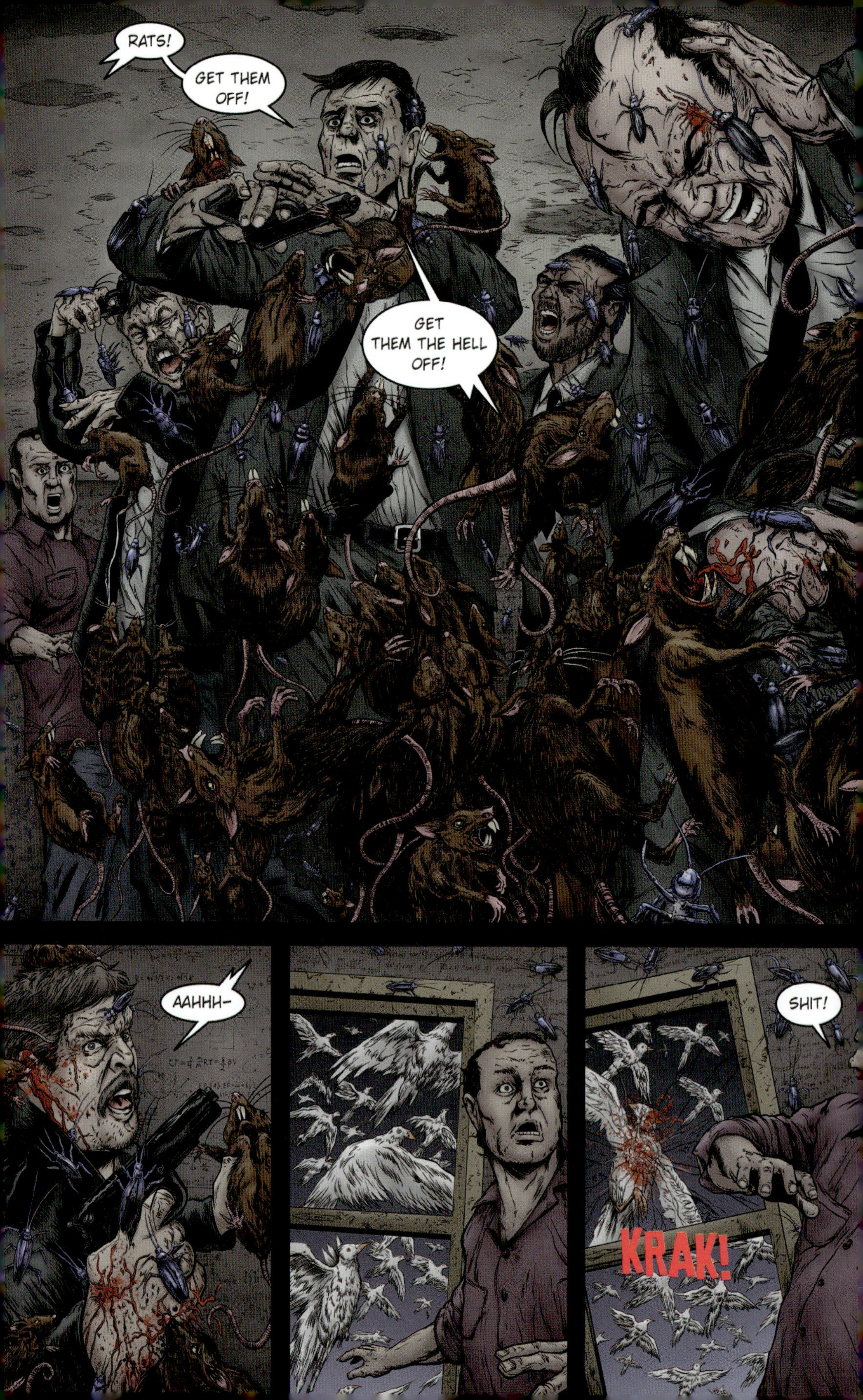
RATS!
GET THEM OFF!
GET THEM THE HELL OFF!
AAHHH-
SHIT!
KRAK!

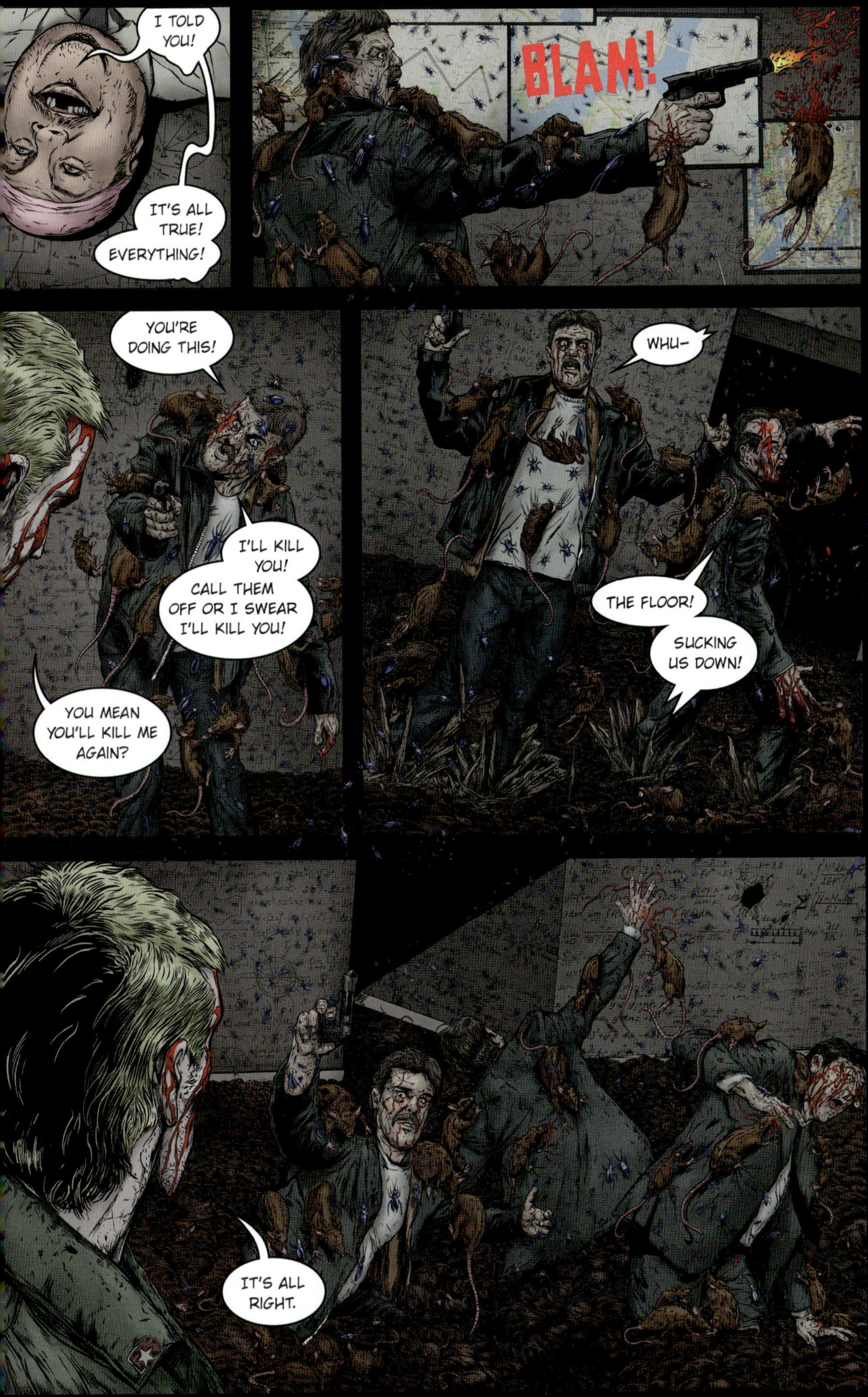
I TOLD YOU!
IT'S ALL TRUE! EVERYTHING!
BLAM!
YOU'RE DOING THIS!
I'LL KILL YOU!
CALL THEM OFF OR I SWEAR I'LL KILL YOU!
YOU MEAN YOU'LL KILL ME AGAIN?
WHU-
THE FLOOR!
SUCKING US DOWN!
IT'S ALL RIGHT.

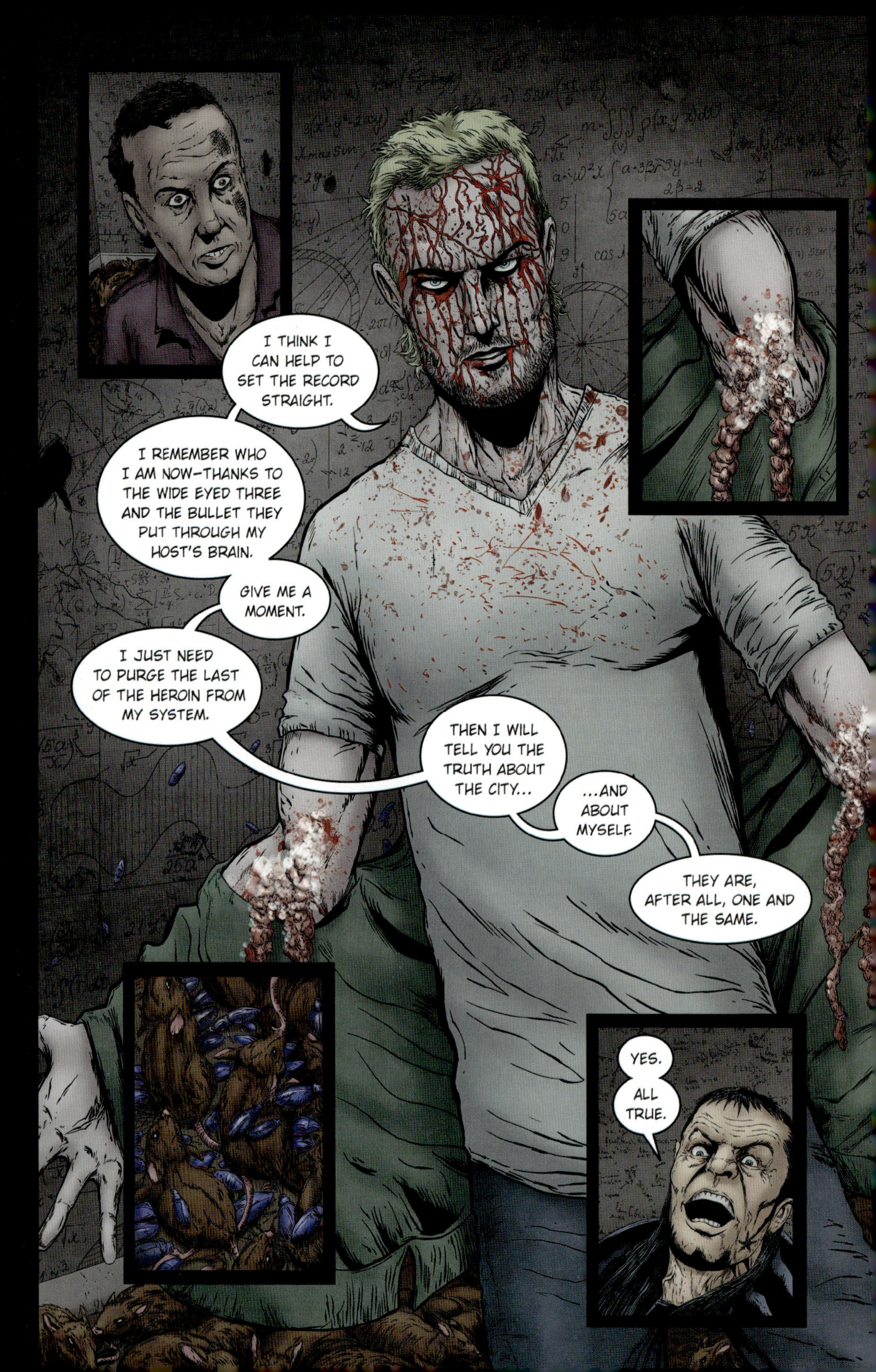
I THINK I CAN HELP TO SET THE RECORD STRAIGHT.
I REMEMBER WHO I AM NOW—THANKS TO THE WIDE EYED THREE AND THE BULLET THEY PUT THROUGH MY HOST'S BRAIN.
GIVE ME A MOMENT.
I JUST NEED TO PURGE THE LAST OF THE HEROIN FROM MY SYSTEM.
THEN I WILL TELL YOU THE TRUTH ABOUT THE CITY...
...AND ABOUT MYSELF.
THEY ARE, AFTER ALL, ONE AND THE SAME.
YES.
ALL TRUE.

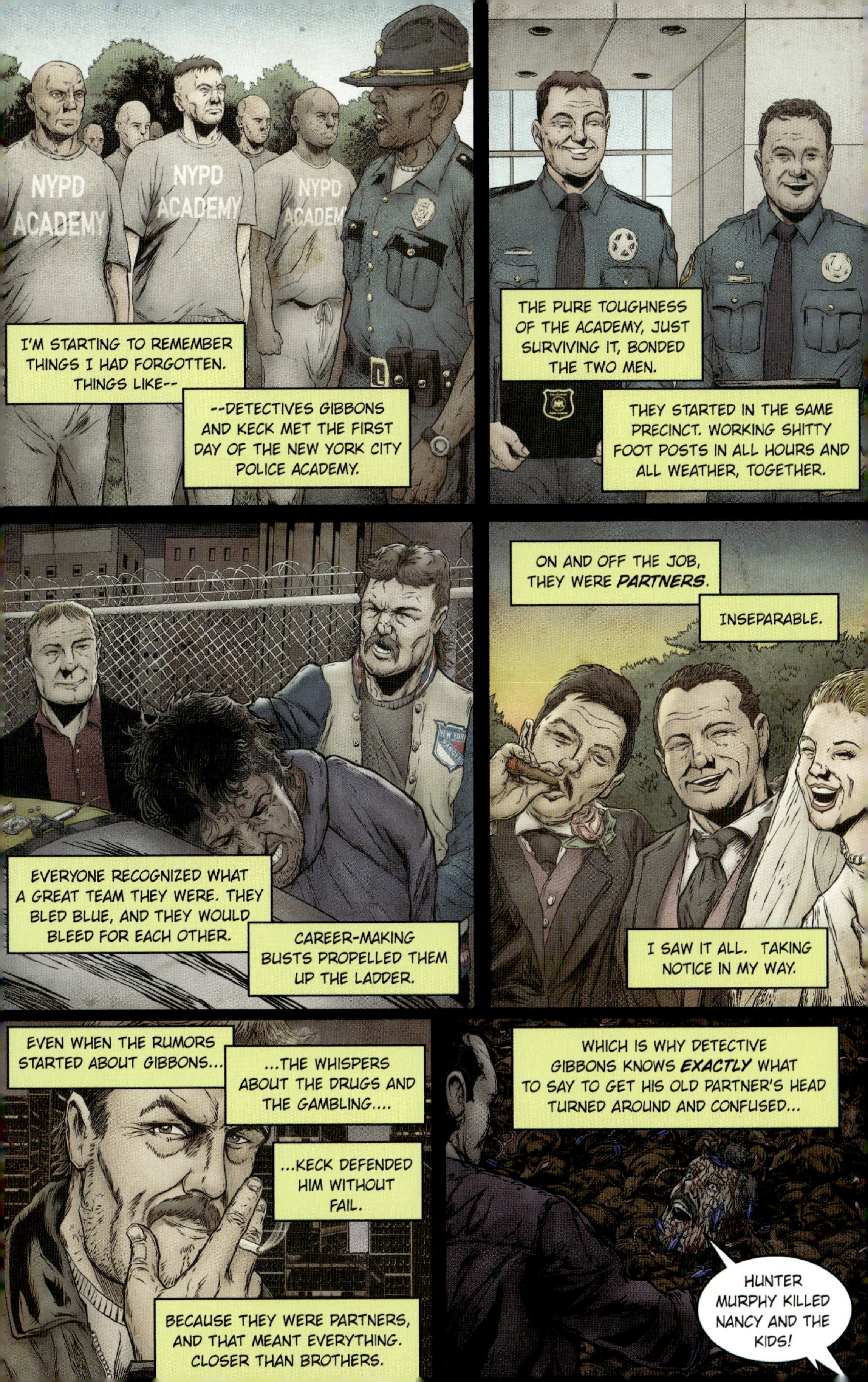

I'M STARTING TO REMEMBER THINGS I HAD FORGOTTEN. THINGS LIKE--
--DETECTIVES GIBBONS AND KECK MET THE FIRST DAY OF THE NEW YORK CITY POLICE ACADEMY.
NYPD ACADEMY
THE PURE TOUGHNESS OF THE ACADEMY, JUST SURVIVING IT, BONDED THE TWO MEN.
THEY STARTED IN THE SAME PRECINCT. WORKING SHITTY FOOT POSTS IN ALL HOURS AND ALL WEATHER, TOGETHER.
EVERYONE RECOGNIZED WHAT A GREAT TEAM THEY WERE. THEY BLED BLUE, AND THEY WOULD BLEED FOR EACH OTHER.
CAREER-MAKING BUSTS PROPELLED THEM UP THE LADDER.
ON AND OFF THE JOB, THEY WERE *PARTNERS*.
INSEPARABLE.
I SAW IT ALL. TAKING NOTICE IN MY WAY.
EVEN WHEN THE RUMORS STARTED ABOUT GIBBONS...
...THE WHISPERS ABOUT THE DRUGS AND THE GAMBLING....
...KECK DEFENDED HIM WITHOUT FAIL.
BECAUSE THEY WERE PARTNERS, AND THAT MEANT EVERYTHING. CLOSER THAN BROTHERS.
WHICH IS WHY DETECTIVE GIBBONS KNOWS *EXACTLY* WHAT TO SAY TO GET HIS OLD PARTNER'S HEAD TURNED AROUND AND CONFUSED...
HUNTER MURPHY KILLED NANCY AND THE KIDS!

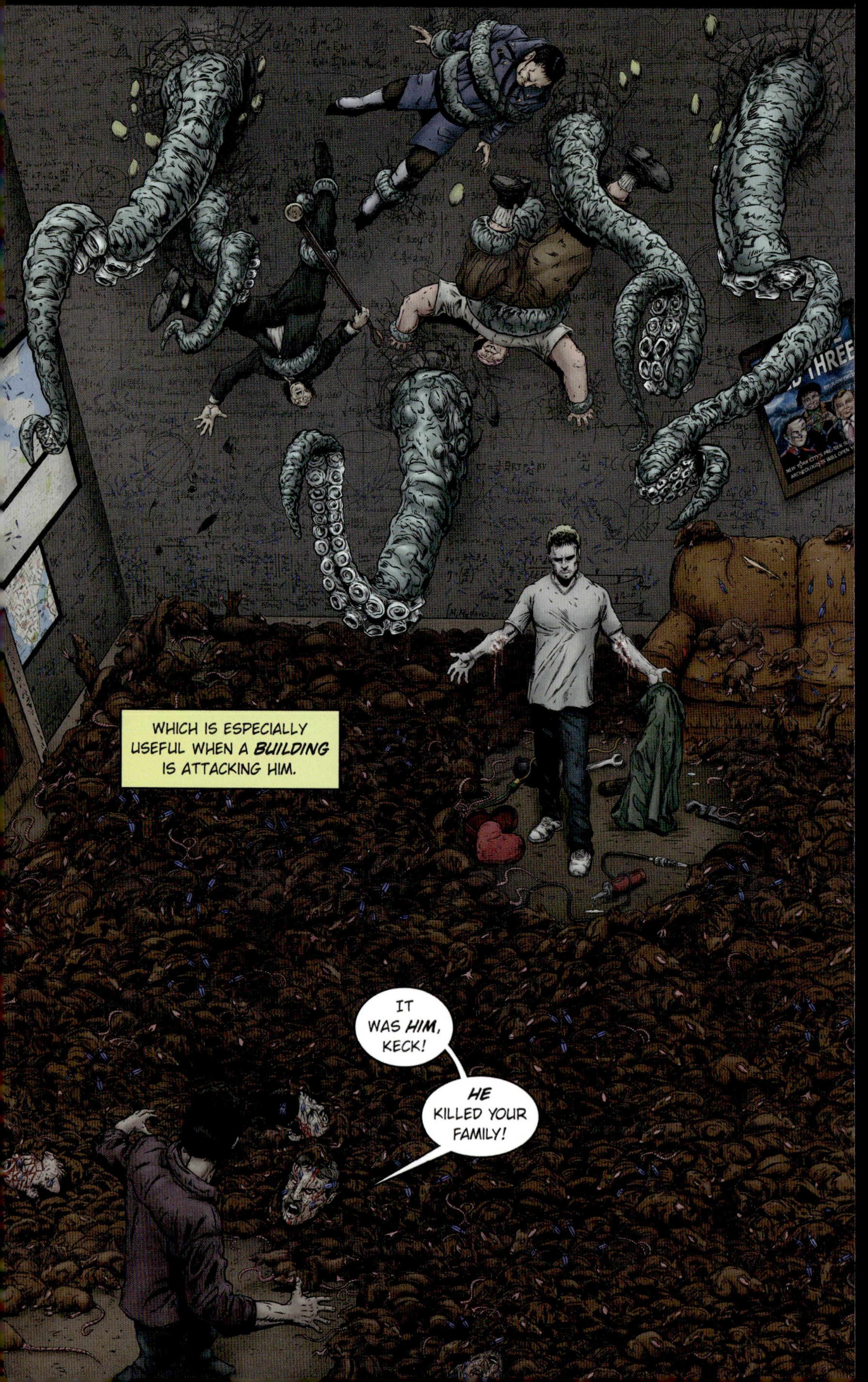
WHICH IS ESPECIALLY USEFUL WHEN A *BUILDING* IS ATTACKING HIM.
IT WAS *HIM*, KECK!
HE KILLED YOUR FAMILY!

GIBBONS IS NOT WRONG. HE KNOWS KECK WELL. IT WORKS.

WHAT?!?!

IT'S *TRUE*, PARTNER!

THAT'S WHY I KILLED HIM! FOR *NANCY*!

HE CAN'T BE KILLED!

HAHAHA HAHAHAHAHA HAHA!

KECK LOSES HIS SHIT INSTANTLY.

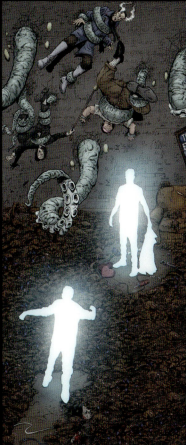

HAHAHA HAHAHAHAHA HAHA!

WHERE THE FUCK DID THEY GO?

WHAT'S GOING ON HERE?

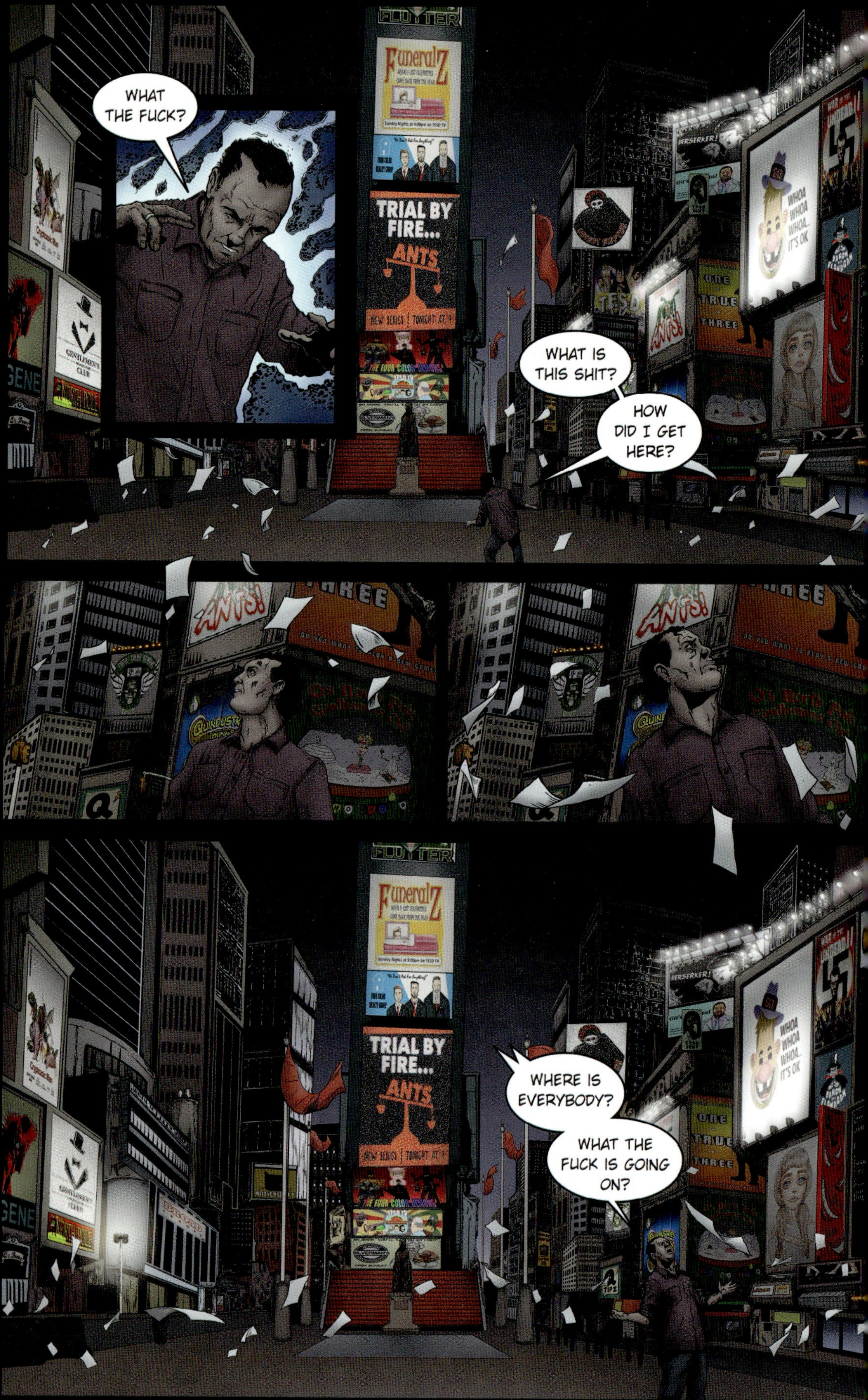

WHAT THE FUCK?
WHAT IS THIS SHIT?
HOW DID I GET HERE?
WHERE IS EVERYBODY?
WHAT THE FUCK IS GOING ON?

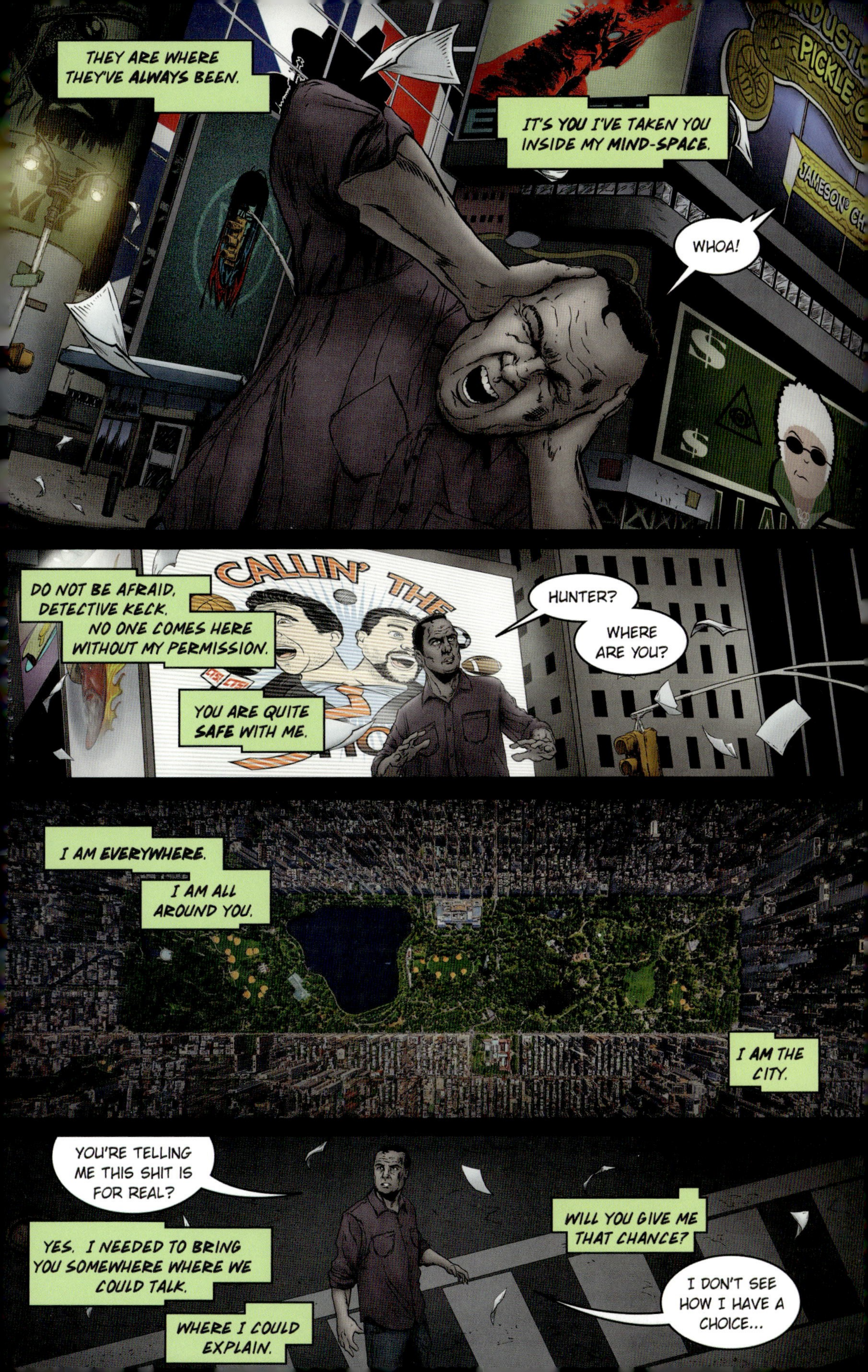
THEY ARE WHERE THEY'VE ALWAYS BEEN.
IT'S YOU I'VE TAKEN YOU INSIDE MY MIND-SPACE.
WHOA!
DO NOT BE AFRAID, DETECTIVE KECK.
NO ONE COMES HERE WITHOUT MY PERMISSION.
YOU ARE QUITE SAFE WITH ME.
HUNTER?
WHERE ARE YOU?
I AM EVERYWHERE.
I AM ALL AROUND YOU.
I AM THE CITY.
YOU'RE TELLING ME THIS SHIT IS FOR REAL?
YES. I NEEDED TO BRING YOU SOMEWHERE WHERE WE COULD TALK.
WHERE I COULD EXPLAIN.
WILL YOU GIVE ME THAT CHANCE?
I DON'T SEE HOW I HAVE A CHOICE...

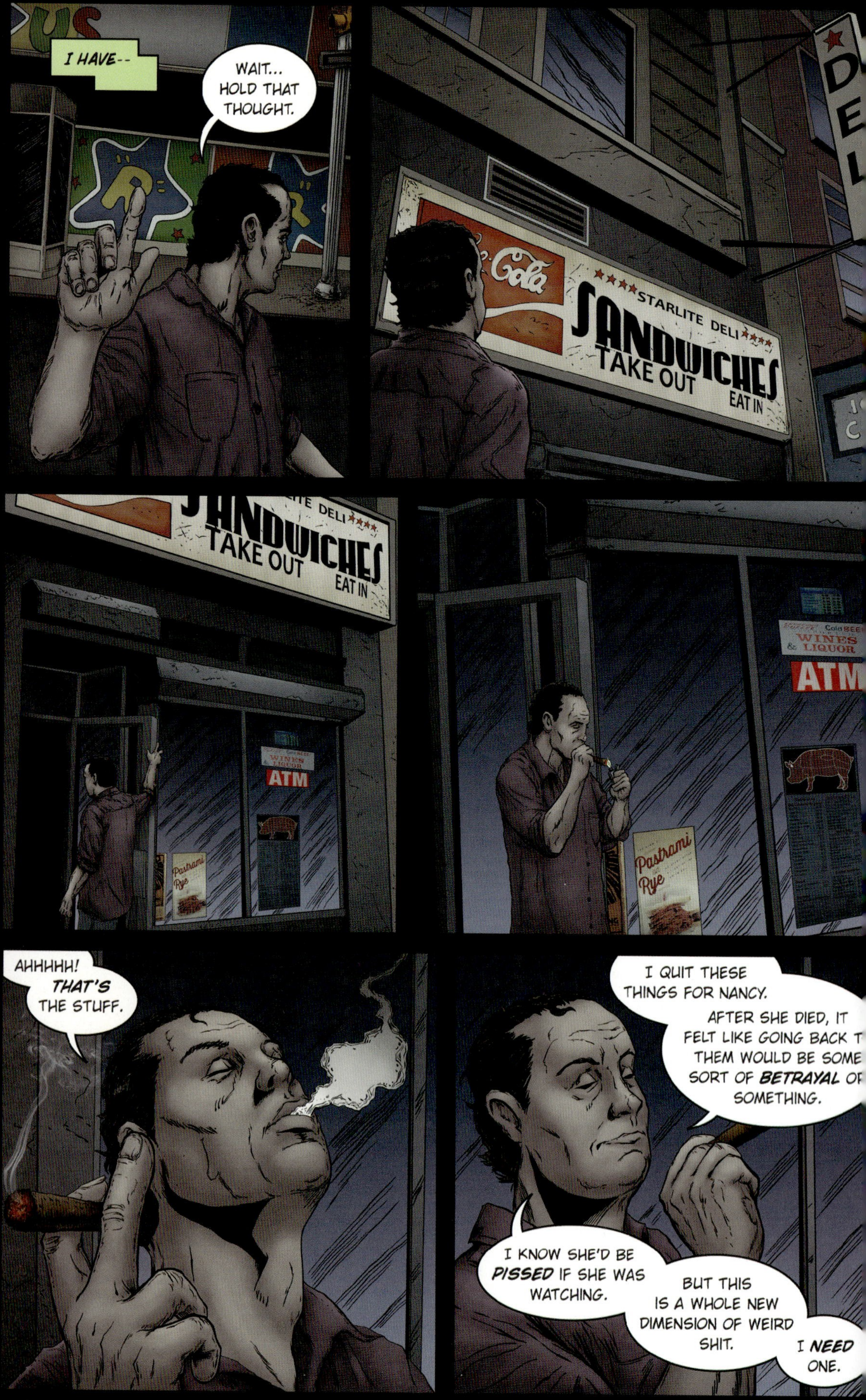

I HAVE--
WAIT... HOLD THAT THOUGHT.
STARLITE DELI
SANDWICHES
TAKE OUT
EAT IN
SANDWICHES
TAKE OUT
EAT IN
WINES & LIQUOR
ATM
Pastrami Rye
Cold BEER
WINES & LIQUOR
ATM
Pastrami Rye
AHHHHH! *THAT'S* THE STUFF.
I QUIT THESE THINGS FOR NANCY.
AFTER SHE DIED, IT FELT LIKE GOING BACK T THEM WOULD BE SOME SORT OF *BETRAYAL* OF SOMETHING.
I KNOW SHE'D BE *PISSED* IF SHE WAS WATCHING.
BUT THIS IS A WHOLE NEW DIMENSION OF WEIRD SHIT.
I *NEED* ONE.

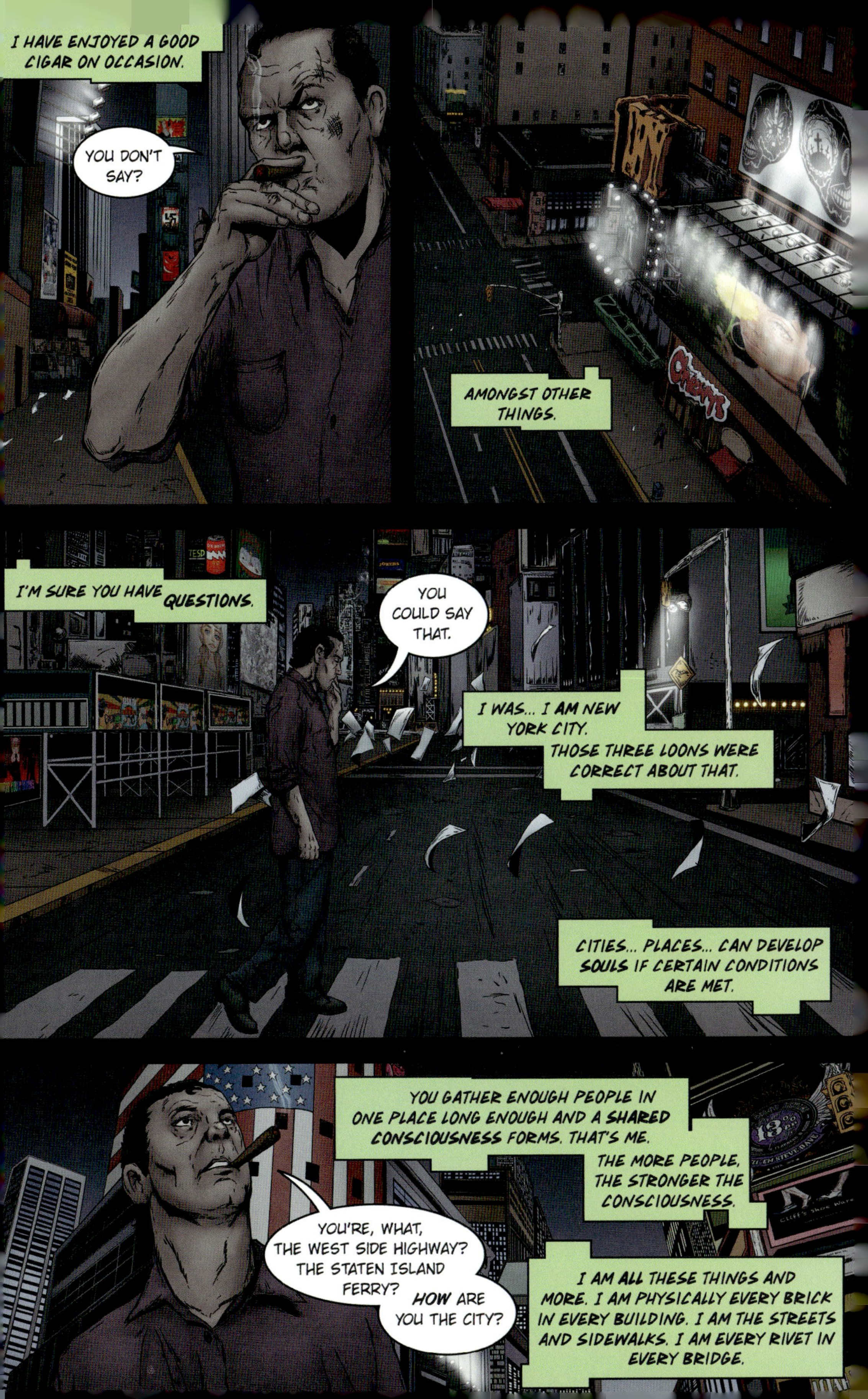
I HAVE ENJOYED A GOOD CIGAR ON OCCASION.
YOU DON'T SAY?
AMONGST OTHER THINGS.
I'M SURE YOU HAVE QUESTIONS.
YOU COULD SAY THAT.
I WAS... I AM NEW YORK CITY.
THOSE THREE LOONS WERE CORRECT ABOUT THAT.
CITIES... PLACES... CAN DEVELOP SOULS IF CERTAIN CONDITIONS ARE MET.
YOU GATHER ENOUGH PEOPLE IN ONE PLACE LONG ENOUGH AND A SHARED CONSCIOUSNESS FORMS. THAT'S ME.
THE MORE PEOPLE, THE STRONGER THE CONSCIOUSNESS.
YOU'RE, WHAT, THE WEST SIDE HIGHWAY? THE STATEN ISLAND FERRY? HOW ARE YOU THE CITY?
I AM ALL THESE THINGS AND MORE. I AM PHYSICALLY EVERY BRICK IN EVERY BUILDING. I AM THE STREETS AND SIDEWALKS. I AM EVERY RIVET IN EVERY BRIDGE.

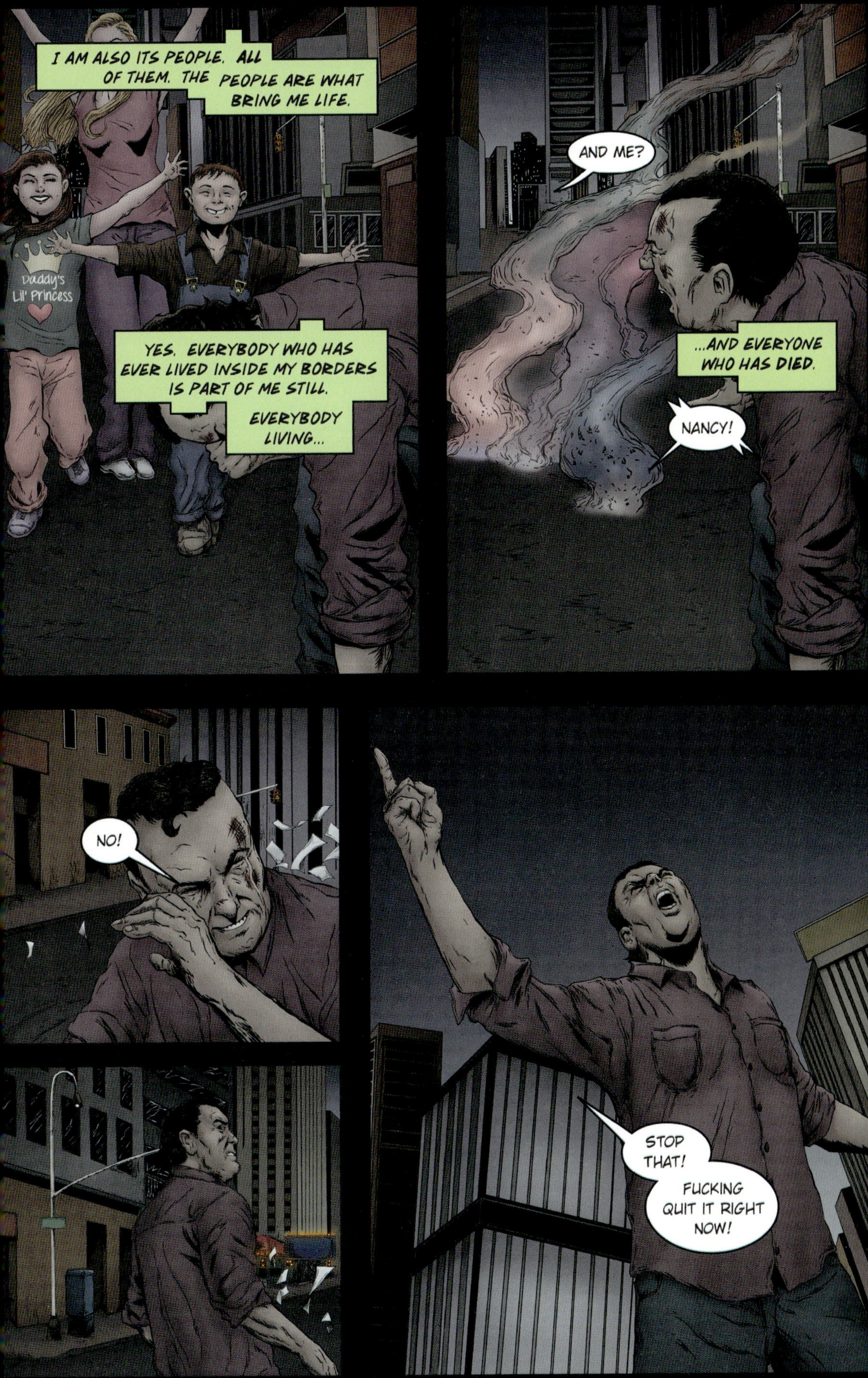
I AM ALSO ITS PEOPLE. ALL OF THEM. THE PEOPLE ARE WHAT BRING ME LIFE.
Daddy's Lil' Princess
YES. EVERYBODY WHO HAS EVER LIVED INSIDE MY BORDERS IS PART OF ME STILL.
EVERYBODY LIVING...
AND ME?
...AND EVERYONE WHO HAS DIED.
NANCY!
NO!
STOP THAT!
FUCKING QUIT IT RIGHT NOW!

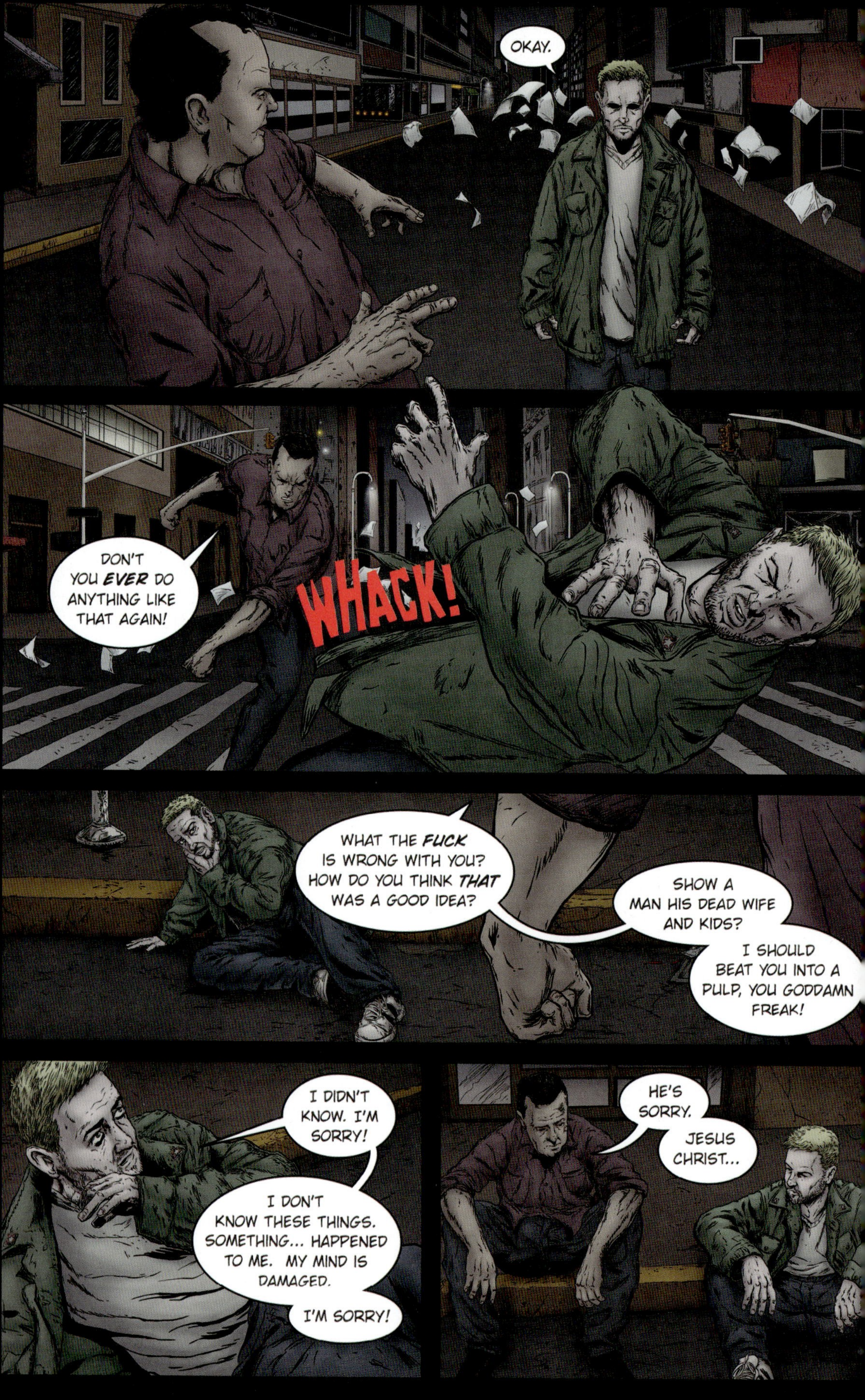
OKAY.
DON'T YOU EVER DO ANYTHING LIKE THAT AGAIN!
WHACK!
WHAT THE FUCK IS WRONG WITH YOU? HOW DO YOU THINK THAT WAS A GOOD IDEA?
SHOW A MAN HIS DEAD WIFE AND KIDS?
I SHOULD BEAT YOU INTO A PULP, YOU GODDAMN FREAK!
I DIDN'T KNOW. I'M SORRY!
I DON'T KNOW THESE THINGS. SOMETHING... HAPPENED TO ME. MY MIND IS DAMAGED.
I'M SORRY!
HE'S SORRY.
JESUS CHRIST...

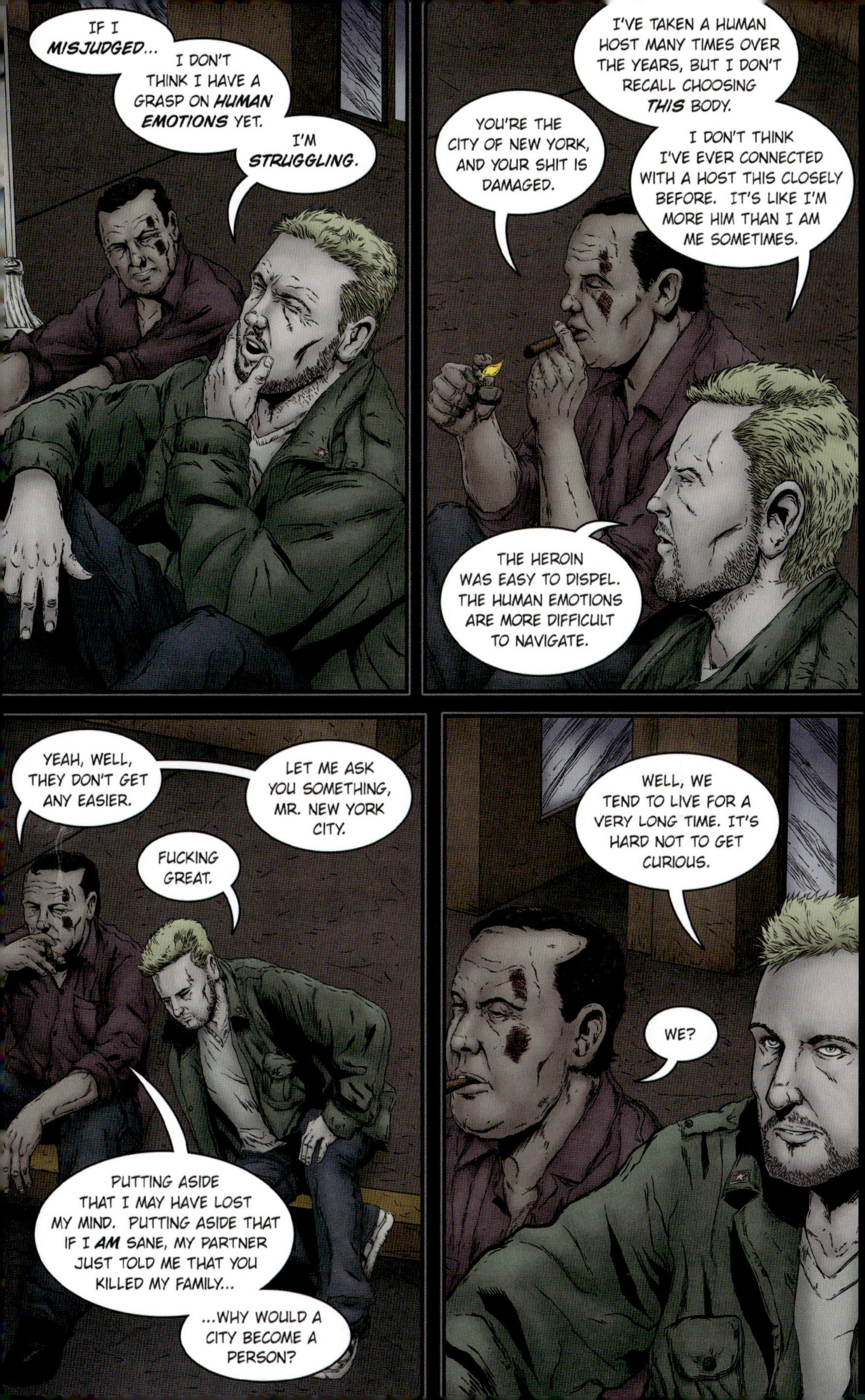
IF I MISJUDGED...
I DON'T THINK I HAVE A GRASP ON HUMAN EMOTIONS YET.
I'M STRUGGLING.
I'VE TAKEN A HUMAN HOST MANY TIMES OVER THE YEARS, BUT I DON'T RECALL CHOOSING THIS BODY.
YOU'RE THE CITY OF NEW YORK, AND YOUR SHIT IS DAMAGED.
I DON'T THINK I'VE EVER CONNECTED WITH A HOST THIS CLOSELY BEFORE. IT'S LIKE I'M MORE HIM THAN I AM ME SOMETIMES.
THE HEROIN WAS EASY TO DISPEL. THE HUMAN EMOTIONS ARE MORE DIFFICULT TO NAVIGATE.
YEAH, WELL, THEY DON'T GET ANY EASIER.
LET ME ASK YOU SOMETHING, MR. NEW YORK CITY.
FUCKING GREAT.
PUTTING ASIDE THAT I MAY HAVE LOST MY MIND. PUTTING ASIDE THAT IF I AM SANE, MY PARTNER JUST TOLD ME THAT YOU KILLED MY FAMILY...
...WHY WOULD A CITY BECOME A PERSON?
WELL, WE TEND TO LIVE FOR A VERY LONG TIME. IT'S HARD NOT TO GET CURIOUS.
WE?

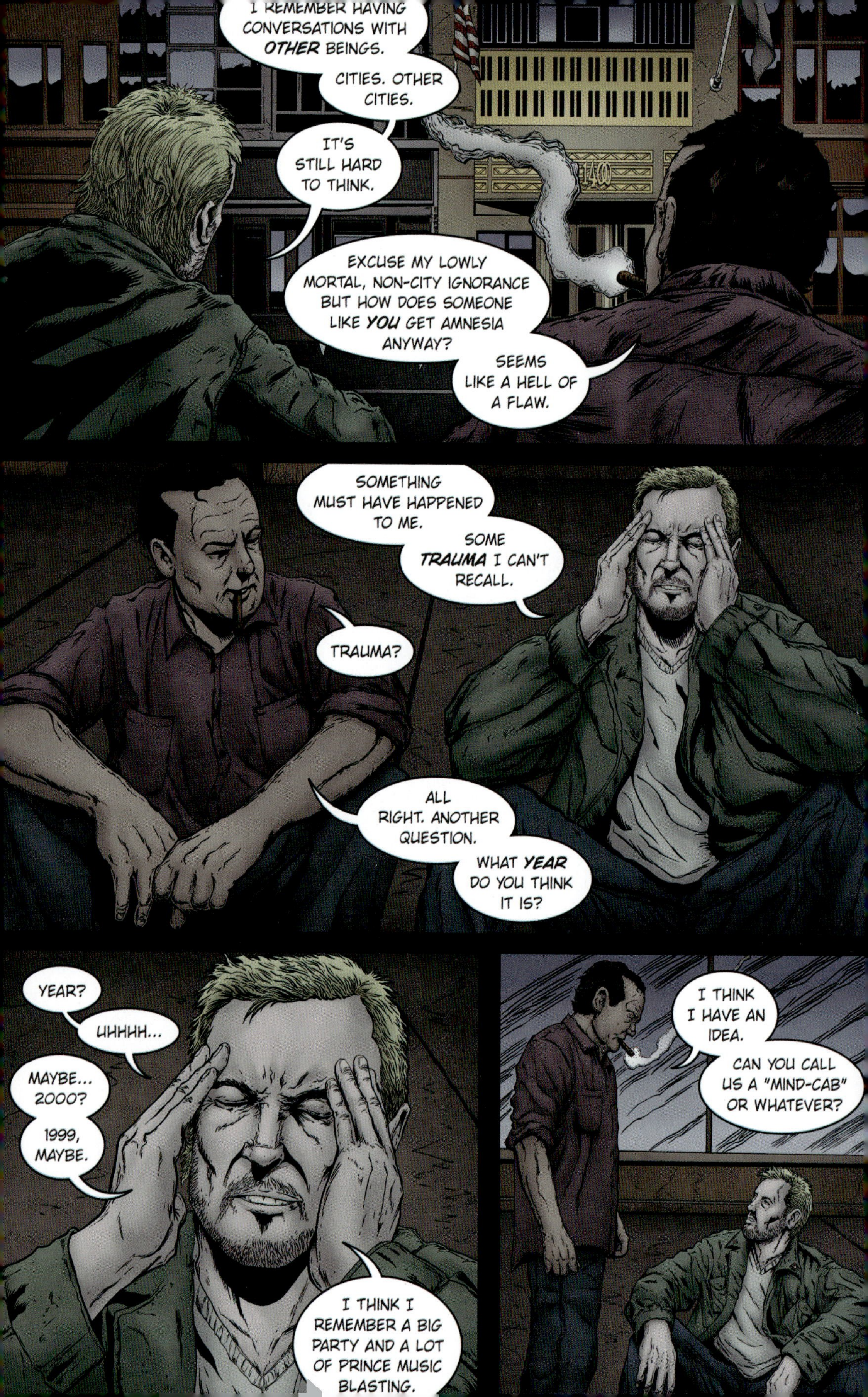
I REMEMBER HAVING CONVERSATIONS WITH OTHER BEINGS.
CITIES. OTHER CITIES.
IT'S STILL HARD TO THINK.
EXCUSE MY LOWLY MORTAL, NON-CITY IGNORANCE BUT HOW DOES SOMEONE LIKE YOU GET AMNESIA ANYWAY?
SEEMS LIKE A HELL OF A FLAW.
SOMETHING MUST HAVE HAPPENED TO ME.
SOME TRAUMA I CAN'T RECALL.
TRAUMA?
ALL RIGHT. ANOTHER QUESTION.
WHAT YEAR DO YOU THINK IT IS?
YEAR?
UHHHH...
MAYBE... 2000?
1999, MAYBE.
I THINK I REMEMBER A BIG PARTY AND A LOT OF PRINCE MUSIC BLASTING.
I THINK I HAVE AN IDEA.
CAN YOU CALL US A "MIND-CAB" OR WHATEVER?

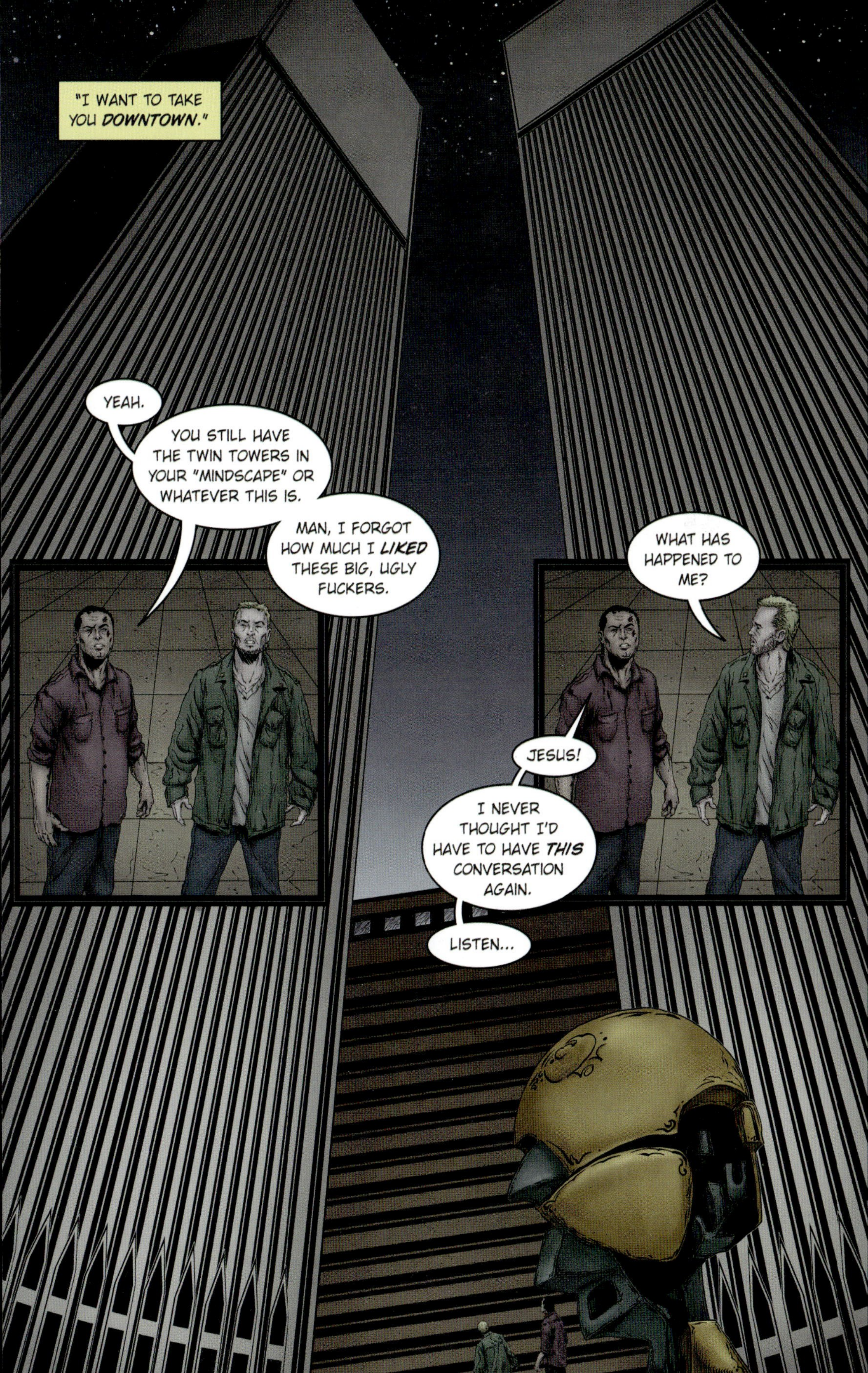
"I WANT TO TAKE YOU DOWNTOWN."
YEAH.
YOU STILL HAVE THE TWIN TOWERS IN YOUR "MINDSCAPE" OR WHATEVER THIS IS.
MAN, I FORGOT HOW MUCH I LIKED THESE BIG, UGLY FUCKERS.
WHAT HAS HAPPENED TO ME?
JESUS!
I NEVER THOUGHT I'D HAVE TO HAVE THIS CONVERSATION AGAIN.
LISTEN...

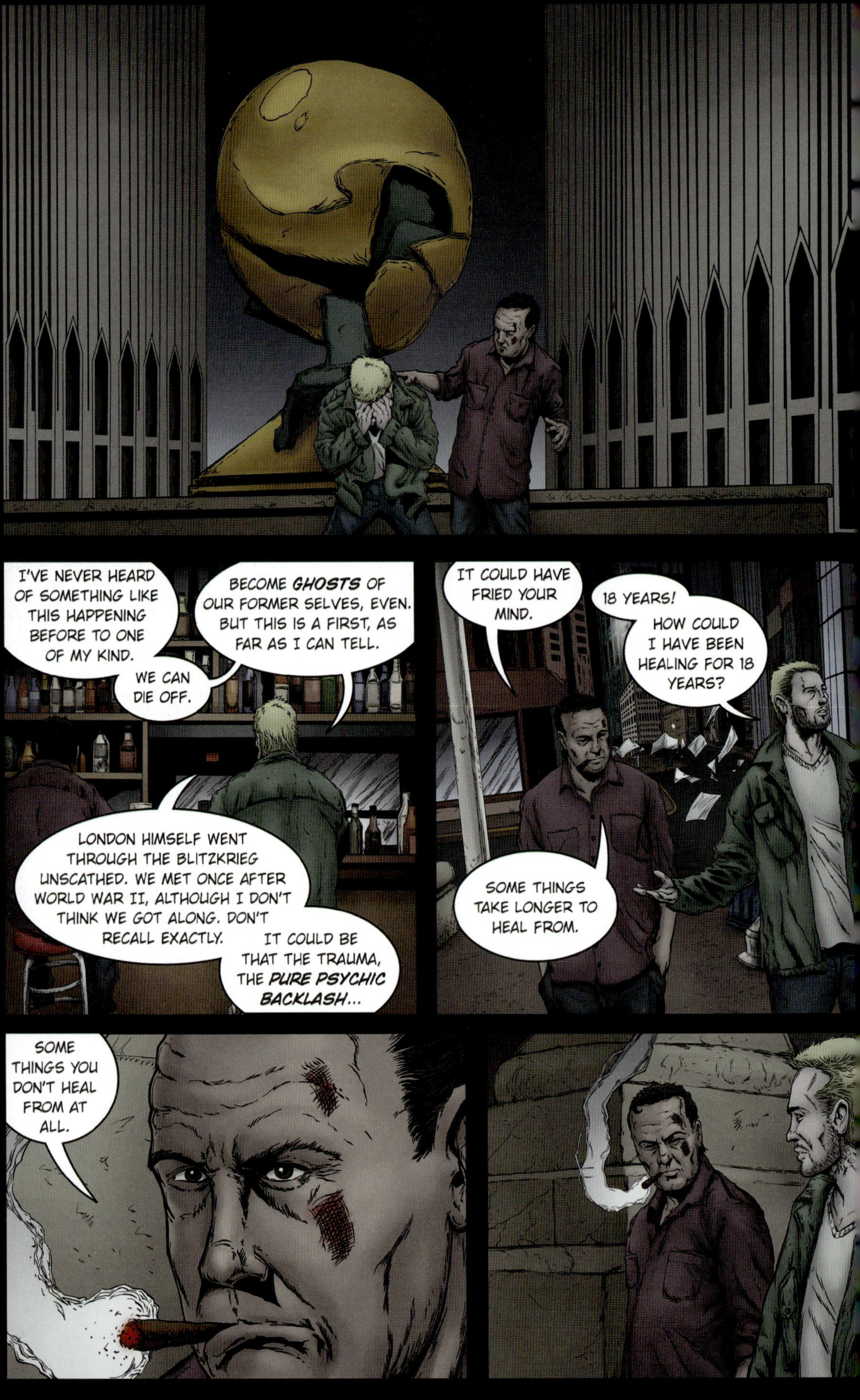
I'VE NEVER HEARD OF SOMETHING LIKE THIS HAPPENING BEFORE TO ONE OF MY KIND.
WE CAN DIE OFF.
BECOME GHOSTS OF OUR FORMER SELVES, EVEN. BUT THIS IS A FIRST, AS FAR AS I CAN TELL.
LONDON HIMSELF WENT THROUGH THE BLITZKRIEG UNSCATHED. WE MET ONCE AFTER WORLD WAR II, ALTHOUGH I DON'T THINK WE GOT ALONG. DON'T RECALL EXACTLY.
IT COULD BE THAT THE TRAUMA, THE PURE PSYCHIC BACKLASH...
IT COULD HAVE FRIED YOUR MIND.
18 YEARS!
HOW COULD I HAVE BEEN HEALING FOR 18 YEARS?
SOME THINGS TAKE LONGER TO HEAL FROM.
SOME THINGS YOU DON'T HEAL FROM AT ALL.

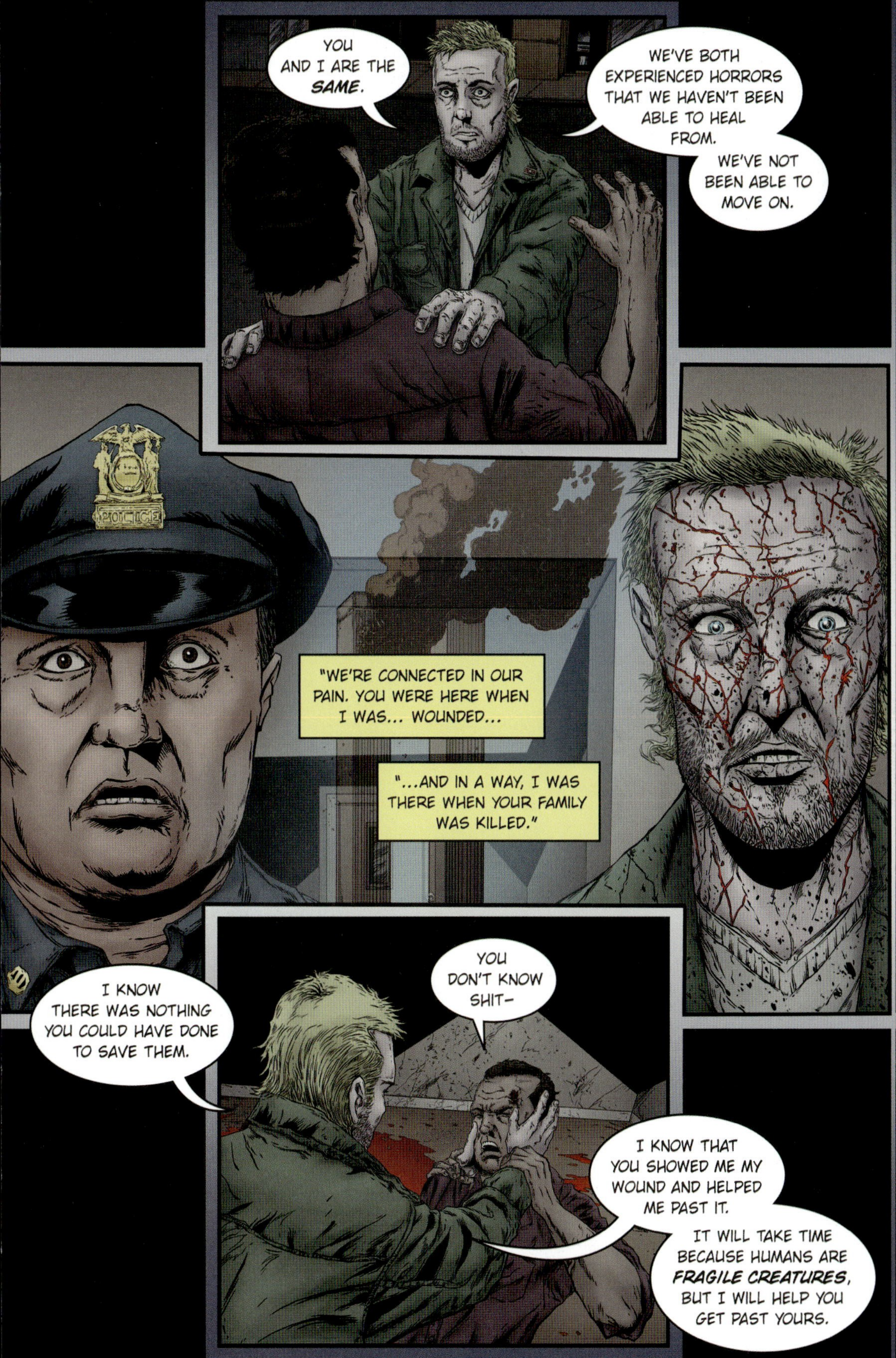
YOU AND I ARE THE ***SAME***.
WE'VE BOTH EXPERIENCED HORRORS THAT WE HAVEN'T BEEN ABLE TO HEAL FROM.
WE'VE NOT BEEN ABLE TO MOVE ON.
POLICE
"WE'RE CONNECTED IN OUR PAIN. YOU WERE HERE WHEN I WAS... WOUNDED...
"...AND IN A WAY, I WAS THERE WHEN YOUR FAMILY WAS KILLED."
I KNOW THERE WAS NOTHING YOU COULD HAVE DONE TO SAVE THEM.
YOU DON'T KNOW SHIT–
I KNOW THAT YOU SHOWED ME MY WOUND AND HELPED ME PAST IT.
IT WILL TAKE TIME BECAUSE HUMANS ARE ***FRAGILE CREATURES***, BUT I WILL HELP YOU GET PAST YOURS.

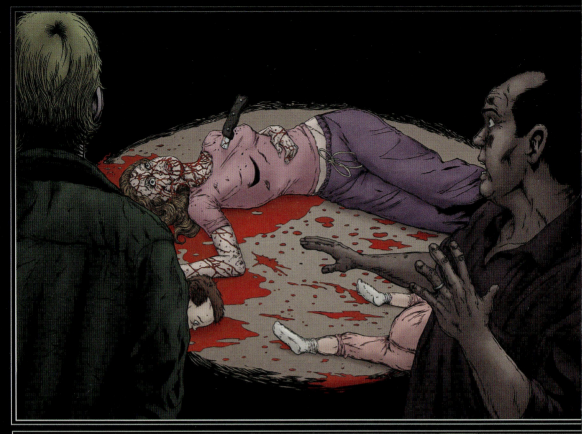

AH, NANCY, BABY...

...I'M SO SORRY...

...SO SORRY I LET THIS HAPPEN.

BUT YOU DIDN'T.

I DID THIS... THIS BODY... BEFORE I CLAIMED IT.

THIS IS NOT YOUR FAULT.

IT'S CALLED GUILT.

YOU WANT TO PASS AS HUMAN, YOU'D BEST START PRACTICING.

I...

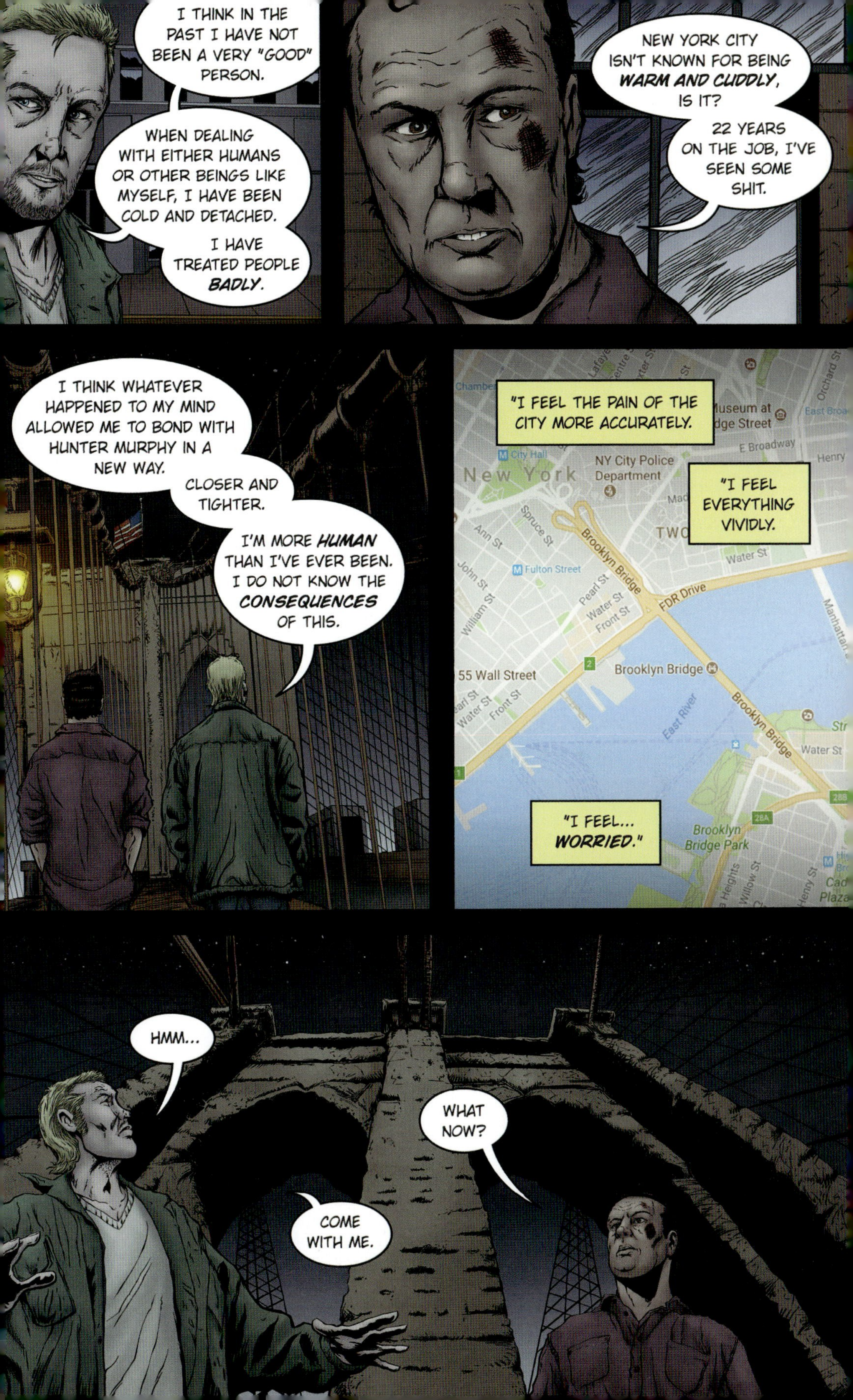
I THINK IN THE PAST I HAVE NOT BEEN A VERY "GOOD" PERSON.
WHEN DEALING WITH EITHER HUMANS OR OTHER BEINGS LIKE MYSELF, I HAVE BEEN COLD AND DETACHED.
I HAVE TREATED PEOPLE **BADLY**.
NEW YORK CITY ISN'T KNOWN FOR BEING ***WARM AND CUDDLY***, IS IT?
22 YEARS ON THE JOB, I'VE SEEN SOME SHIT.
I THINK WHATEVER HAPPENED TO MY MIND ALLOWED ME TO BOND WITH HUNTER MURPHY IN A NEW WAY.
CLOSER AND TIGHTER.
I'M MORE ***HUMAN*** THAN I'VE EVER BEEN. I DO NOT KNOW THE ***CONSEQUENCES*** OF THIS.
"I FEEL THE PAIN OF THE CITY MORE ACCURATELY.
"I FEEL EVERYTHING VIVIDLY.
New York
City Hall
NY City Police Department
Brooklyn Bridge
Fulton Street
FDR Drive
55 Wall Street
East River
Brooklyn Bridge Park
"I FEEL... ***WORRIED***."
HMM...
WHAT NOW?
COME WITH ME.

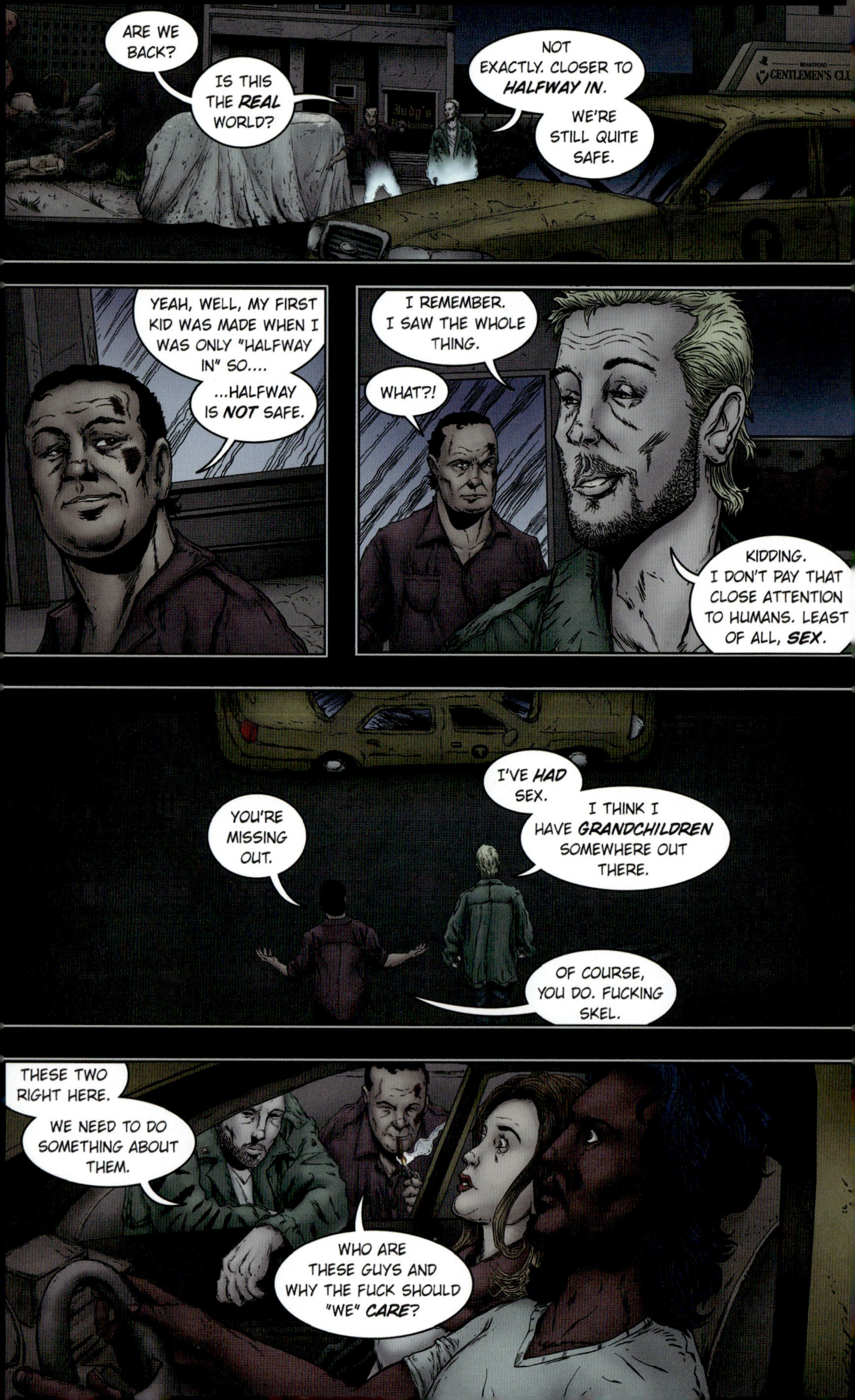
ARE WE BACK?
IS THIS THE REAL WORLD?
NOT EXACTLY. CLOSER TO HALFWAY IN.
WE'RE STILL QUITE SAFE.
GENTLEMEN'S CLU
YEAH, WELL, MY FIRST KID WAS MADE WHEN I WAS ONLY "HALFWAY IN" SO....
...HALFWAY IS NOT SAFE.
I REMEMBER. I SAW THE WHOLE THING.
WHAT?!
KIDDING. I DON'T PAY THAT CLOSE ATTENTION TO HUMANS. LEAST OF ALL, SEX.
YOU'RE MISSING OUT.
I'VE HAD SEX.
I THINK I HAVE GRANDCHILDREN SOMEWHERE OUT THERE.
OF COURSE, YOU DO. FUCKING SKEL.
THESE TWO RIGHT HERE.
WE NEED TO DO SOMETHING ABOUT THEM.
WHO ARE THESE GUYS AND WHY THE FUCK SHOULD "WE" CARE?

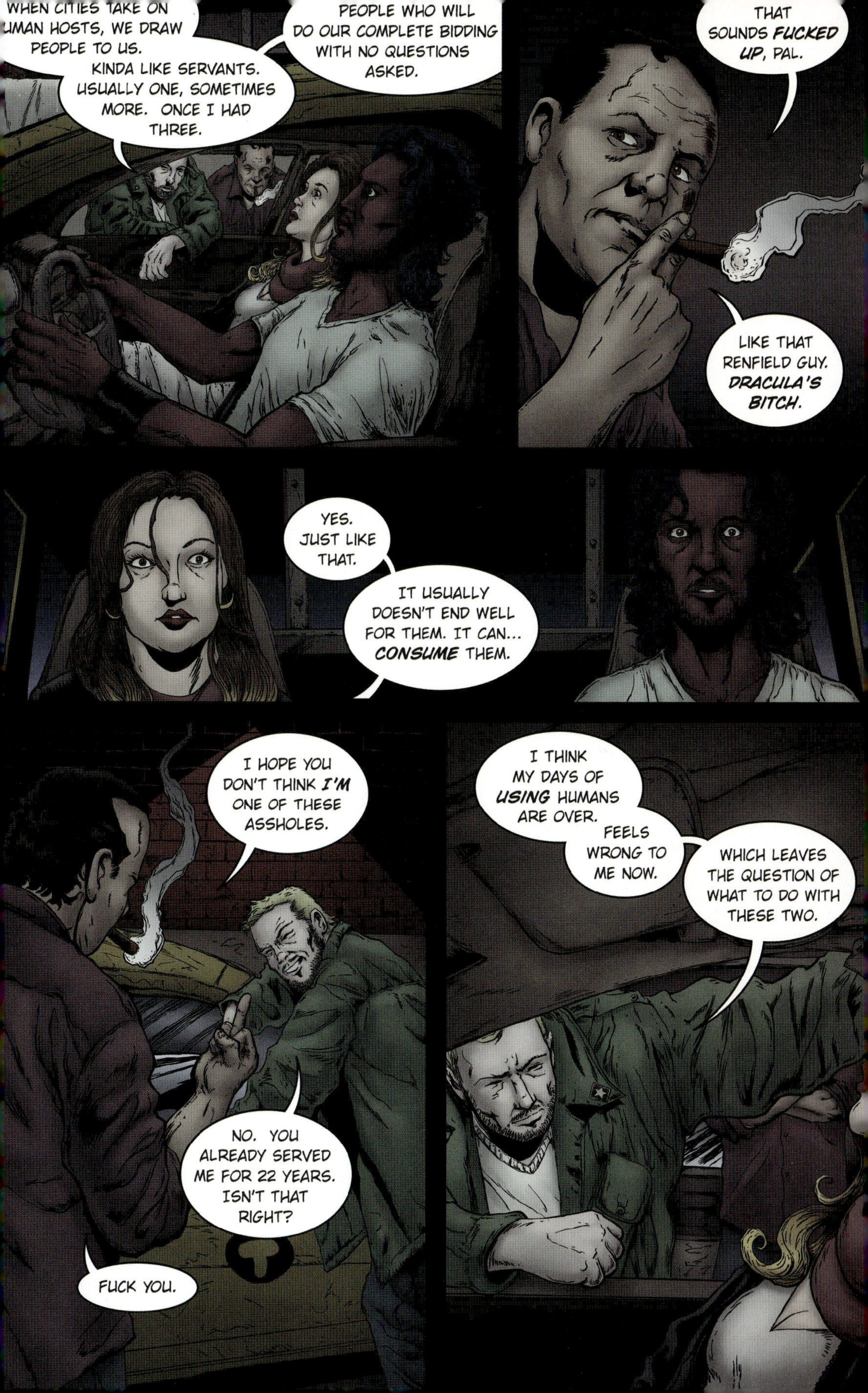
WHEN CITIES TAKE ON
UMAN HOSTS, WE DRAW PEOPLE TO US.
KINDA LIKE SERVANTS. USUALLY ONE, SOMETIMES MORE. ONCE I HAD THREE.
PEOPLE WHO WILL DO OUR COMPLETE BIDDING WITH NO QUESTIONS ASKED.
THAT SOUNDS FUCKED UP, PAL.
LIKE THAT RENFIELD GUY. DRACULA'S BITCH.
YES. JUST LIKE THAT.
IT USUALLY DOESN'T END WELL FOR THEM. IT CAN... CONSUME THEM.
I HOPE YOU DON'T THINK I'M ONE OF THESE ASSHOLES.
NO. YOU ALREADY SERVED ME FOR 22 YEARS. ISN'T THAT RIGHT?
FUCK YOU.
I THINK MY DAYS OF USING HUMANS ARE OVER.
FEELS WRONG TO ME NOW.
WHICH LEAVES THE QUESTION OF WHAT TO DO WITH THESE TWO.

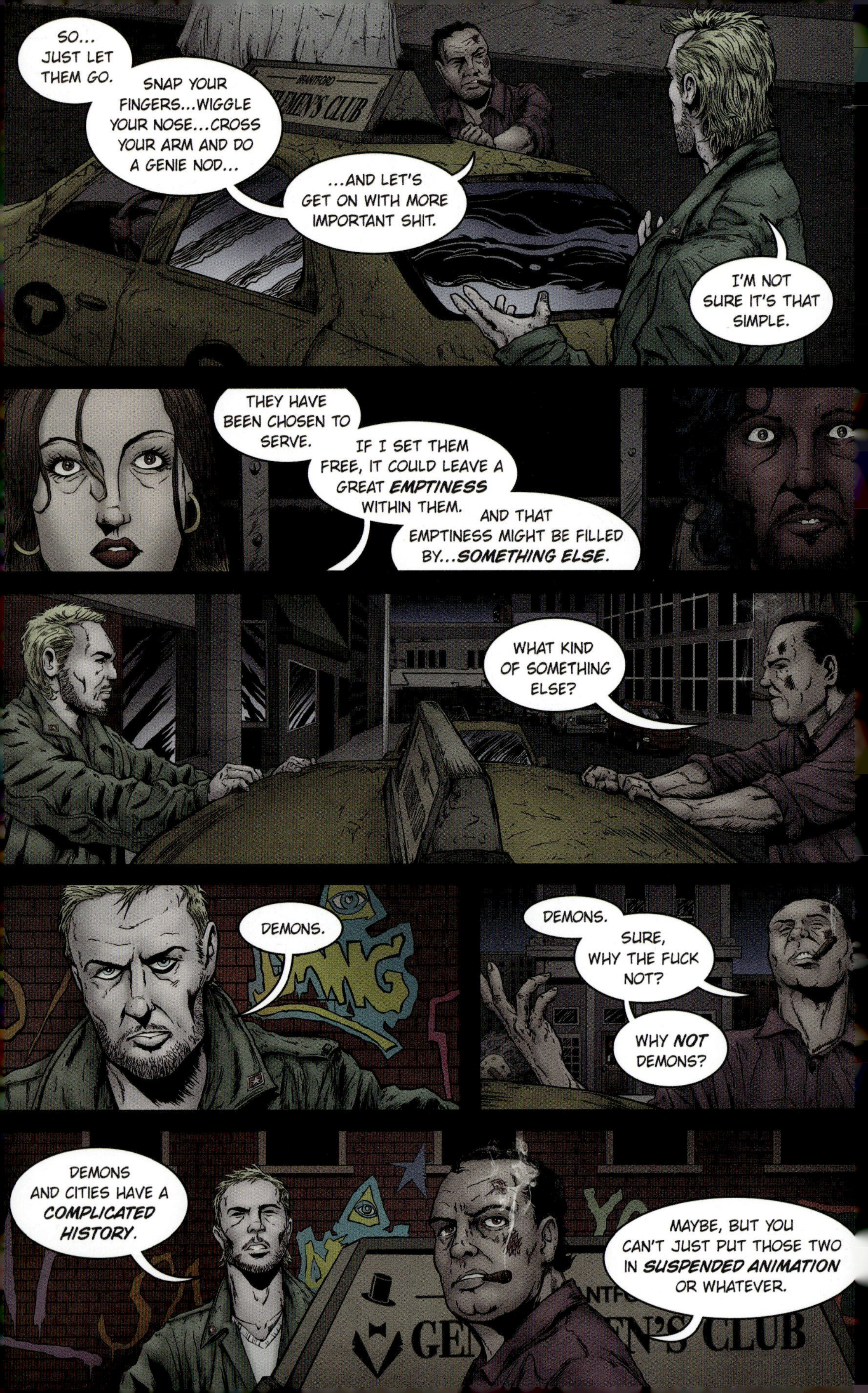
SO... JUST LET THEM GO.
SNAP YOUR FINGERS...WIGGLE YOUR NOSE...CROSS YOUR ARM AND DO A GENIE NOD...
...AND LET'S GET ON WITH MORE IMPORTANT SHIT.
I'M NOT SURE IT'S THAT SIMPLE.
THEY HAVE BEEN CHOSEN TO SERVE.
IF I SET THEM FREE, IT COULD LEAVE A GREAT EMPTINESS WITHIN THEM.
AND THAT EMPTINESS MIGHT BE FILLED BY...SOMETHING ELSE.
WHAT KIND OF SOMETHING ELSE?
DEMONS.
DEMONS.
SURE, WHY THE FUCK NOT?
WHY NOT DEMONS?
DEMONS AND CITIES HAVE A COMPLICATED HISTORY.
MAYBE, BUT YOU CAN'T JUST PUT THOSE TWO IN SUSPENDED ANIMATION OR WHATEVER.

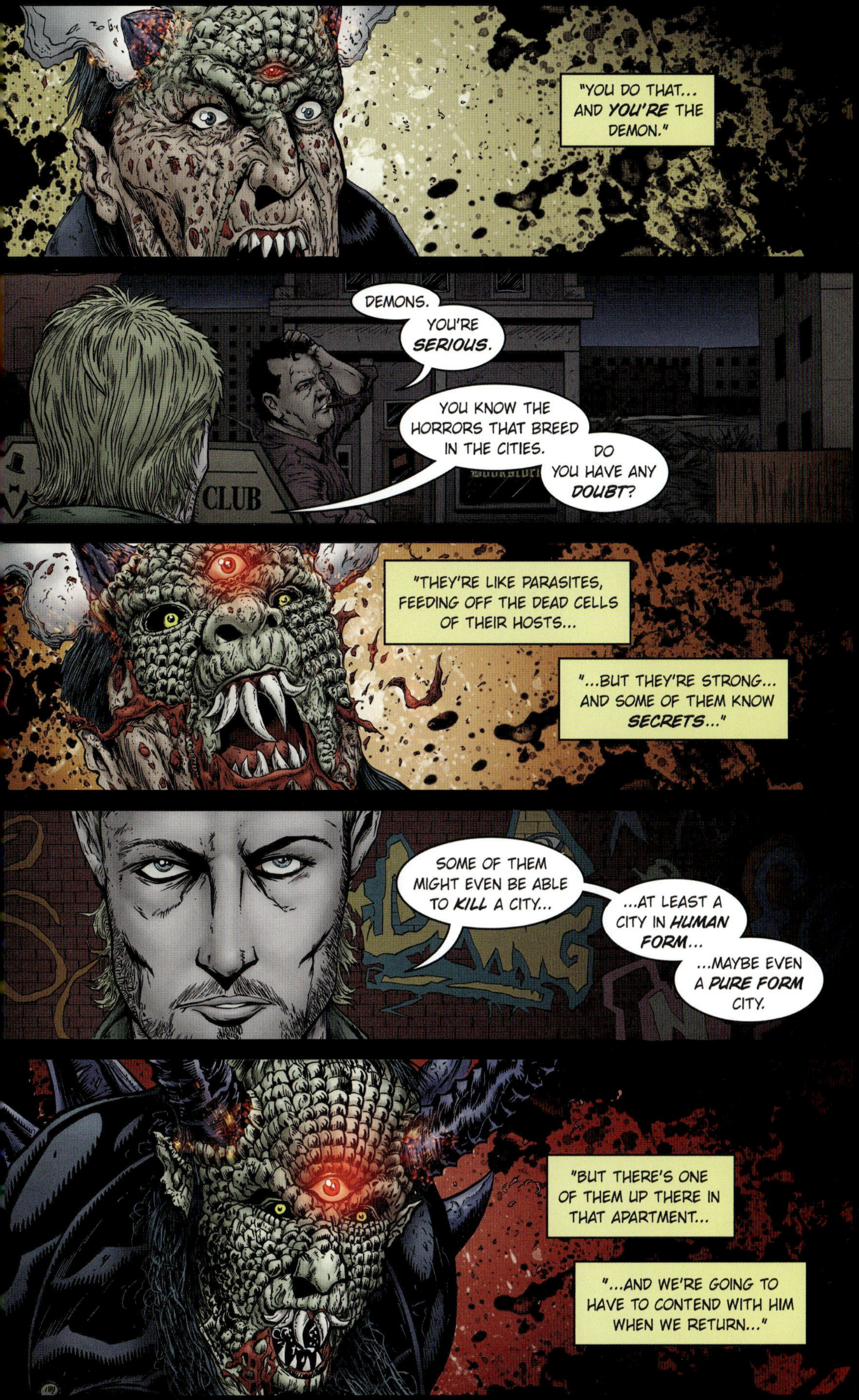
"YOU DO THAT... AND YOU'RE THE DEMON."
DEMONS. YOU'RE SERIOUS.
YOU KNOW THE HORRORS THAT BREED IN THE CITIES.
DO YOU HAVE ANY DOUBT?
CLUB
"THEY'RE LIKE PARASITES, FEEDING OFF THE DEAD CELLS OF THEIR HOSTS...
"...BUT THEY'RE STRONG... AND SOME OF THEM KNOW SECRETS..."
SOME OF THEM MIGHT EVEN BE ABLE TO KILL A CITY...
...AT LEAST A CITY IN HUMAN FORM...
...MAYBE EVEN A PURE FORM CITY.
"BUT THERE'S ONE OF THEM UP THERE IN THAT APARTMENT...
"...AND WE'RE GOING TO HAVE TO CONTEND WITH HIM WHEN WE RETURN..."

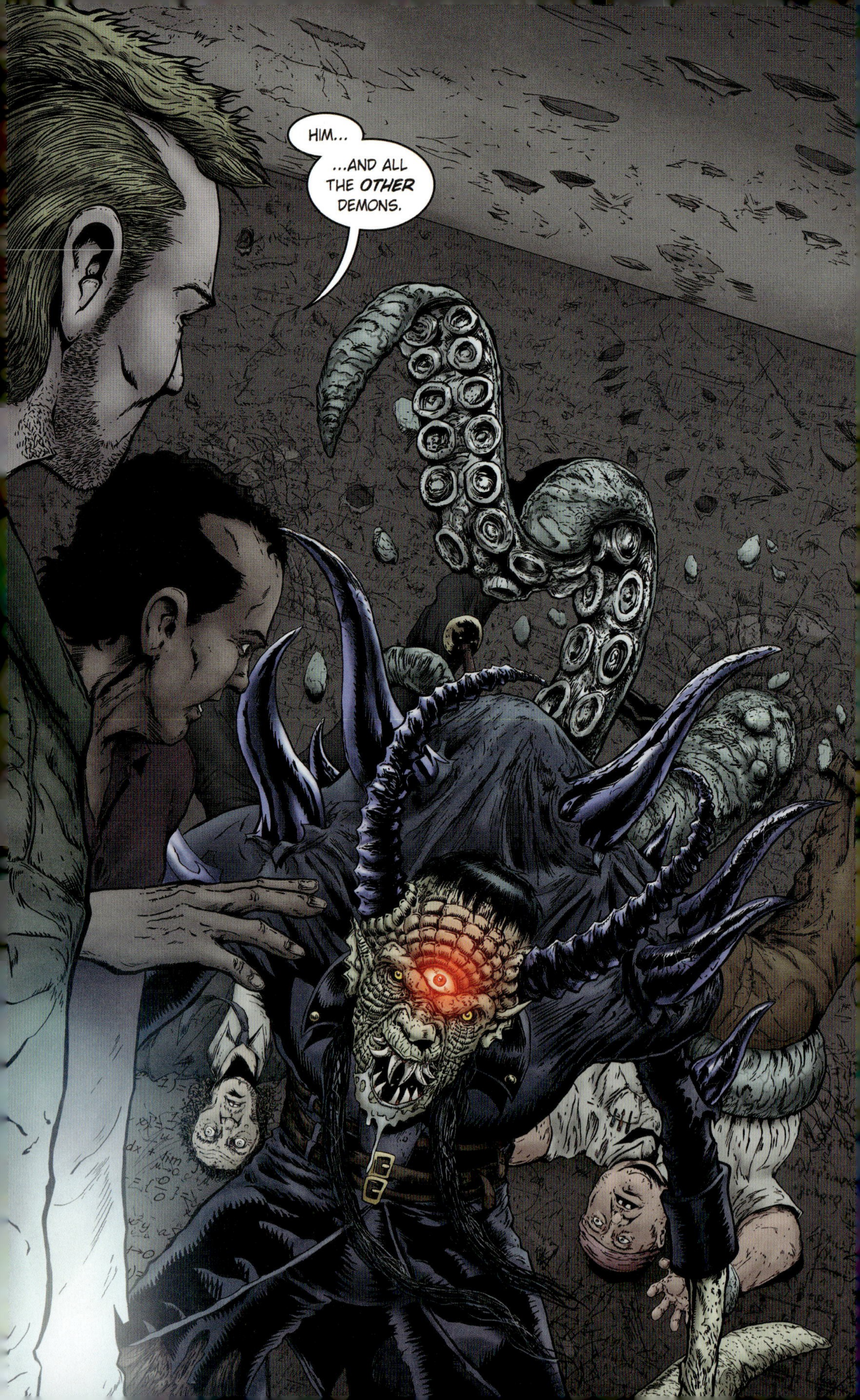
HIM...
...AND ALL THE *OTHER* DEMONS.

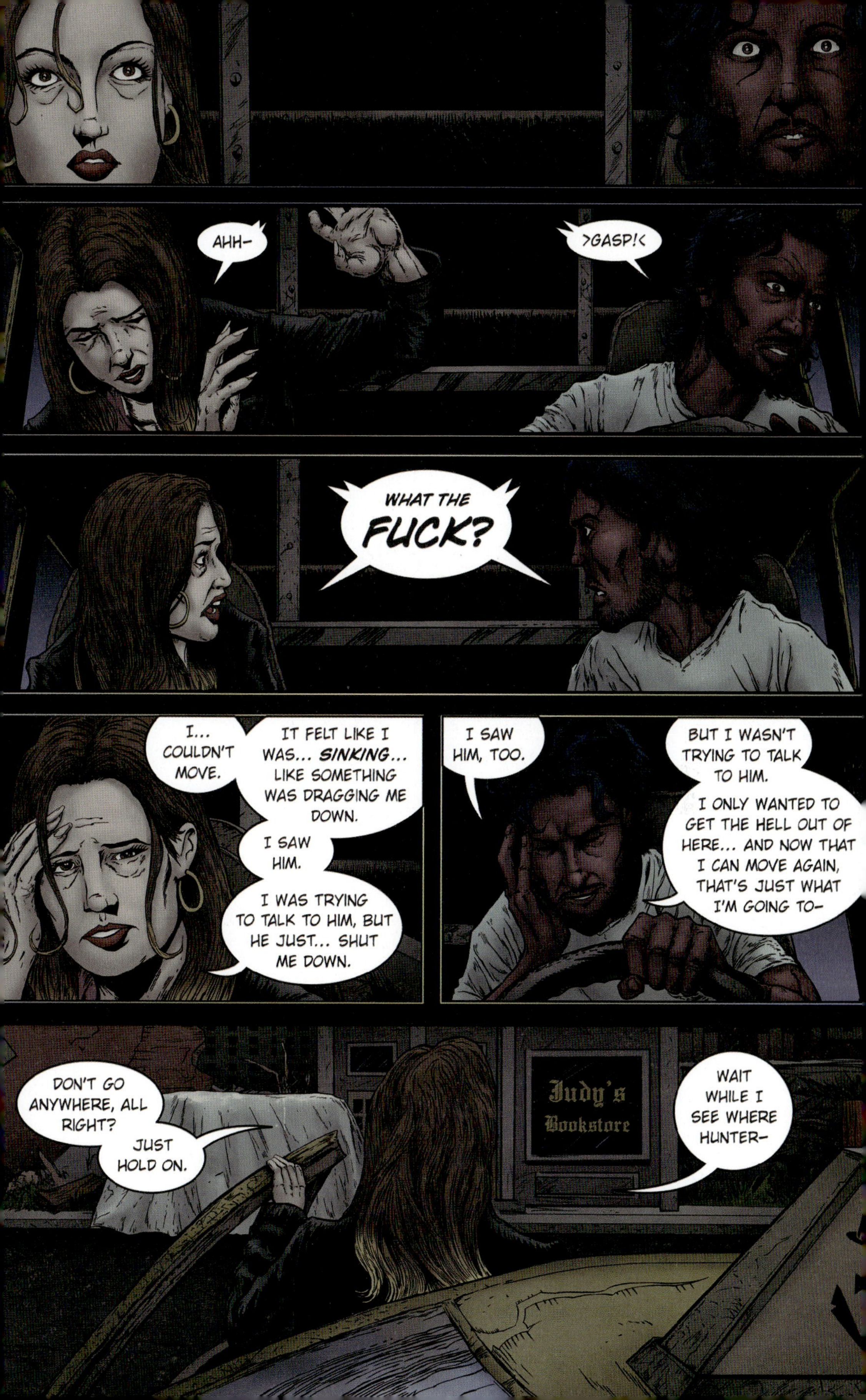
AHH-
>GASP!<
WHAT THE FUCK?
I... COULDN'T MOVE.
IT FELT LIKE I WAS... SINKING... LIKE SOMETHING WAS DRAGGING ME DOWN.
I SAW HIM.
I WAS TRYING TO TALK TO HIM, BUT HE JUST... SHUT ME DOWN.
I SAW HIM, TOO.
BUT I WASN'T TRYING TO TALK TO HIM.
I ONLY WANTED TO GET THE HELL OUT OF HERE... AND NOW THAT I CAN MOVE AGAIN, THAT'S JUST WHAT I'M GOING TO-
DON'T GO ANYWHERE, ALL RIGHT?
JUST HOLD ON.
Judy's Bookstore
WAIT WHILE I SEE WHERE HUNTER-

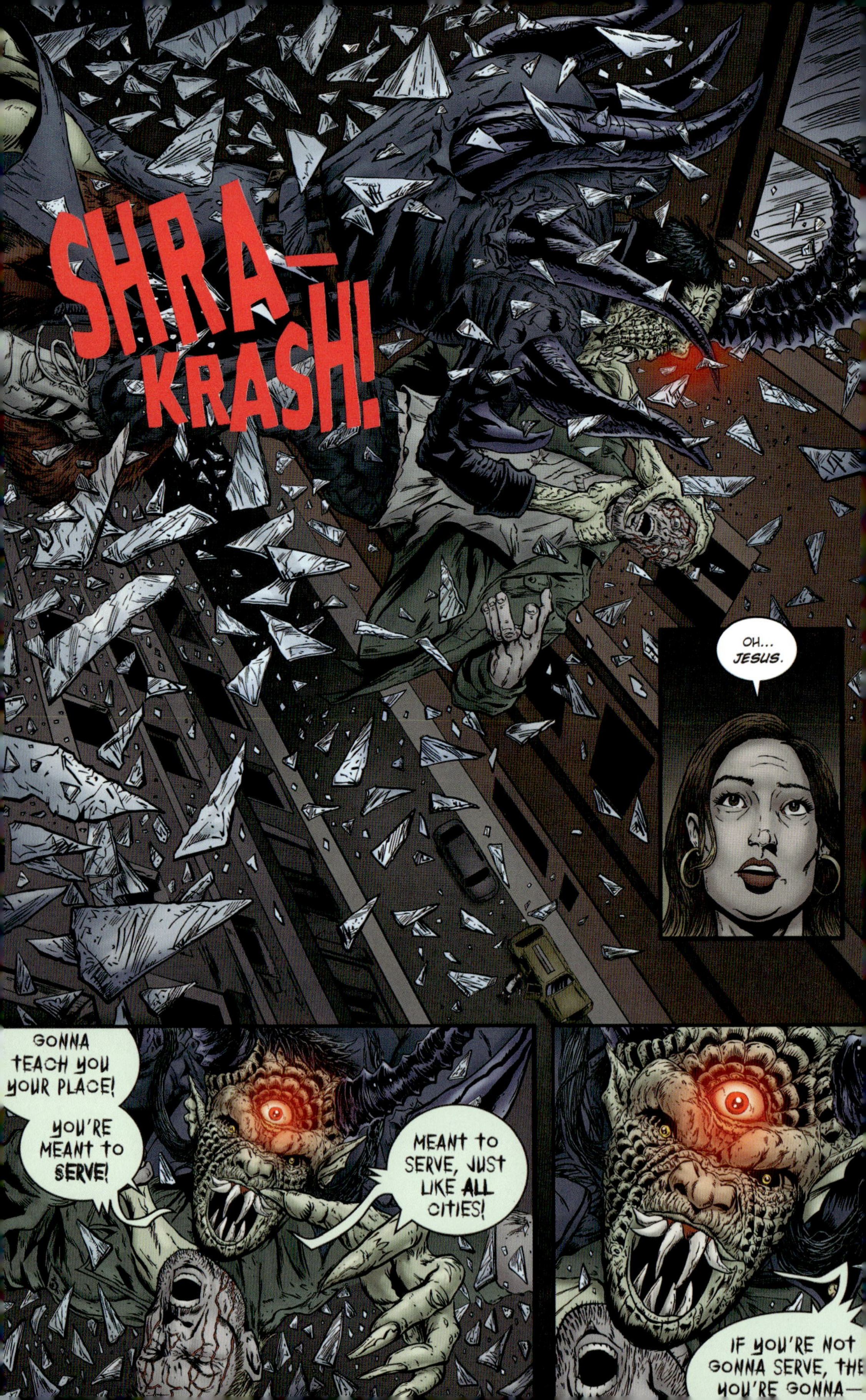
SHRA—
KRASH!
OH... JESUS.
GONNA TEACH YOU YOUR PLACE!
YOU'RE MEANT TO SERVE!
MEANT TO SERVE, JUST LIKE ALL CITIES!
IF YOU'RE NOT GONNA SERVE, THE YOU'RE GONNA—

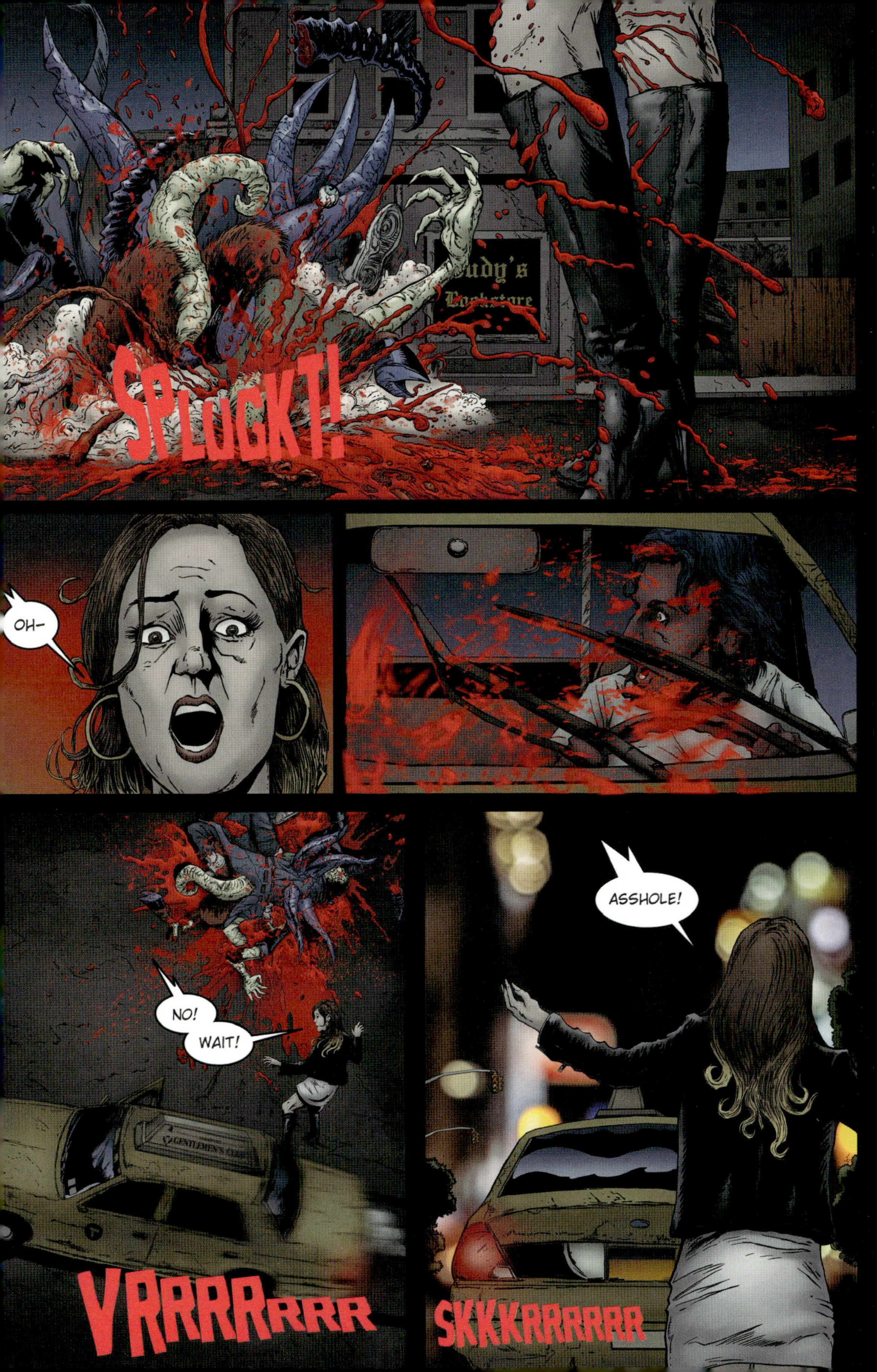
SPLUGKT!
OH-
NO!
WAIT!
VRRRRrrr
ASSHOLE!
SKKRRRRRR

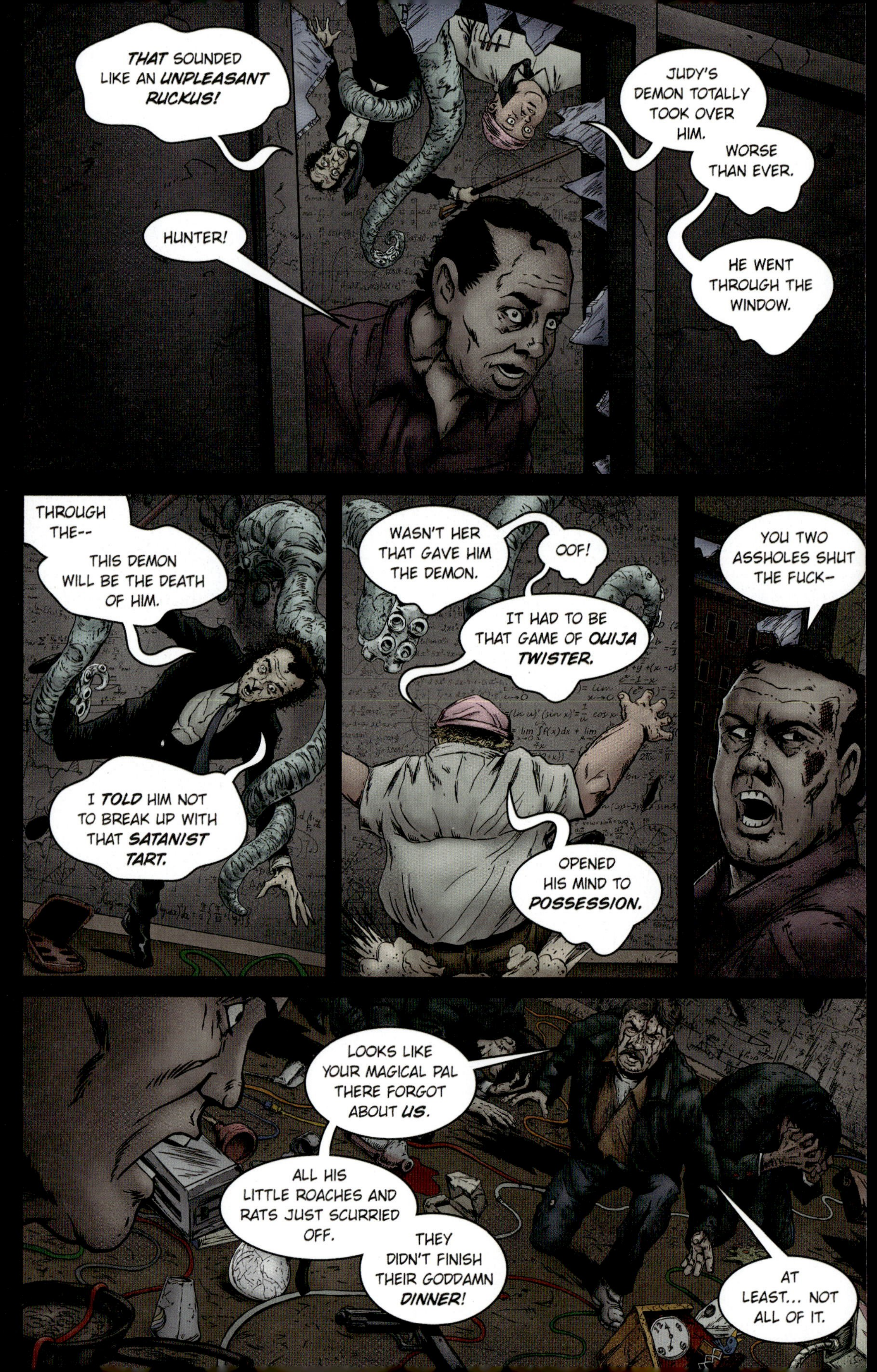
THAT SOUNDED LIKE AN UNPLEASANT RUCKUS!
JUDY'S DEMON TOTALLY TOOK OVER HIM.
WORSE THAN EVER.
HUNTER!
HE WENT THROUGH THE WINDOW.
THROUGH THE--
THIS DEMON WILL BE THE DEATH OF HIM.
I TOLD HIM NOT TO BREAK UP WITH THAT SATANIST TART.
WASN'T HER THAT GAVE HIM THE DEMON.
OOF!
IT HAD TO BE THAT GAME OF OUIJA TWISTER.
OPENED HIS MIND TO POSSESSION.
YOU TWO ASSHOLES SHUT THE FUCK-
LOOKS LIKE YOUR MAGICAL PAL THERE FORGOT ABOUT US.
ALL HIS LITTLE ROACHES AND RATS JUST SCURRIED OFF.
THEY DIDN'T FINISH THEIR GODDAMN DINNER!
AT LEAST... NOT ALL OF IT.

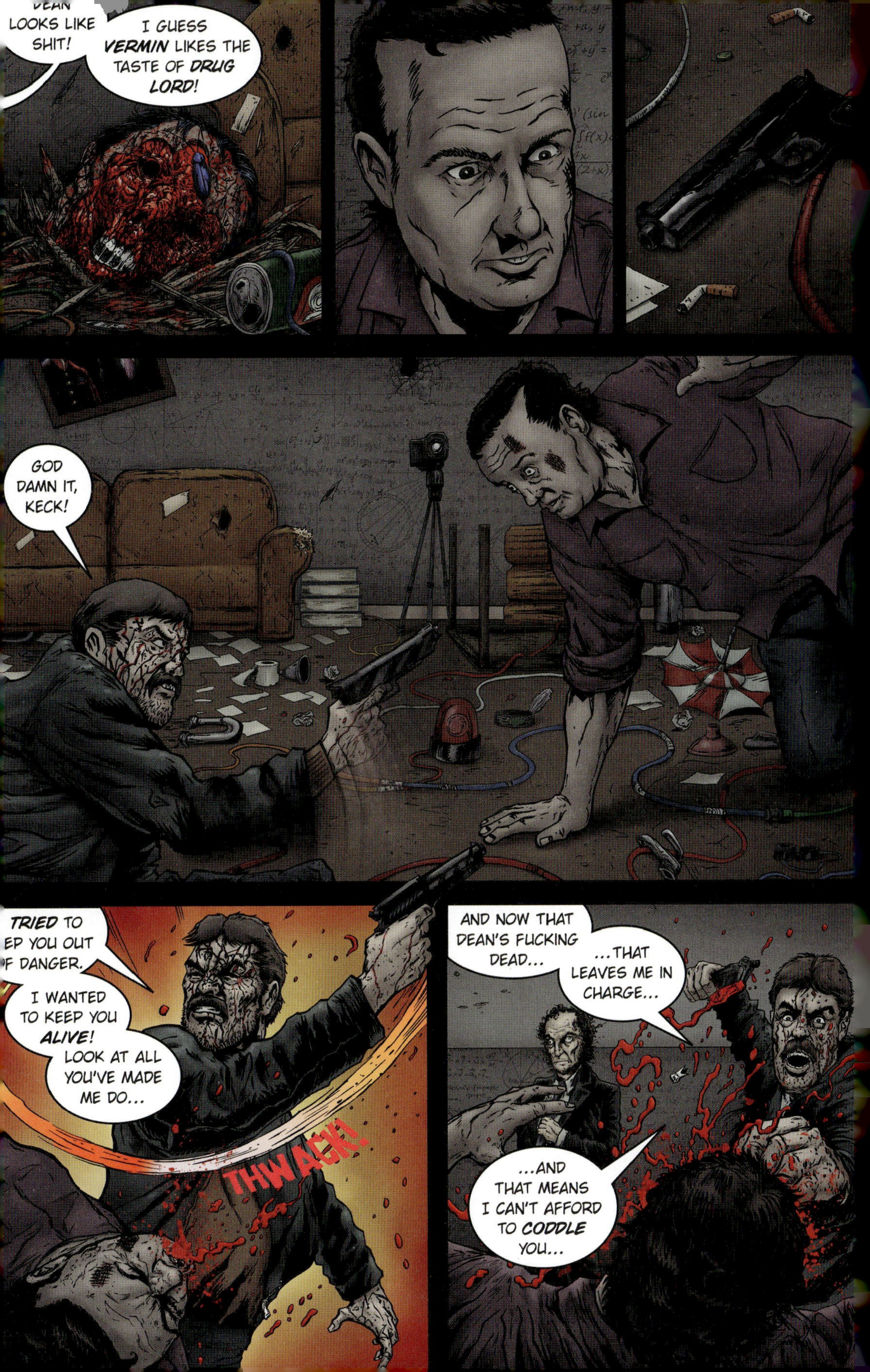
DEAN LOOKS LIKE SHIT!
I GUESS VERMIN LIKES THE TASTE OF DRUG LORD!
GOD DAMN IT, KECK!
TRIED TO EP YOU OUT F DANGER.
I WANTED TO KEEP YOU ALIVE!
LOOK AT ALL YOU'VE MADE ME DO...
THWACK!
AND NOW THAT DEAN'S FUCKING DEAD...
...THAT LEAVES ME IN CHARGE...
...AND THAT MEANS I CAN'T AFFORD TO CODDLE YOU...

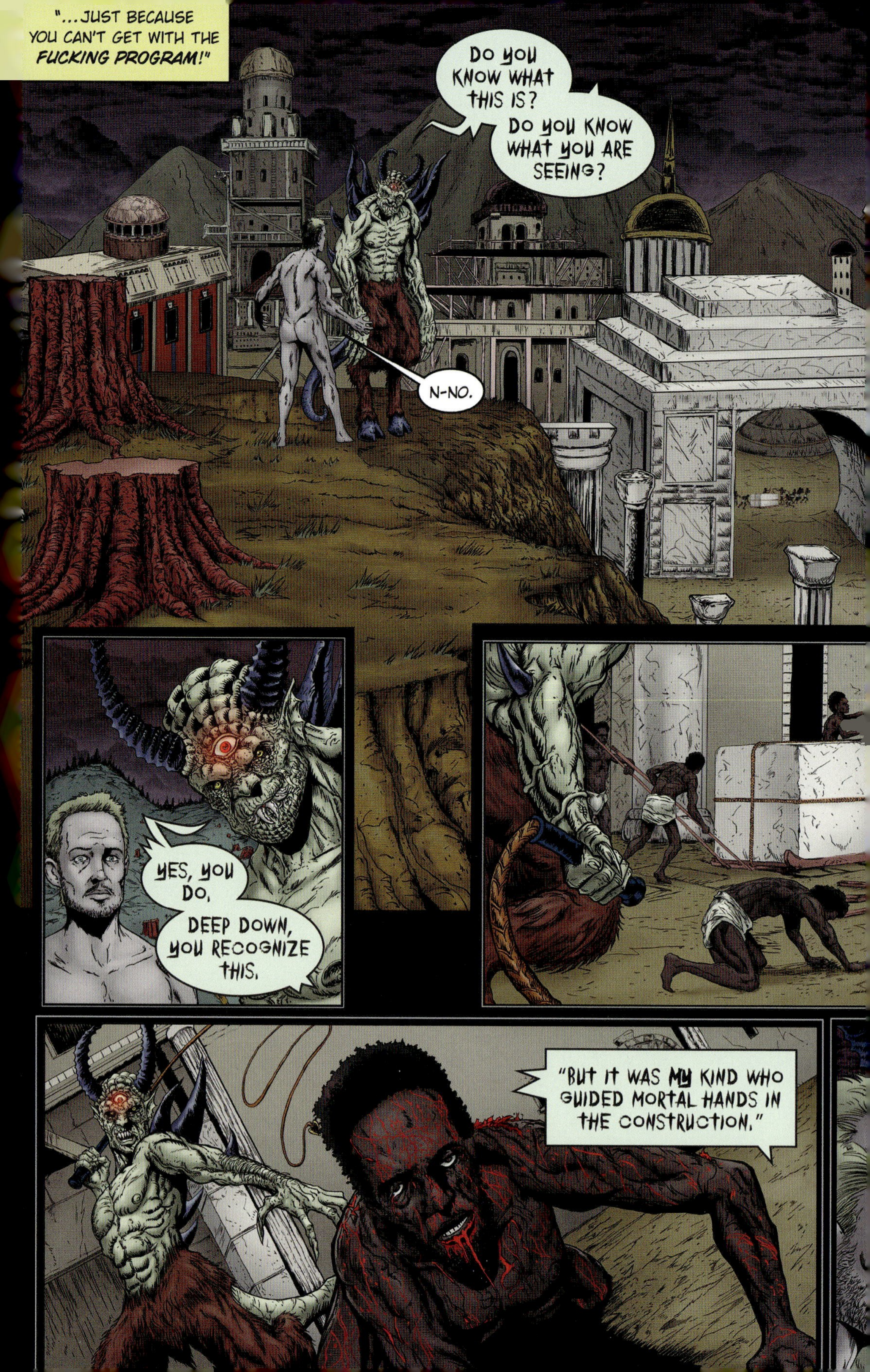
"...JUST BECAUSE YOU CAN'T GET WITH THE FUCKING PROGRAM!"
DO YOU KNOW WHAT THIS IS?
DO YOU KNOW WHAT YOU ARE SEEING?
N-NO.
YES, YOU DO.
DEEP DOWN, YOU RECOGNIZE THIS.
"BUT IT WAS MY KIND WHO GUIDED MORTAL HANDS IN THE CONSTRUCTION."

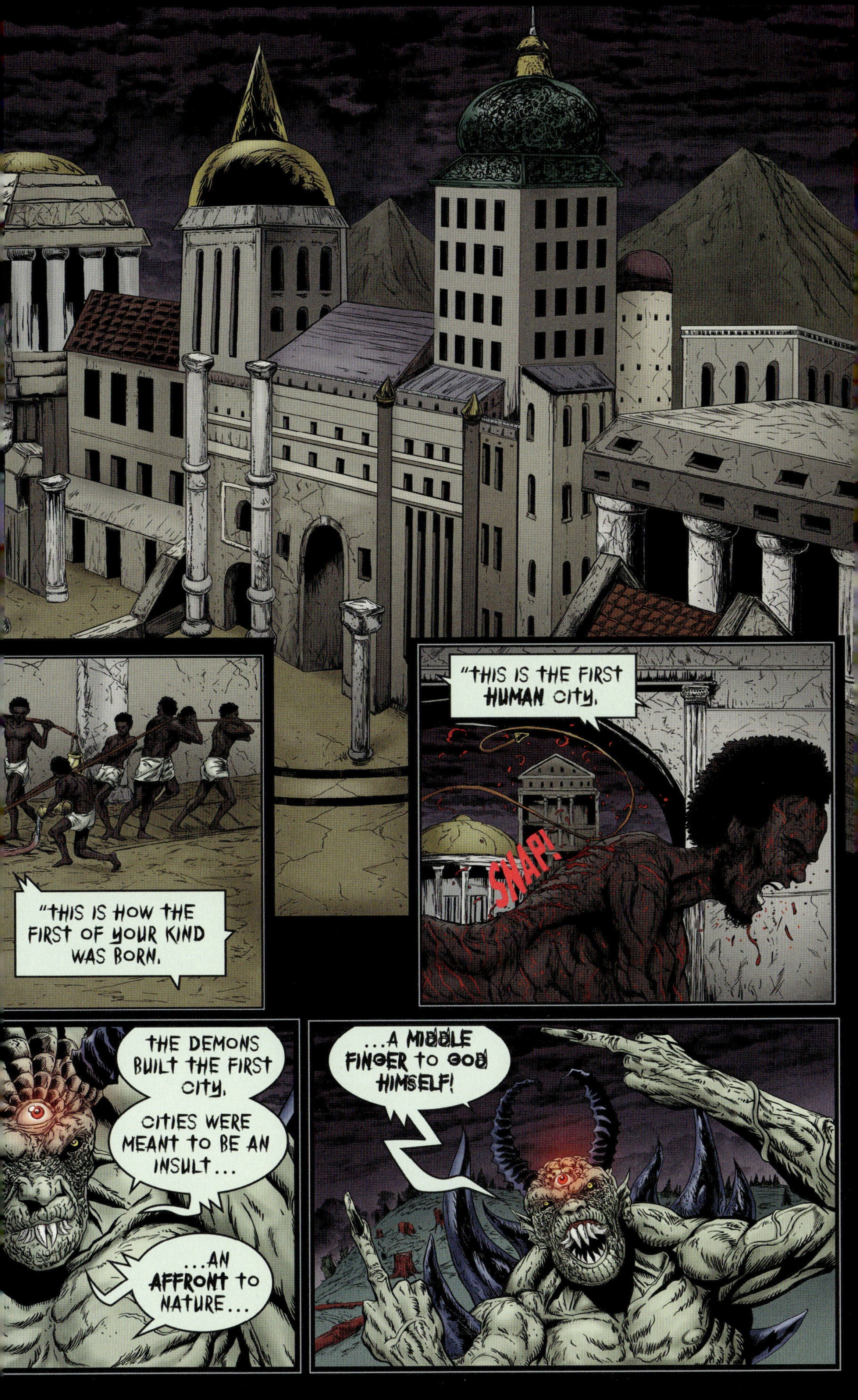
"THIS IS THE FIRST HUMAN CITY.
SNAP!
"THIS IS HOW THE FIRST OF YOUR KIND WAS BORN.
THE DEMONS BUILT THE FIRST CITY.
CITIES WERE MEANT TO BE AN INSULT...
...AN AFFRONT TO NATURE...
...A MIDDLE FINGER TO GOD HIMSELF!

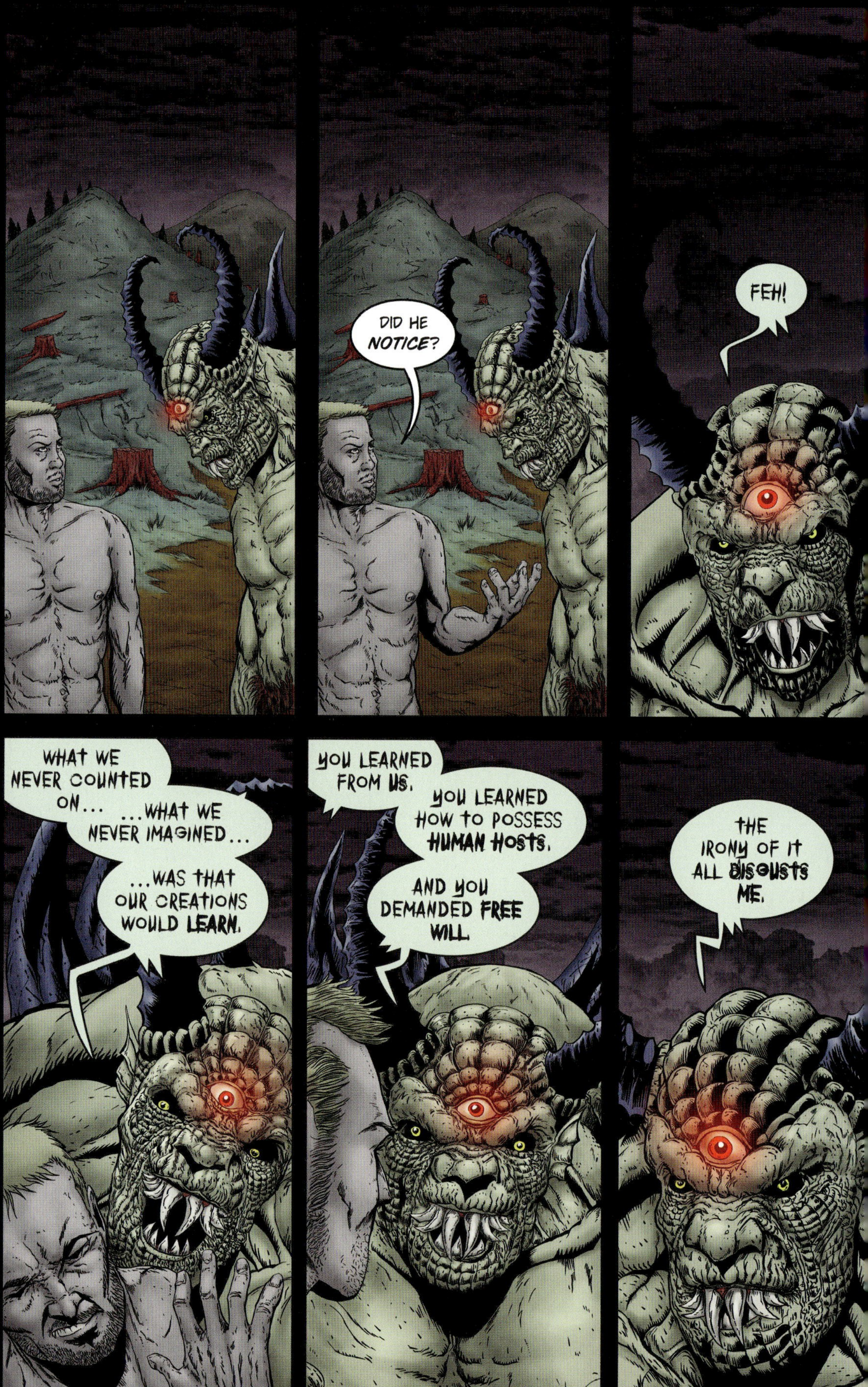
DID HE NOTICE?
FEH!
WHAT WE NEVER COUNTED ON... ...WHAT WE NEVER IMAGINED... ...WAS THAT OUR CREATIONS WOULD LEARN.
YOU LEARNED FROM US.
YOU LEARNED HOW TO POSSESS HUMAN HOSTS.
AND YOU DEMANDED FREE WILL.
THE IRONY OF IT ALL DISGUSTS ME.

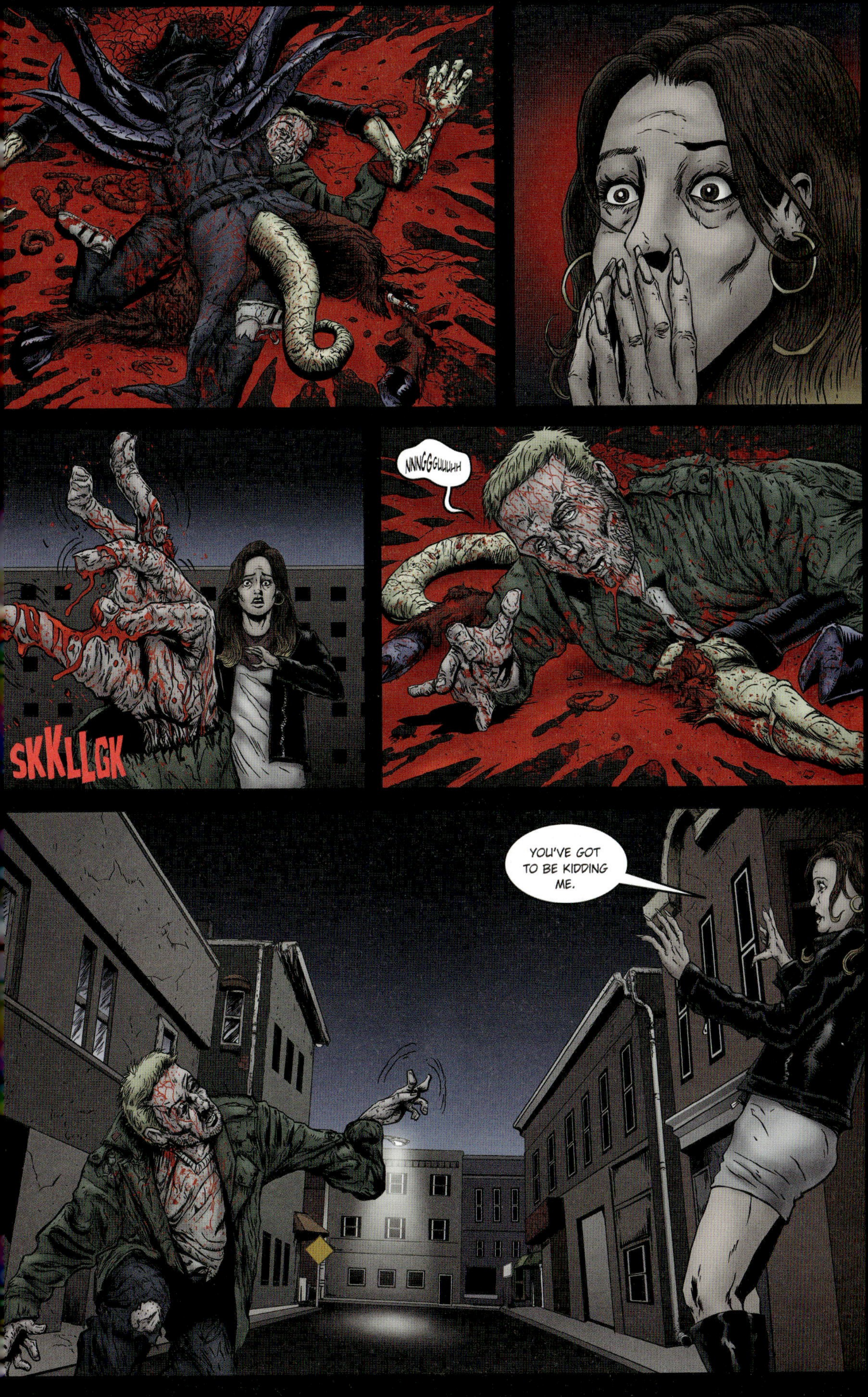
SKKLLGK
NNNGGGUUUHH
YOU'VE GOT TO BE KIDDING ME.

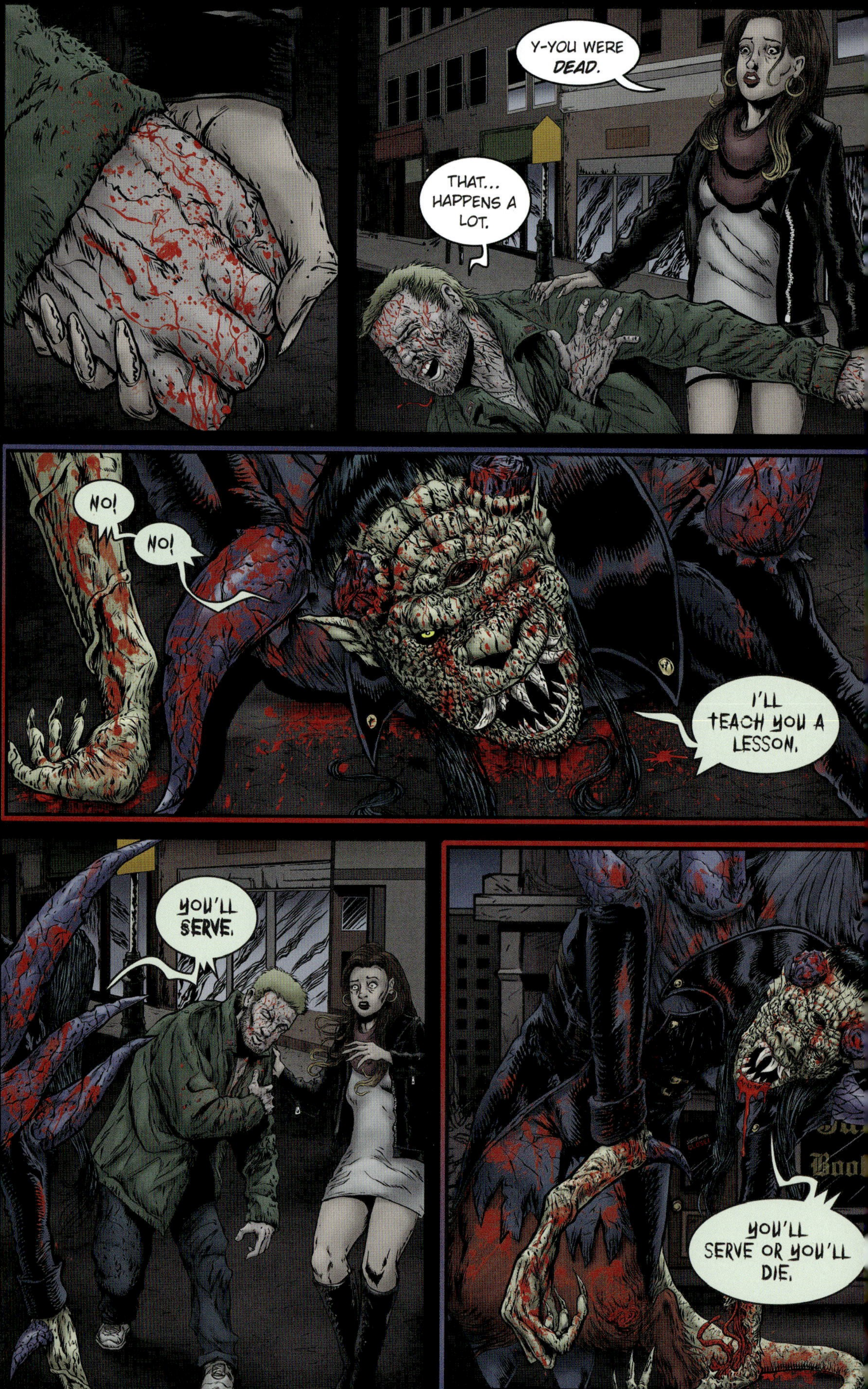
Y-YOU WERE DEAD.
THAT... HAPPENS A LOT.
NO!
NO!
I'LL TEACH YOU A LESSON.
YOU'LL SERVE.
YOU'LL SERVE OR YOU'LL DIE.

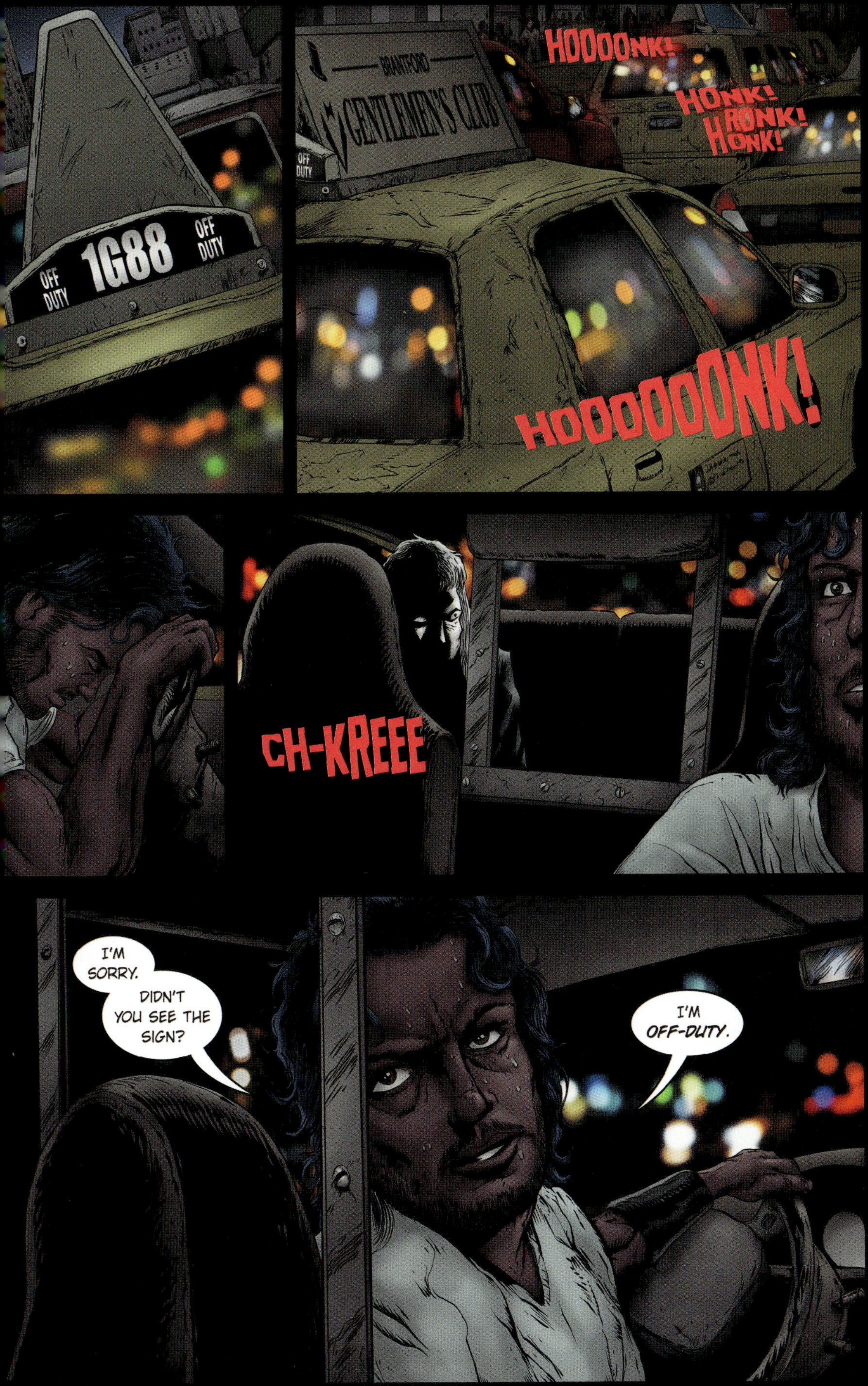
1G88
OFF DUTY
OFF DUTY
BRANTFORD
GENTLEMEN'S CLUB
OFF DUTY
HOOOONK!
HONK!
RONK!
HONK!
HOOOOOONK!
CH-KREEE
I'M SORRY. DIDN'T YOU SEE THE SIGN?
I'M OFF-DUTY.

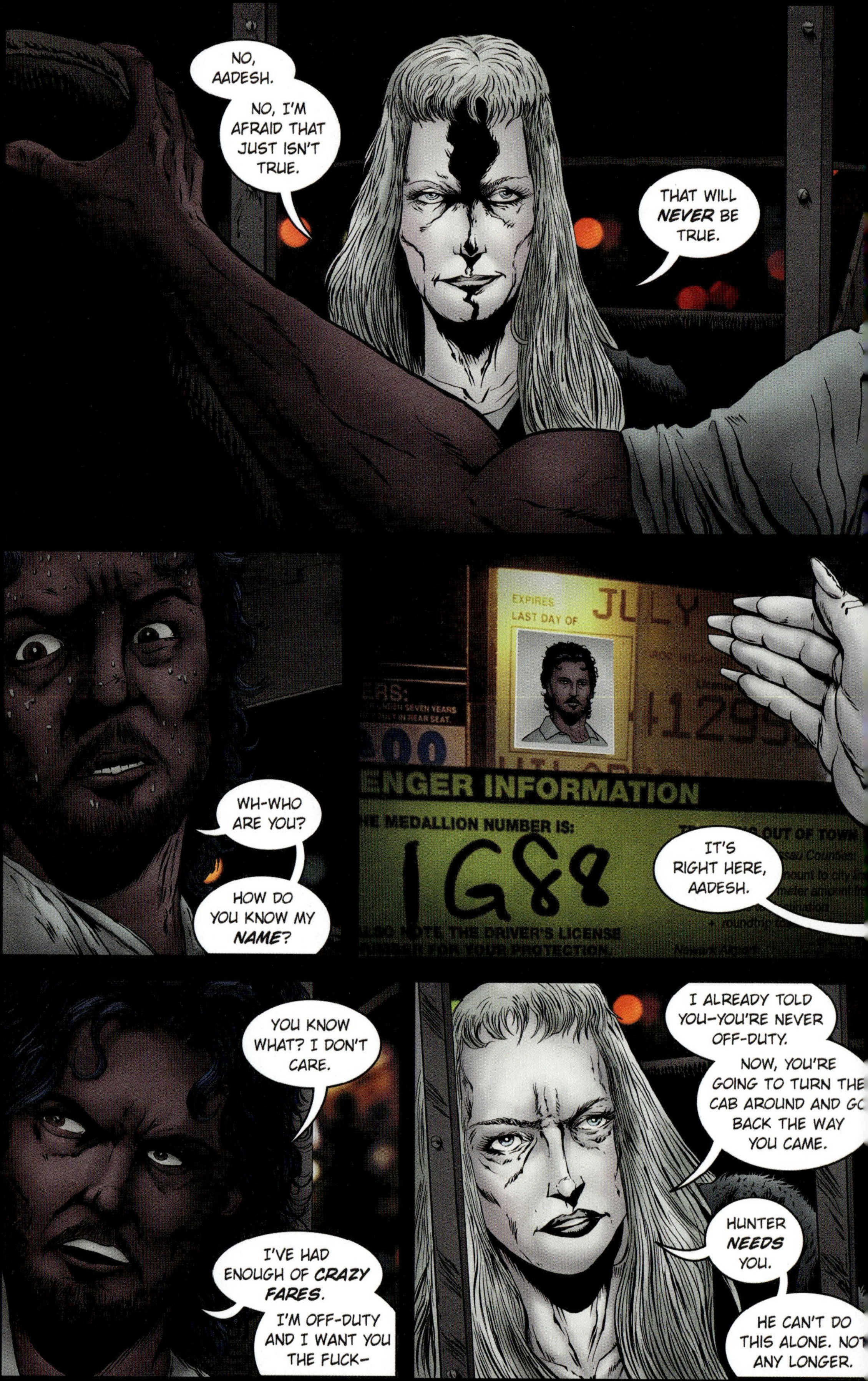
NO, AADESH.
NO, I'M AFRAID THAT JUST ISN'T TRUE.
THAT WILL NEVER BE TRUE.
WH-WHO ARE YOU?
HOW DO YOU KNOW MY NAME?
EXPIRES LAST DAY OF JULY
ENGER INFORMATION
HE MEDALLION NUMBER IS:
1G88
IT'S RIGHT HERE, AADESH.
YOU KNOW WHAT? I DON'T CARE.
I'VE HAD ENOUGH OF CRAZY FARES.
I'M OFF-DUTY AND I WANT YOU THE FUCK-
I ALREADY TOLD YOU-YOU'RE NEVER OFF-DUTY.
NOW, YOU'RE GOING TO TURN THE CAB AROUND AND GO BACK THE WAY YOU CAME.
HUNTER NEEDS YOU.
HE CAN'T DO THIS ALONE. NOT ANY LONGER.

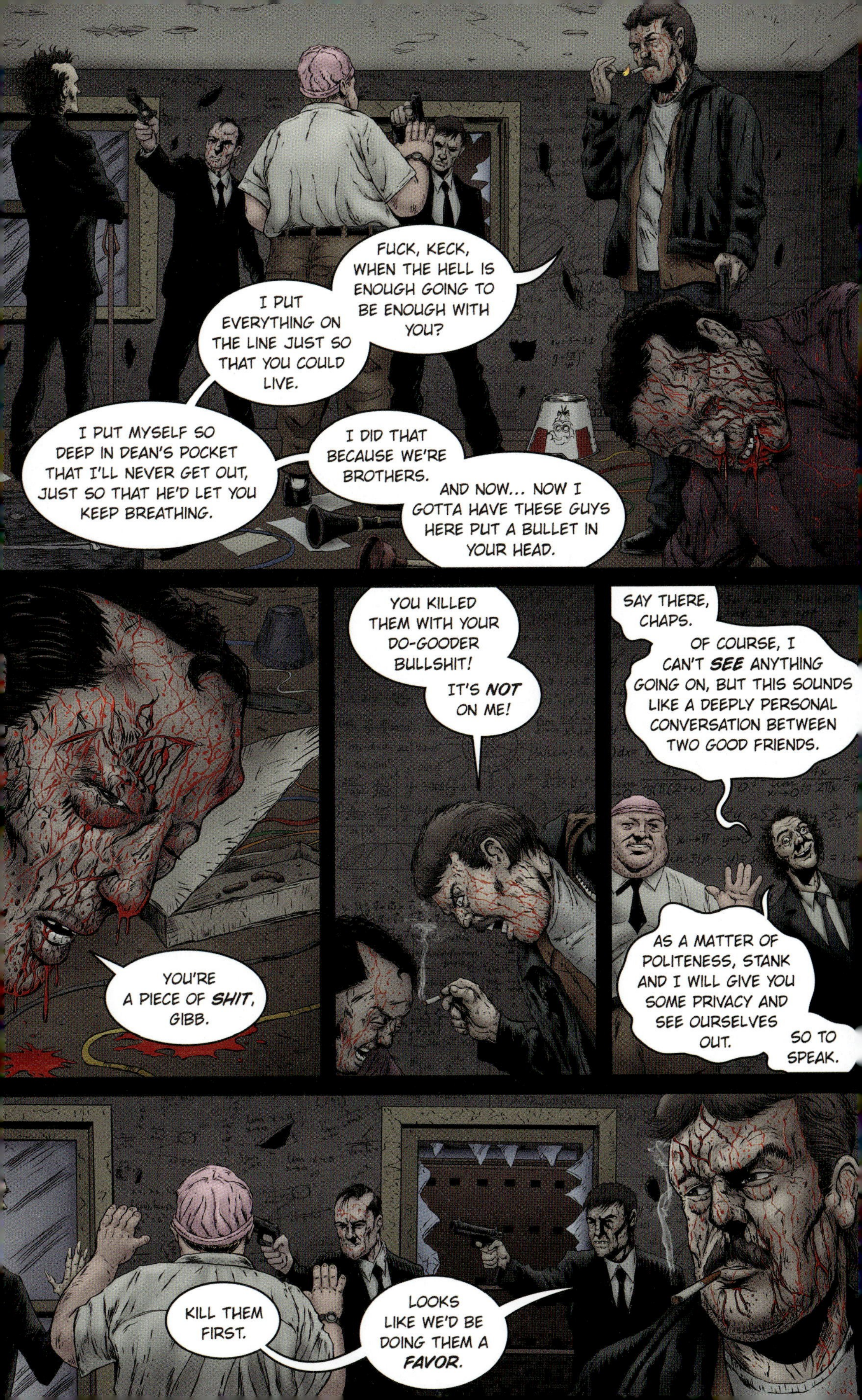
FUCK, KECK, WHEN THE HELL IS ENOUGH GOING TO BE ENOUGH WITH YOU?
I PUT EVERYTHING ON THE LINE JUST SO THAT YOU COULD LIVE.
I PUT MYSELF SO DEEP IN DEAN'S POCKET THAT I'LL NEVER GET OUT, JUST SO THAT HE'D LET YOU KEEP BREATHING.
I DID THAT BECAUSE WE'RE BROTHERS.
AND NOW... NOW I GOTTA HAVE THESE GUYS HERE PUT A BULLET IN YOUR HEAD.
YOU'RE A PIECE OF *SHIT*, GIBB.
YOU KILLED THEM WITH YOUR DO-GOODER BULLSHIT!
IT'S *NOT* ON ME!
SAY THERE, CHAPS.
OF COURSE, I CAN'T *SEE* ANYTHING GOING ON, BUT THIS SOUNDS LIKE A DEEPLY PERSONAL CONVERSATION BETWEEN TWO GOOD FRIENDS.
AS A MATTER OF POLITENESS, STANK AND I WILL GIVE YOU SOME PRIVACY AND SEE OURSELVES OUT.
SO TO SPEAK.
KILL THEM FIRST.
LOOKS LIKE WE'D BE DOING THEM A *FAVOR*.

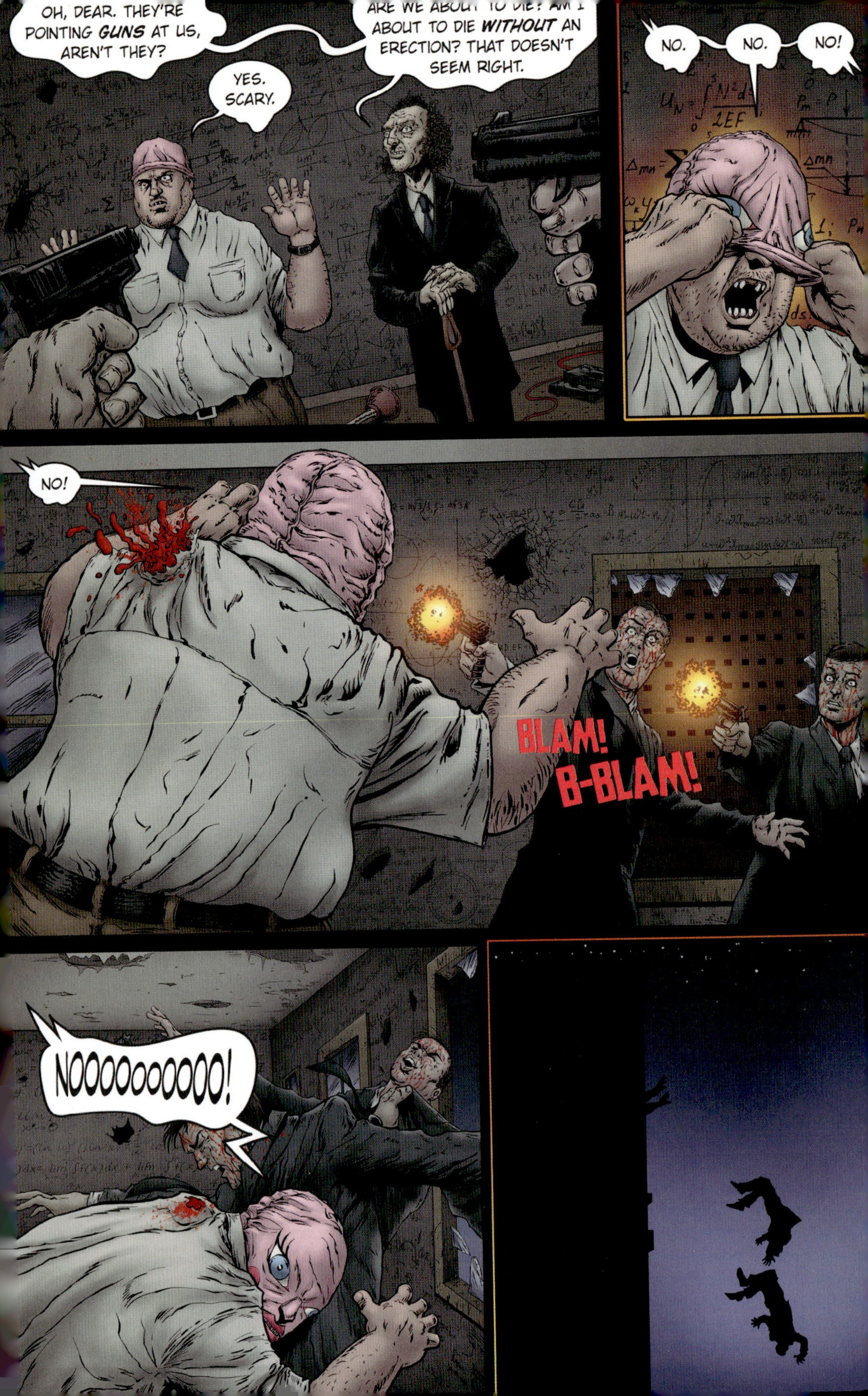

OH, DEAR. THEY'RE POINTING **GUNS** AT US, AREN'T THEY?
YES. SCARY.
ARE WE ABOUT TO DIE? AM I ABOUT TO DIE ***WITHOUT*** AN ERECTION? THAT DOESN'T SEEM RIGHT.
NO.
NO.
NO!
NO!
BLAM!
B-BLAM!
NOOOOOOOOOO!

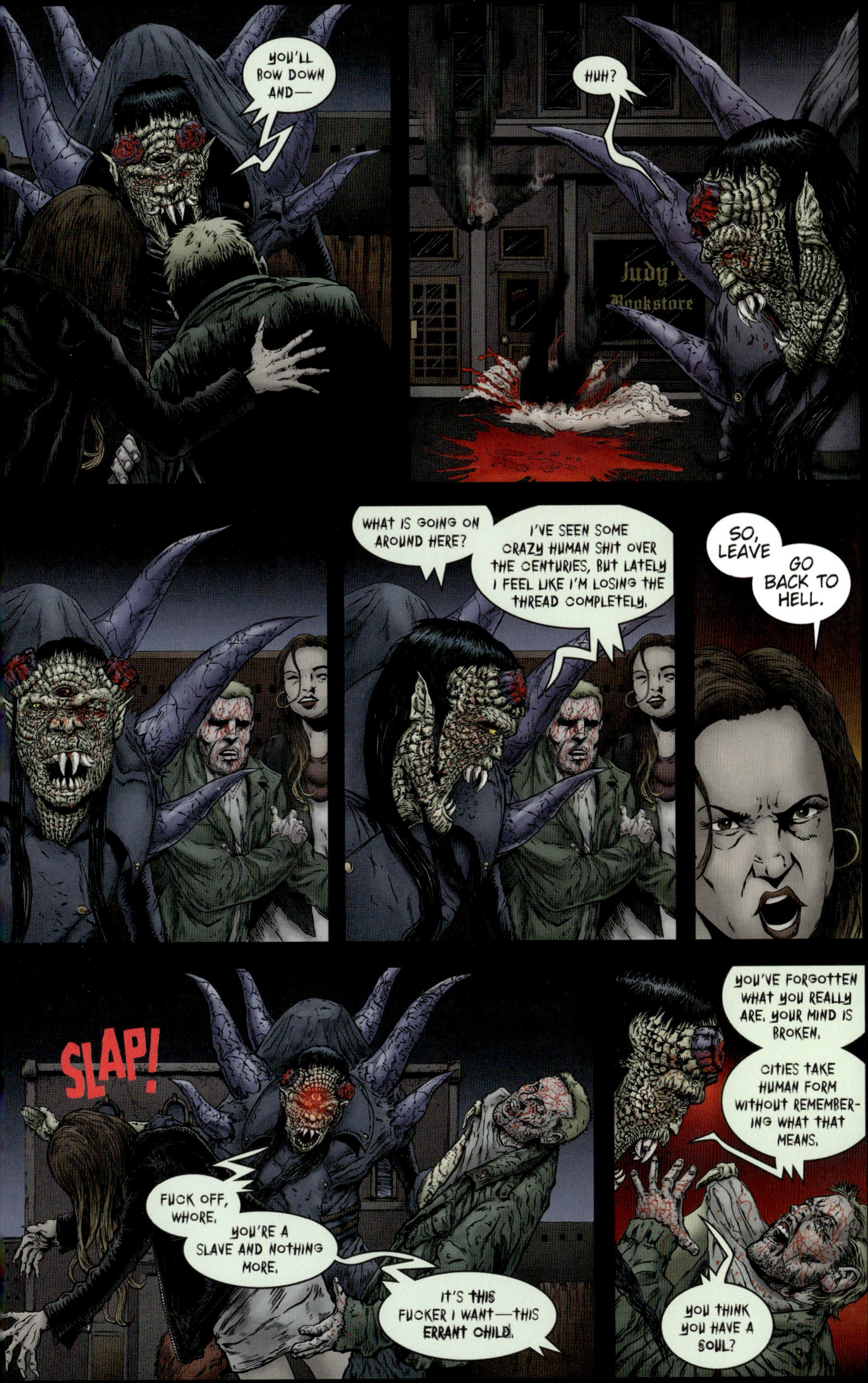
YOU'LL BOW DOWN AND—
HUH?
Judy's Bookstore
WHAT IS GOING ON AROUND HERE?
I'VE SEEN SOME CRAZY HUMAN SHIT OVER THE CENTURIES, BUT LATELY I FEEL LIKE I'M LOSING THE THREAD COMPLETELY.
SO, LEAVE
GO BACK TO HELL.
SLAP!
FUCK OFF, WHORE.
YOU'RE A SLAVE AND NOTHING MORE.
IT'S THIS FUCKER I WANT—THIS ERRANT CHILD.
YOU'VE FORGOTTEN WHAT YOU REALLY ARE. YOUR MIND IS BROKEN.
CITIES TAKE HUMAN FORM WITHOUT REMEMBERING WHAT THAT MEANS.
YOU THINK YOU HAVE A SOUL?

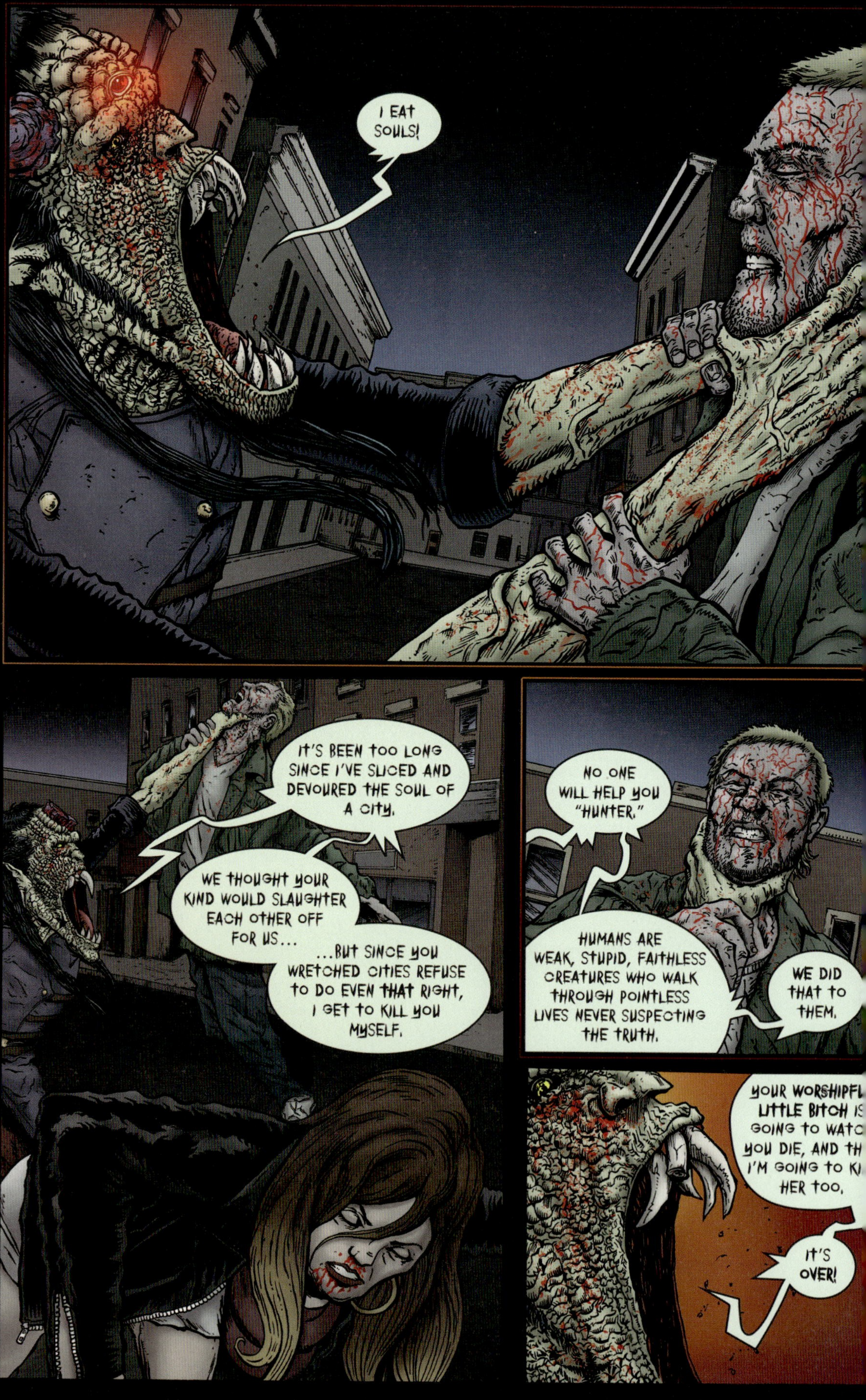
I EAT SOULS!
IT'S BEEN TOO LONG SINCE I'VE SLICED AND DEVOURED THE SOUL OF A CITY.
WE THOUGHT YOUR KIND WOULD SLAUGHTER EACH OTHER OFF FOR US...
...BUT SINCE YOU WRETCHED CITIES REFUSE TO DO EVEN THAT RIGHT, I GET TO KILL YOU MYSELF.
NO ONE WILL HELP YOU "HUNTER."
HUMANS ARE WEAK, STUPID, FAITHLESS CREATURES WHO WALK THROUGH POINTLESS LIVES NEVER SUSPECTING THE TRUTH.
WE DID THAT TO THEM.
YOUR WORSHIPFL LITTLE BITCH IS GOING TO WATC YOU DIE, AND TH I'M GOING TO KI HER TOO.
IT'S OVER!

"YOU HAVE NO ONE LEFT!"

OK, FAT ASS.

I'VE HAD ABOUT ENOUGH WEIRD SHIT FOR TODAY.

TIME TO WRAP THIS UP.

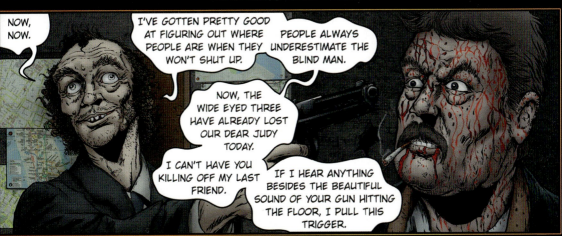

NOW, NOW.

I'VE GOTTEN PRETTY GOOD AT FIGURING OUT WHERE PEOPLE ARE WHEN THEY WON'T SHUT UP.

PEOPLE ALWAYS UNDERESTIMATE THE BLIND MAN.

NOW, THE WIDE EYED THREE HAVE ALREADY LOST OUR DEAR JUDY TODAY.

I CAN'T HAVE YOU KILLING OFF MY LAST FRIEND.

IF I HEAR ANYTHING BESIDES THE BEAUTIFUL SOUND OF YOUR GUN HITTING THE FLOOR, I PULL THIS TRIGGER.

AND YOU BECOME MY NEXT *DATE*.

I'M A *COP*, YOU IDIOT.

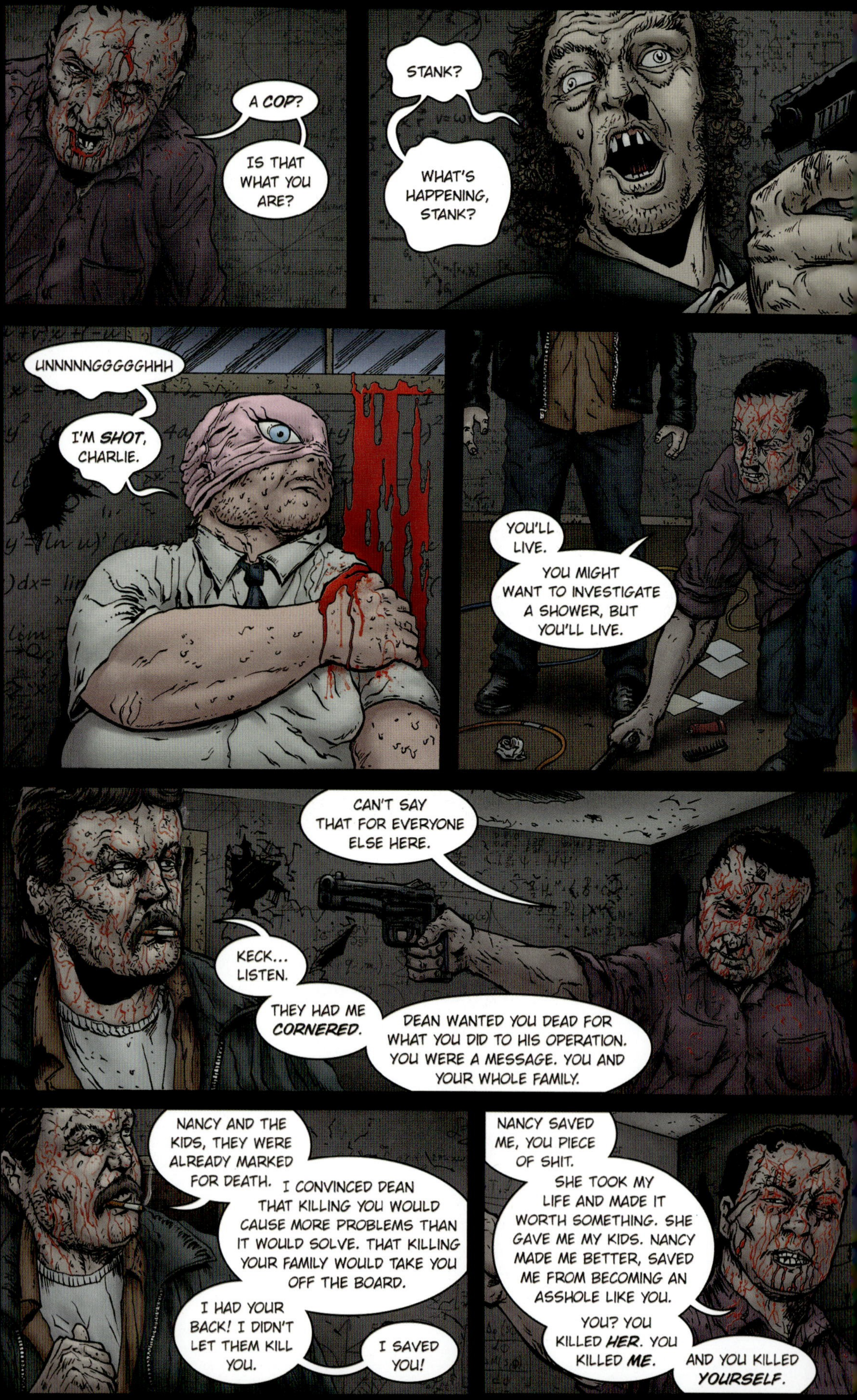

A COP?
IS THAT WHAT YOU ARE?
STANK?
WHAT'S HAPPENING, STANK?
UNNNNNGGGGGHHH
I'M SHOT, CHARLIE.
YOU'LL LIVE.
YOU MIGHT WANT TO INVESTIGATE A SHOWER, BUT YOU'LL LIVE.
CAN'T SAY THAT FOR EVERYONE ELSE HERE.
KECK... LISTEN.
THEY HAD ME CORNERED.
DEAN WANTED YOU DEAD FOR WHAT YOU DID TO HIS OPERATION. YOU WERE A MESSAGE. YOU AND YOUR WHOLE FAMILY.
NANCY AND THE KIDS, THEY WERE ALREADY MARKED FOR DEATH.
I CONVINCED DEAN THAT KILLING YOU WOULD CAUSE MORE PROBLEMS THAN IT WOULD SOLVE. THAT KILLING YOUR FAMILY WOULD TAKE YOU OFF THE BOARD.
I HAD YOUR BACK! I DIDN'T LET THEM KILL YOU.
I SAVED YOU!
NANCY SAVED ME, YOU PIECE OF SHIT.
SHE TOOK MY LIFE AND MADE IT WORTH SOMETHING. SHE GAVE ME MY KIDS. NANCY MADE ME BETTER, SAVED ME FROM BECOMING AN ASSHOLE LIKE YOU.
YOU? YOU KILLED HER. YOU KILLED ME.
AND YOU KILLED YOURSELF.

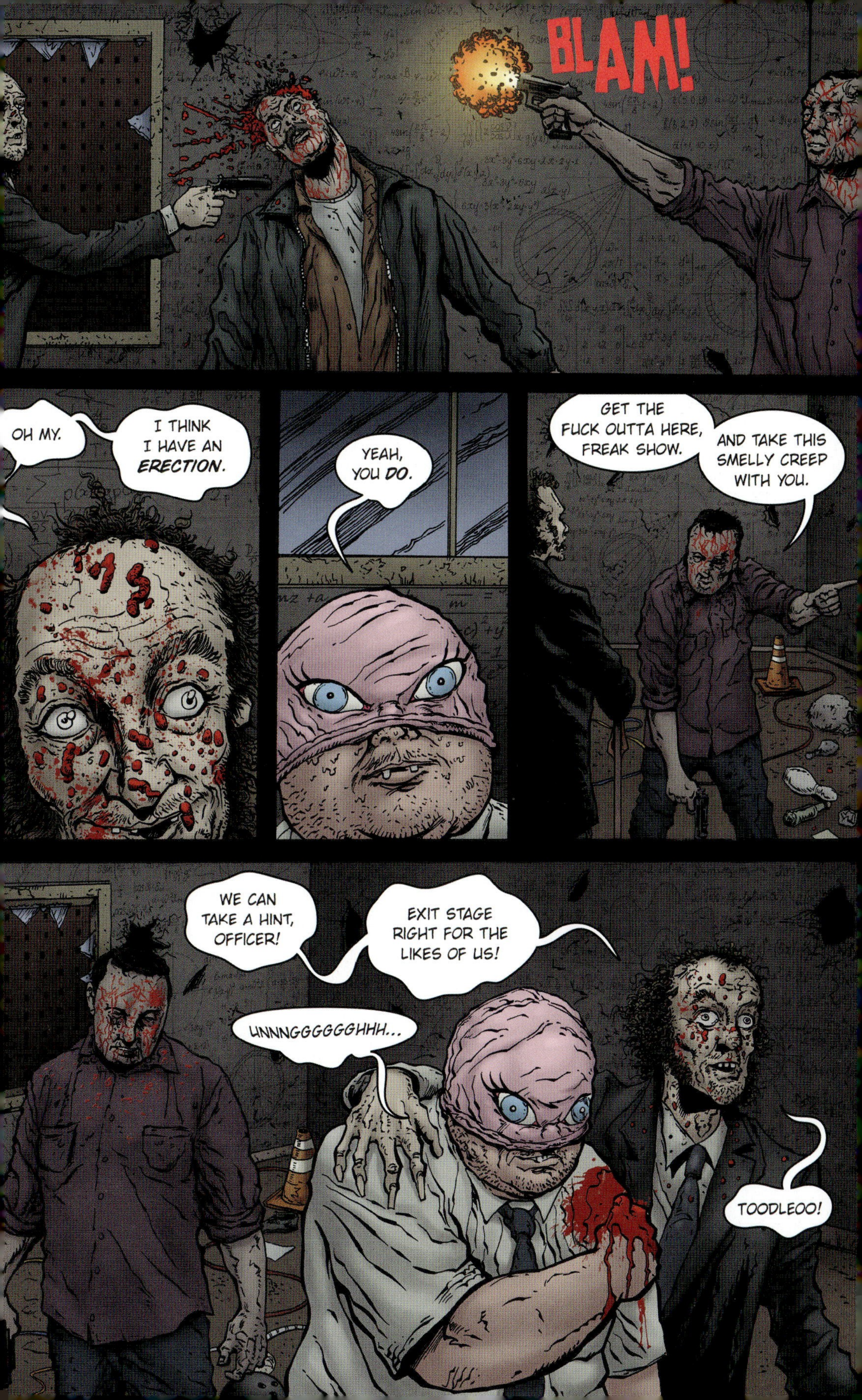
BLAM!
OH MY.
I THINK I HAVE AN ERECTION.
YEAH, YOU DO.
GET THE FUCK OUTTA HERE, FREAK SHOW.
AND TAKE THIS SMELLY CREEP WITH YOU.
WE CAN TAKE A HINT, OFFICER!
EXIT STAGE RIGHT FOR THE LIKES OF US!
UNNNGGGGGGHHH...
TOODLEOO!

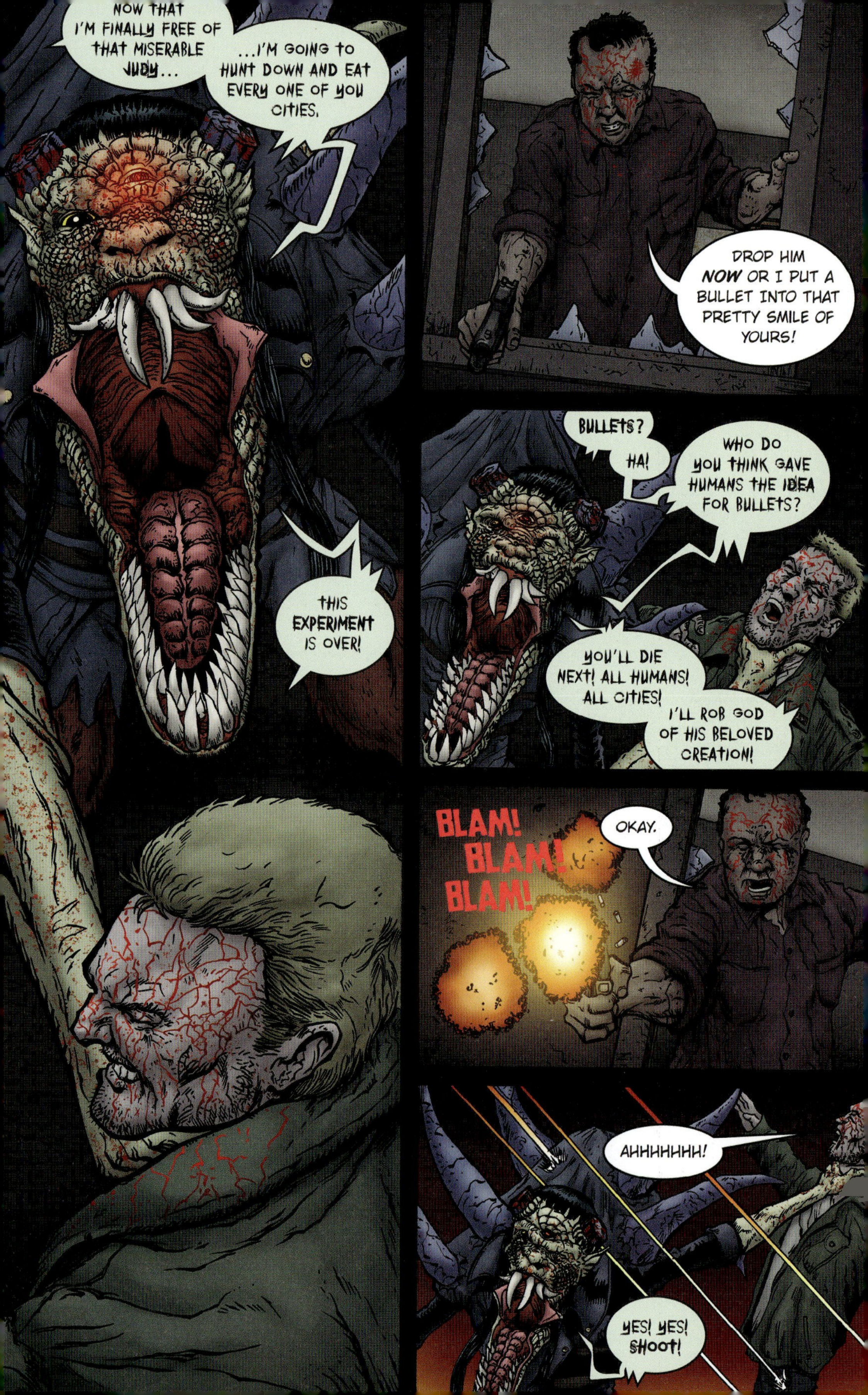

NOW THAT I'M FINALLY FREE OF THAT MISERABLE JUDY...
...I'M GOING TO HUNT DOWN AND EAT EVERY ONE OF YOU CITIES.
THIS EXPERIMENT IS OVER!
DROP HIM NOW OR I PUT A BULLET INTO THAT PRETTY SMILE OF YOURS!
BULLETS?
HA!
WHO DO YOU THINK GAVE HUMANS THE IDEA FOR BULLETS?
YOU'LL DIE NEXT! ALL HUMANS! ALL CITIES!
I'LL ROB GOD OF HIS BELOVED CREATION!
BLAM! BLAM! BLAM!
OKAY.
AHHHHHHH!
YES! YES! SHOOT!

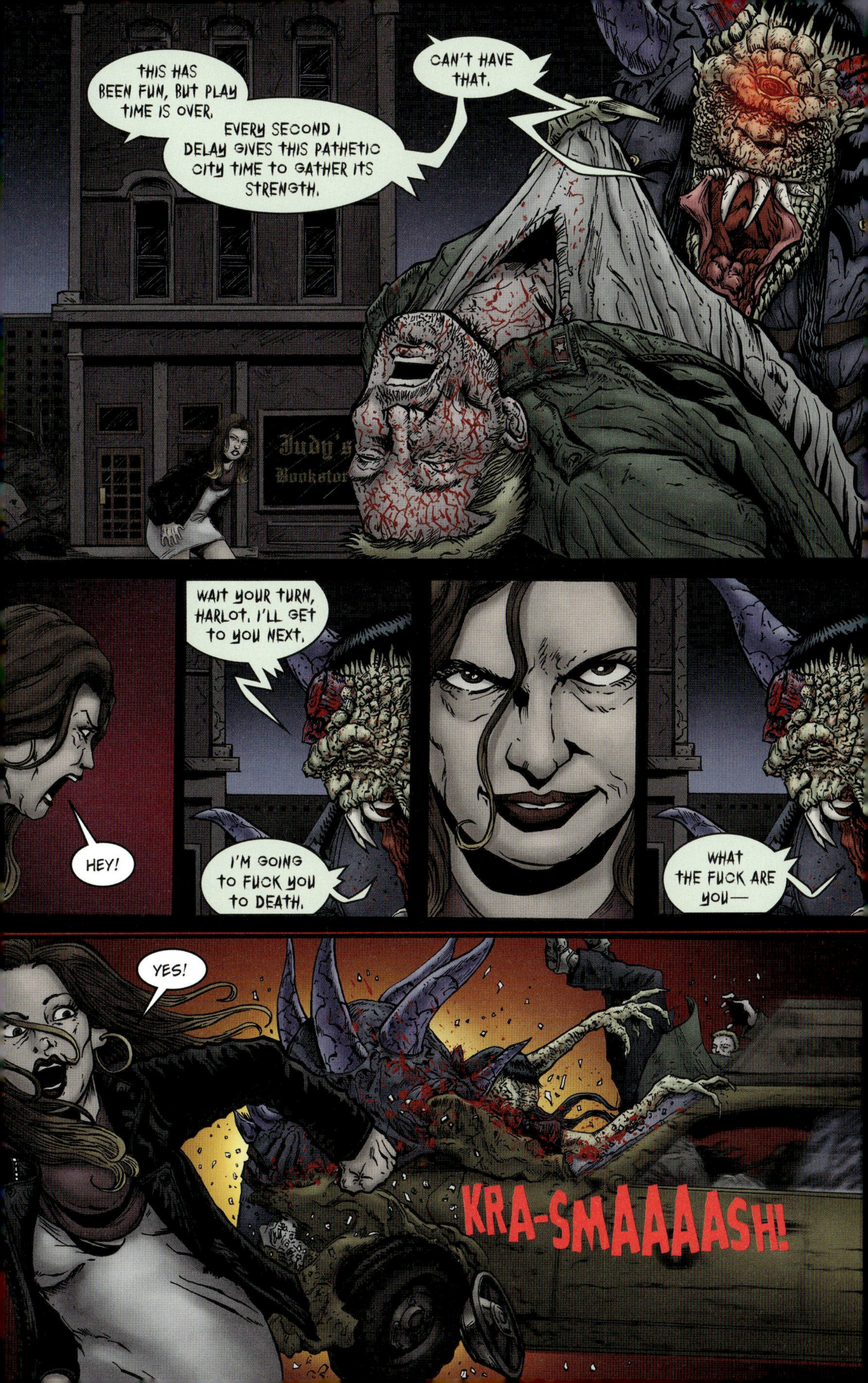

THIS HAS BEEN FUN, BUT PLAY TIME IS OVER.
EVERY SECOND I DELAY GIVES THIS PATHETIC CITY TIME TO GATHER ITS STRENGTH.
CAN'T HAVE THAT.
Judy's Bookstore
HEY!
WAIT YOUR TURN, HARLOT. I'LL GET TO YOU NEXT.
I'M GOING TO FUCK YOU TO DEATH.
WHAT THE FUCK ARE YOU—
YES!
KRA-SMAAAAASH!

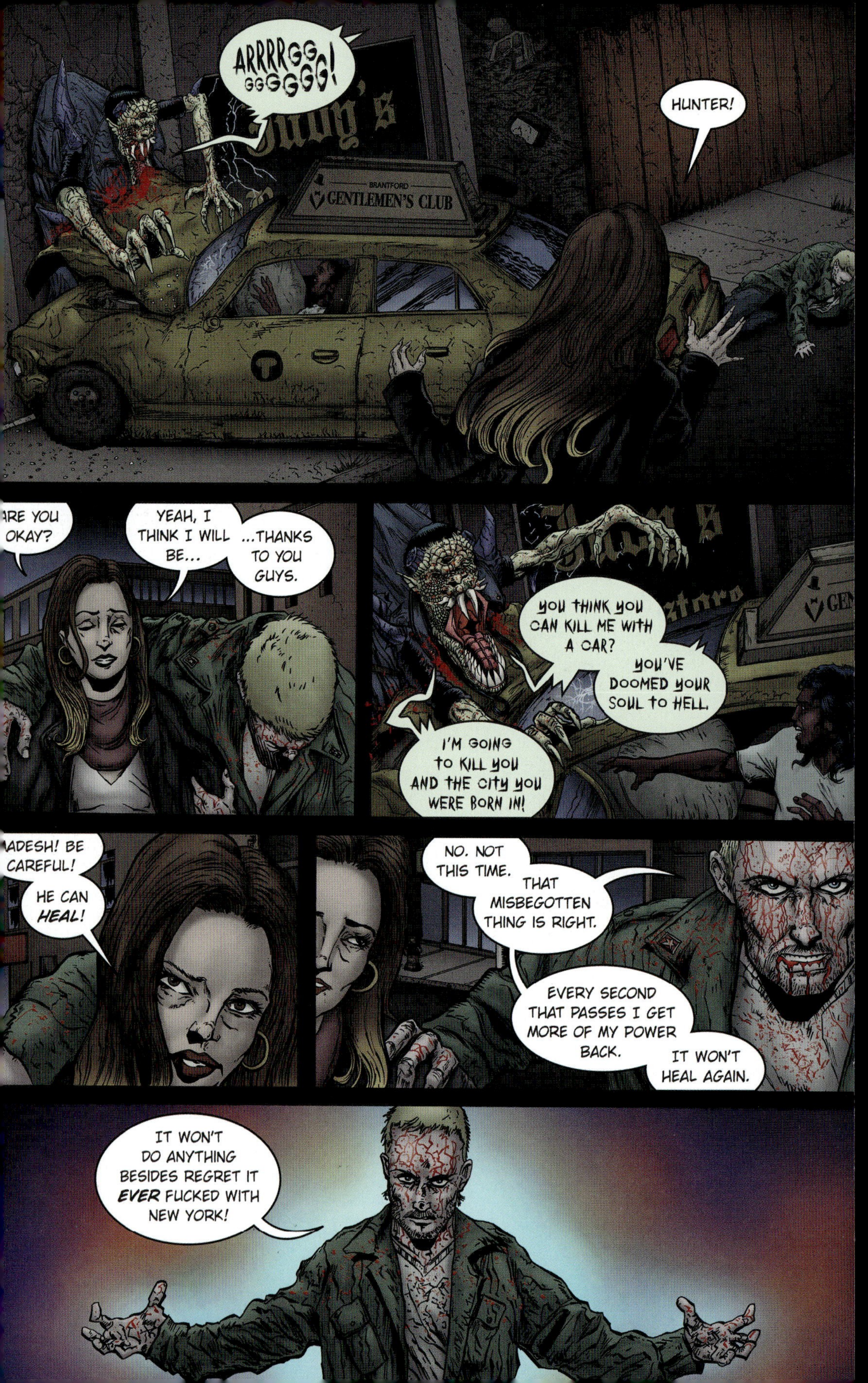
ARRRRGG GGGGGG!
HUNTER!
BRANTFORD GENTLEMEN'S CLUB
ARE YOU OKAY?
YEAH, I THINK I WILL BE...
...THANKS TO YOU GUYS.
YOU THINK YOU CAN KILL ME WITH A CAR?
YOU'VE DOOMED YOUR SOUL TO HELL.
I'M GOING TO KILL YOU AND THE CITY YOU WERE BORN IN!
ADESH! BE CAREFUL!
HE CAN *HEAL*!
NO. NOT THIS TIME.
THAT MISBEGOTTEN THING IS RIGHT.
EVERY SECOND THAT PASSES I GET MORE OF MY POWER BACK.
IT WON'T HEAL AGAIN.
IT WON'T DO ANYTHING BESIDES REGRET IT *EVER* FUCKED WITH NEW YORK!

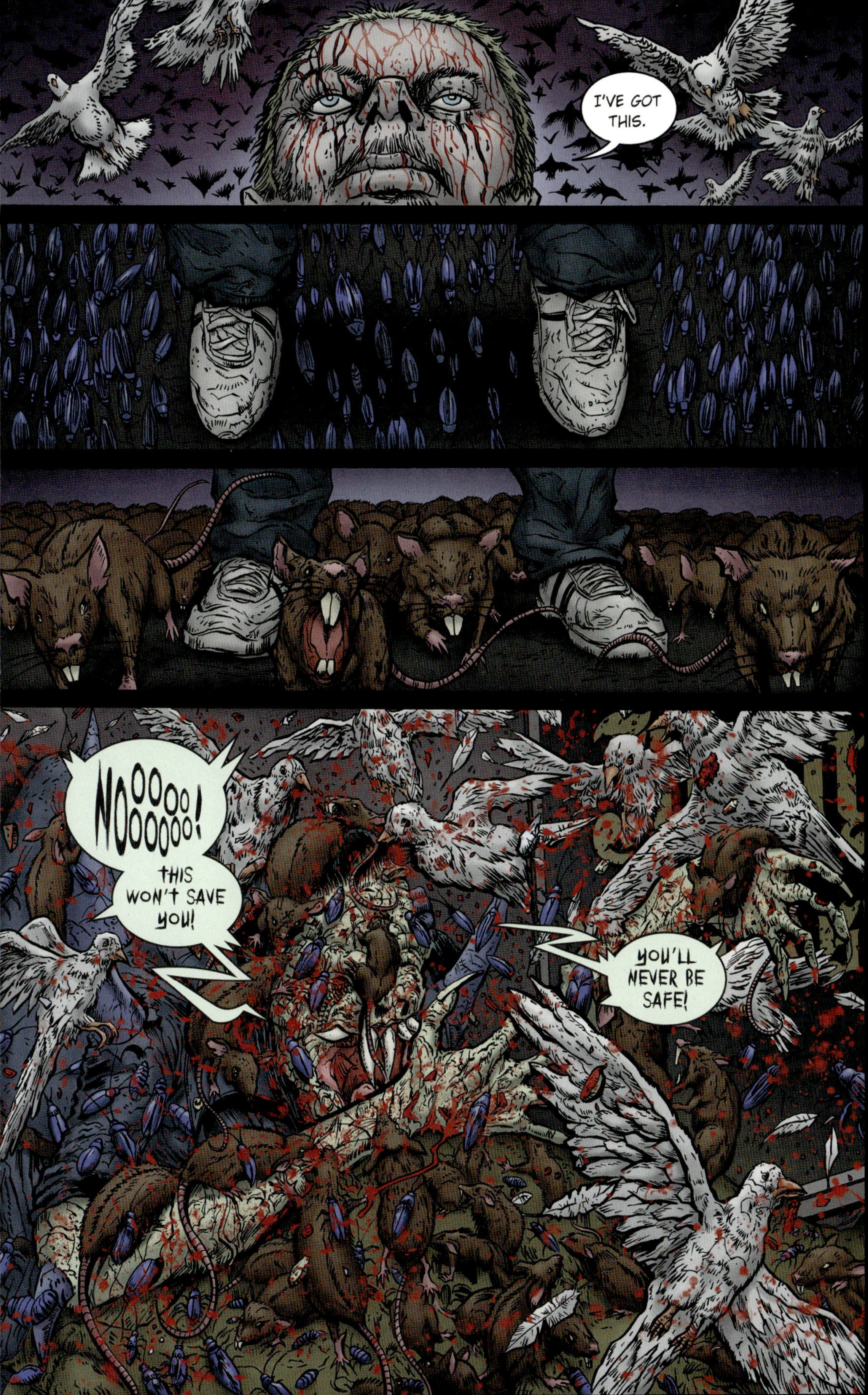
I'VE GOT THIS.
NOOOOO! NOOOOOOO!
THIS WON'T SAVE YOU!
YOU'LL NEVER BE SAFE!

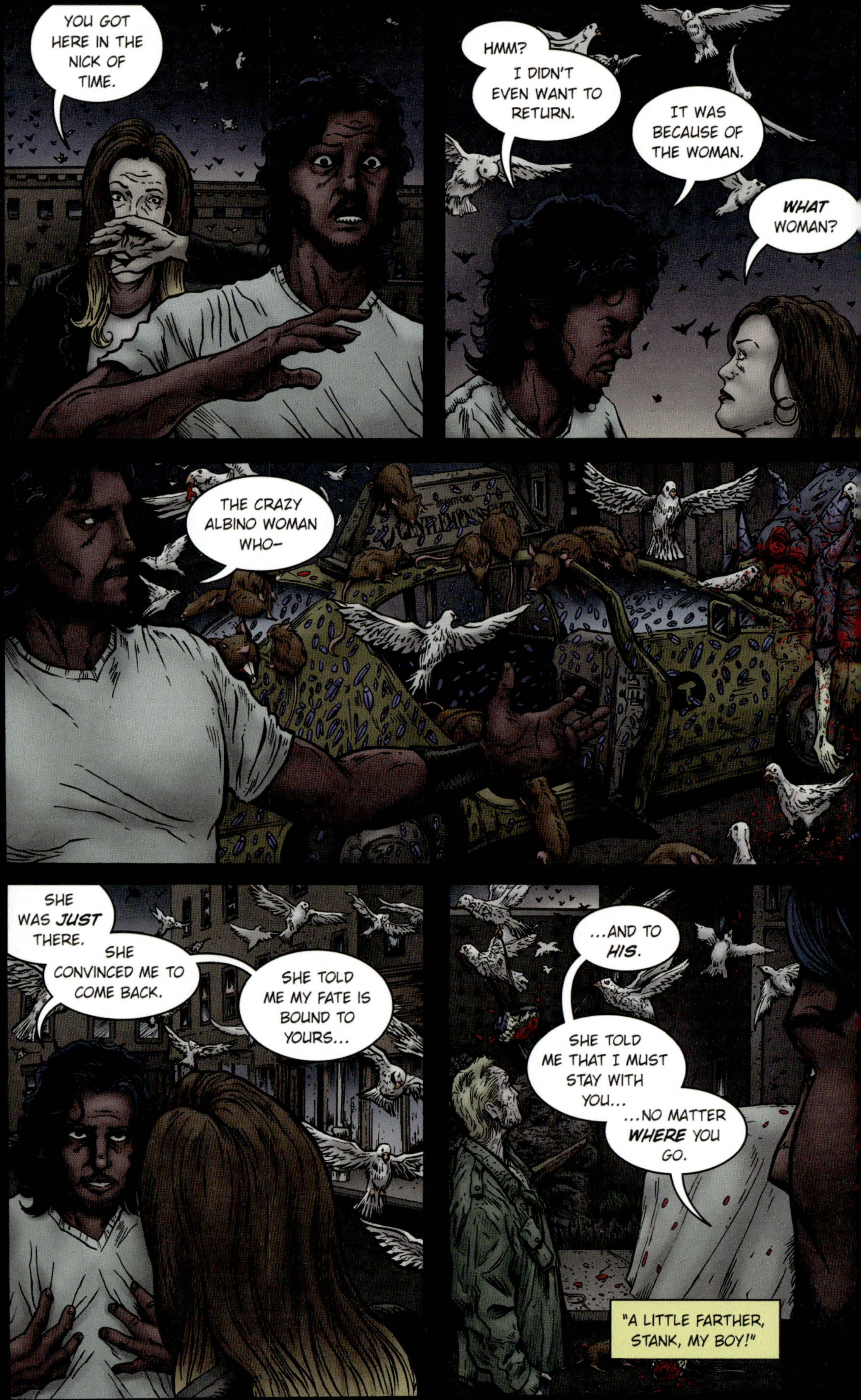
YOU GOT HERE IN THE NICK OF TIME.
HMM?
I DIDN'T EVEN WANT TO RETURN.
IT WAS BECAUSE OF THE WOMAN.
WHAT WOMAN?
THE CRAZY ALBINO WOMAN WHO–
SHE WAS JUST THERE.
SHE CONVINCED ME TO COME BACK.
SHE TOLD ME MY FATE IS BOUND TO YOURS...
...AND TO HIS.
SHE TOLD ME THAT I MUST STAY WITH YOU...
...NO MATTER WHERE YOU GO.
"A LITTLE FARTHER, STANK, MY BOY!"

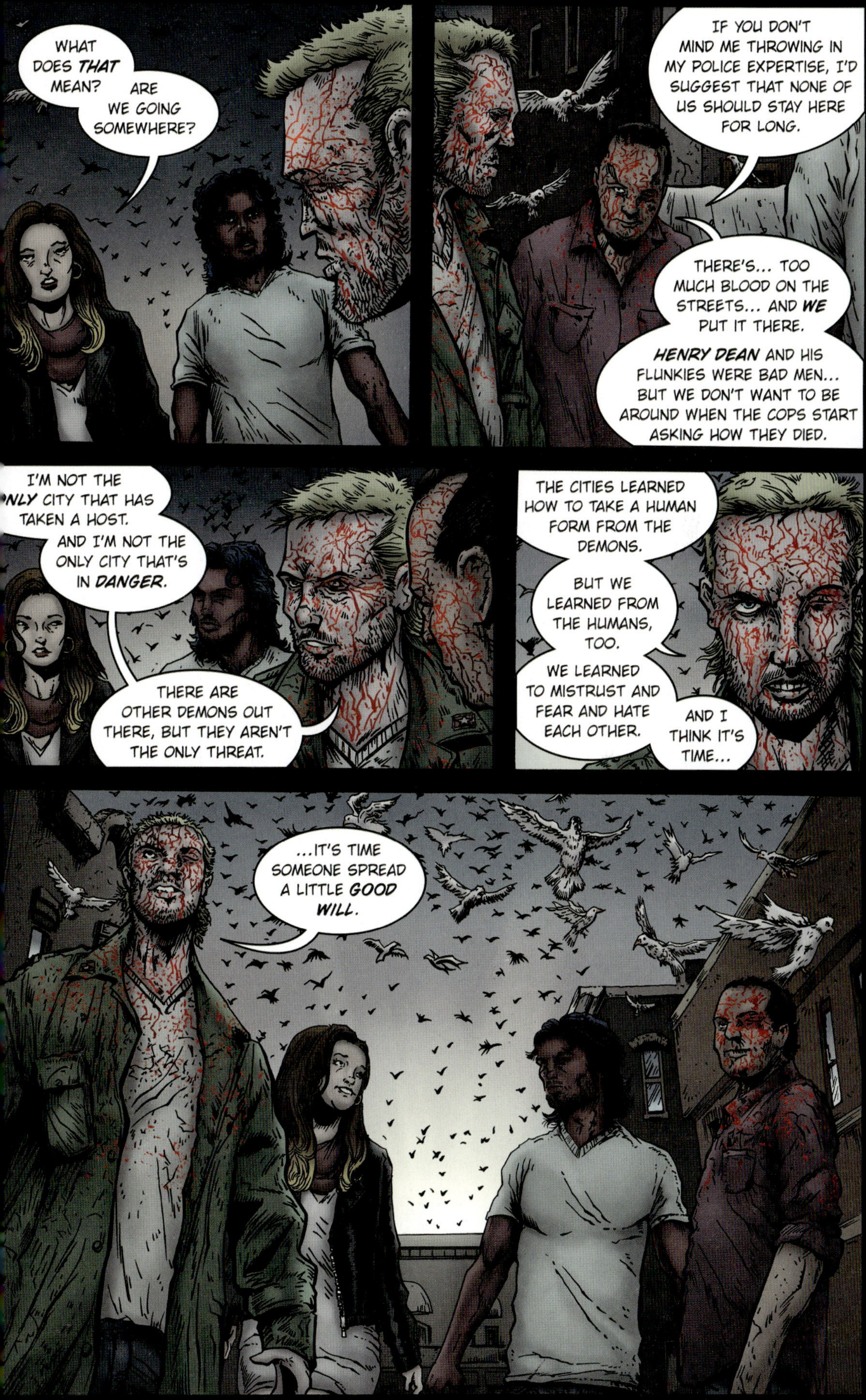

WHAT DOES *THAT* MEAN?
ARE WE GOING SOMEWHERE?
IF YOU DON'T MIND ME THROWING IN MY POLICE EXPERTISE, I'D SUGGEST THAT NONE OF US SHOULD STAY HERE FOR LONG.
THERE'S... TOO MUCH BLOOD ON THE STREETS... AND *WE* PUT IT THERE.
HENRY DEAN AND HIS FLUNKIES WERE BAD MEN... BUT WE DON'T WANT TO BE AROUND WHEN THE COPS START ASKING HOW THEY DIED.
I'M NOT THE *NLY* CITY THAT HAS TAKEN A HOST.
AND I'M NOT THE ONLY CITY THAT'S IN *DANGER*.
THERE ARE OTHER DEMONS OUT THERE, BUT THEY AREN'T THE ONLY THREAT.
THE CITIES LEARNED HOW TO TAKE A HUMAN FORM FROM THE DEMONS.
BUT WE LEARNED FROM THE HUMANS, TOO.
WE LEARNED TO MISTRUST AND FEAR AND HATE EACH OTHER.
AND I THINK IT'S TIME...
...IT'S TIME SOMEONE SPREAD A LITTLE *GOOD WILL*.

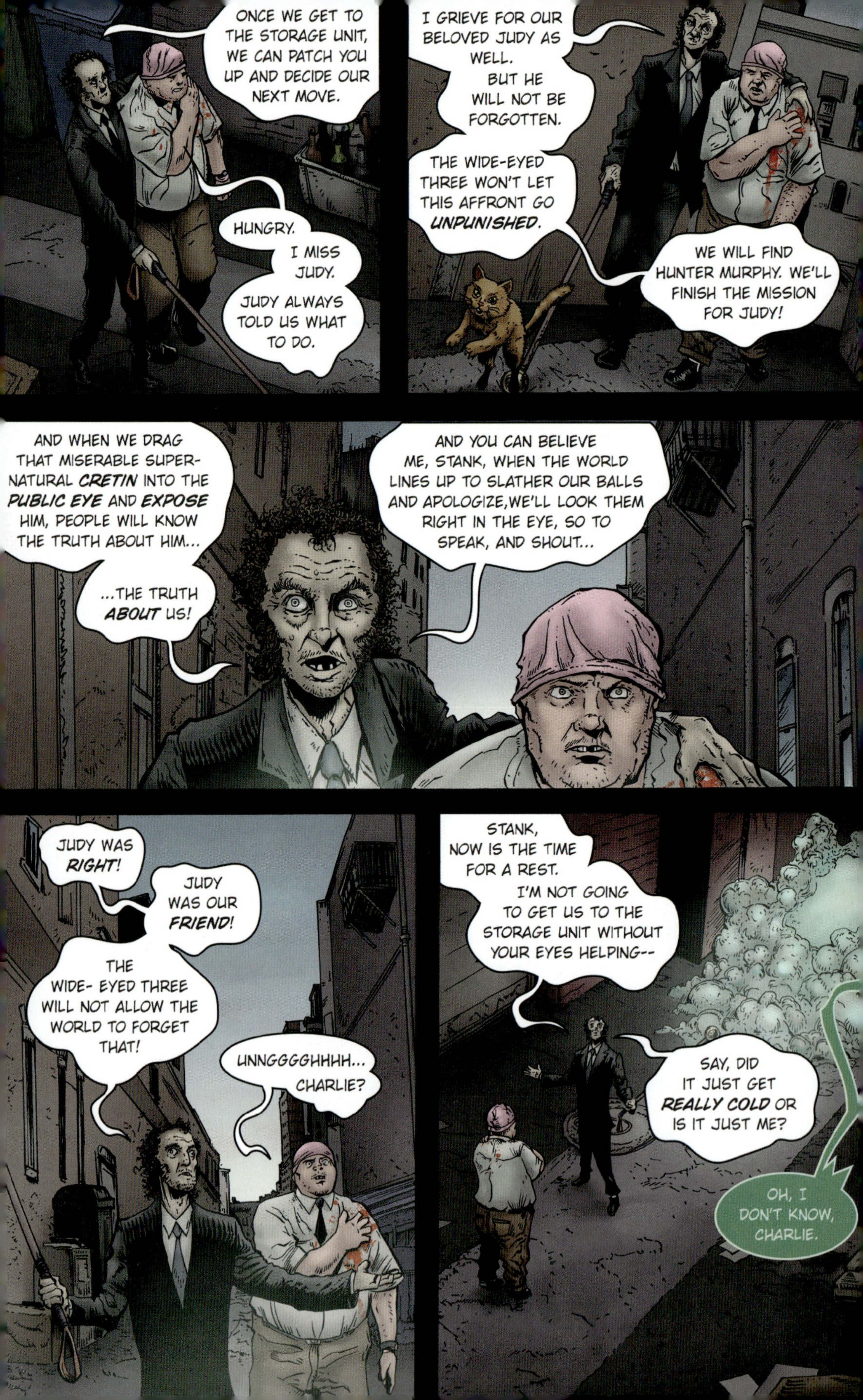
ONCE WE GET TO THE STORAGE UNIT, WE CAN PATCH YOU UP AND DECIDE OUR NEXT MOVE.
HUNGRY.
I MISS JUDY.
JUDY ALWAYS TOLD US WHAT TO DO.
I GRIEVE FOR OUR BELOVED JUDY AS WELL.
BUT HE WILL NOT BE FORGOTTEN.
THE WIDE-EYED THREE WON'T LET THIS AFFRONT GO ***UNPUNISHED***.
WE WILL FIND HUNTER MURPHY. WE'LL FINISH THE MISSION FOR JUDY!
AND WHEN WE DRAG THAT MISERABLE SUPER-NATURAL ***CRETIN*** INTO THE ***PUBLIC EYE*** AND ***EXPOSE*** HIM, PEOPLE WILL KNOW THE TRUTH ABOUT HIM...
...THE TRUTH ***ABOUT*** US!
AND YOU CAN BELIEVE ME, STANK, WHEN THE WORLD LINES UP TO SLATHER OUR BALLS AND APOLOGIZE, WE'LL LOOK THEM RIGHT IN THE EYE, SO TO SPEAK, AND SHOUT...
JUDY WAS ***RIGHT***!
JUDY WAS OUR ***FRIEND***!
THE WIDE- EYED THREE WILL NOT ALLOW THE WORLD TO FORGET THAT!
UNNGGGGHHHH... CHARLIE?
STANK, NOW IS THE TIME FOR A REST.
I'M NOT GOING TO GET US TO THE STORAGE UNIT WITHOUT YOUR EYES HELPING--
SAY, DID IT JUST GET ***REALLY COLD*** OR IS IT JUST ME?
OH, I DON'T KNOW, CHARLIE.

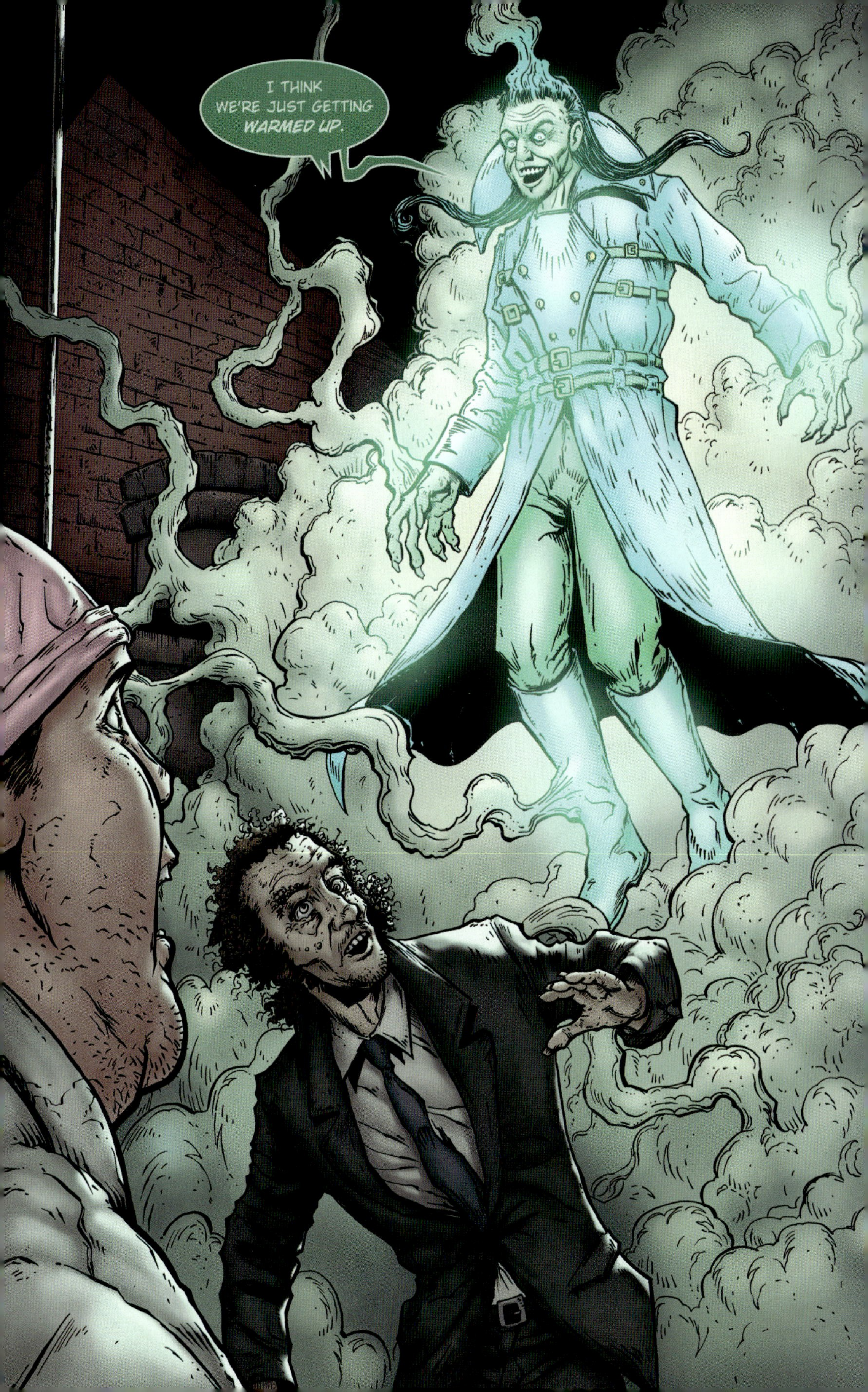
I THINK WE'RE JUST GETTING WARMED UP.

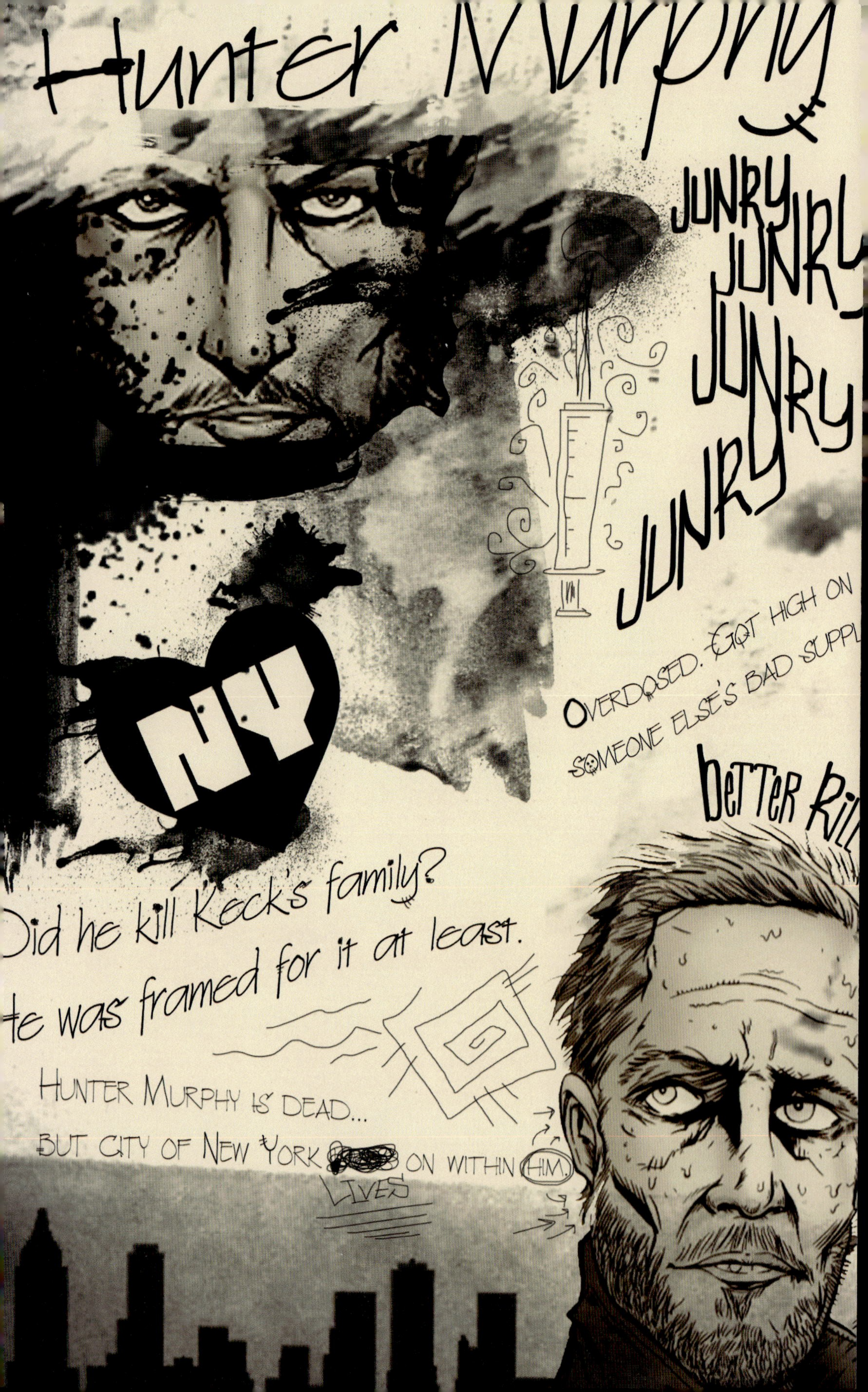

Hunter Murphy
JUNRY JUNRY JUNRY JUNRY JUNRY
NY
OVERDOSED. GOT HIGH ON SOMEONE ELSE'S BAD SUPPL
better Kil
Did he kill Keck's family?
He was framed for it at least.
HUNTER MURPHY IS DEAD...
BUT CITY OF NEW YORK LIVES ON WITHIN HIM.

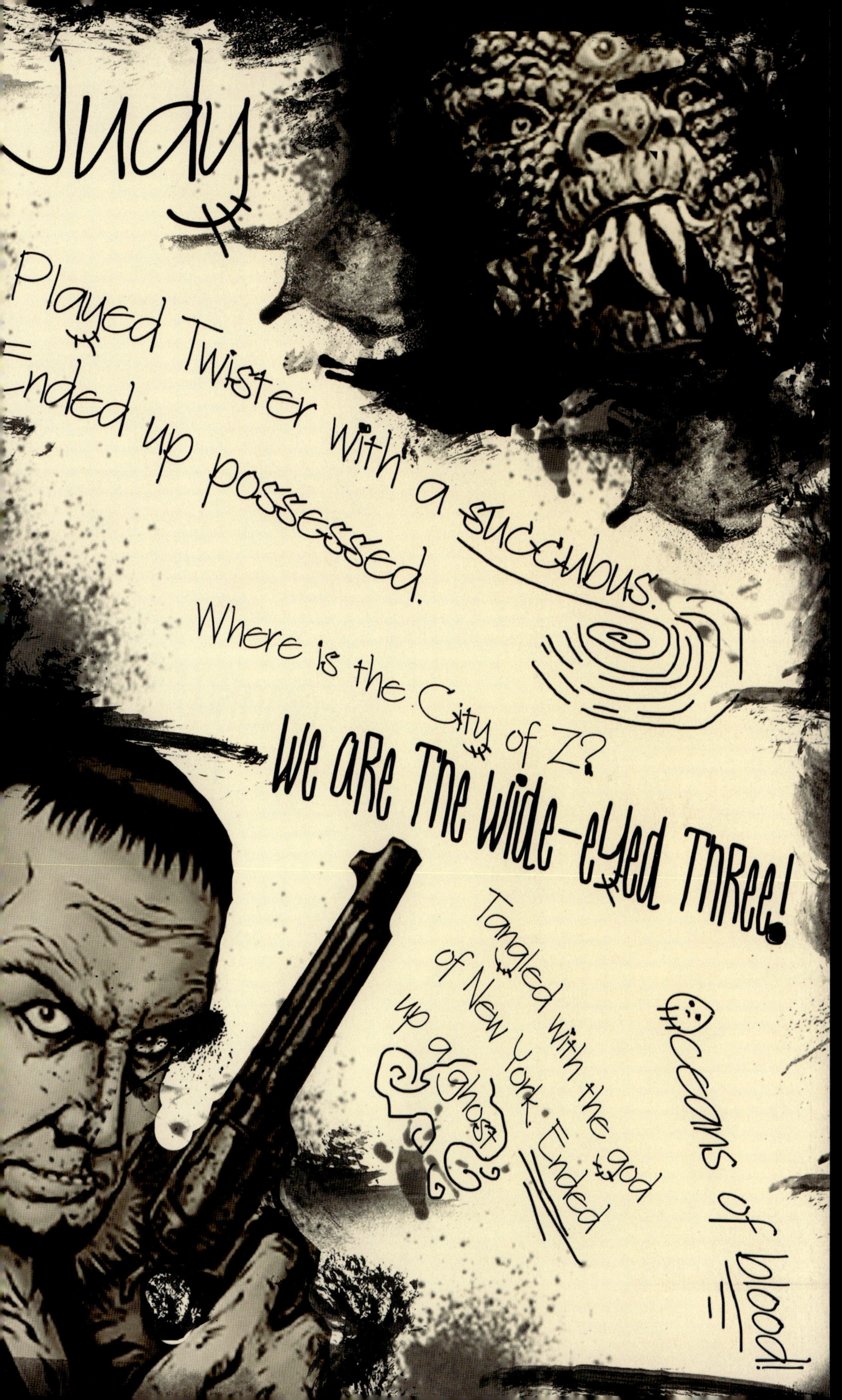
Judy
Played Twister with a succubus.
Ended up possessed.
Where is the City of Z?
We ARe The Wide-eyed ThRee!
Tangled with the god of New York. Ended up a ghost
Oceans of blood!

RANSOM KECK
The MAN.
Decorated officer...
puppet on a string.
Last good cop on the force.
CONGRATS ON YOU
big bust!
LIVES ON A HOUSEBOAT.
LIKE A COP FROM AN ACTION MOVIE,
ONLY MORE OUT OF SHAPE.
LOVES A GOOD CIGAR

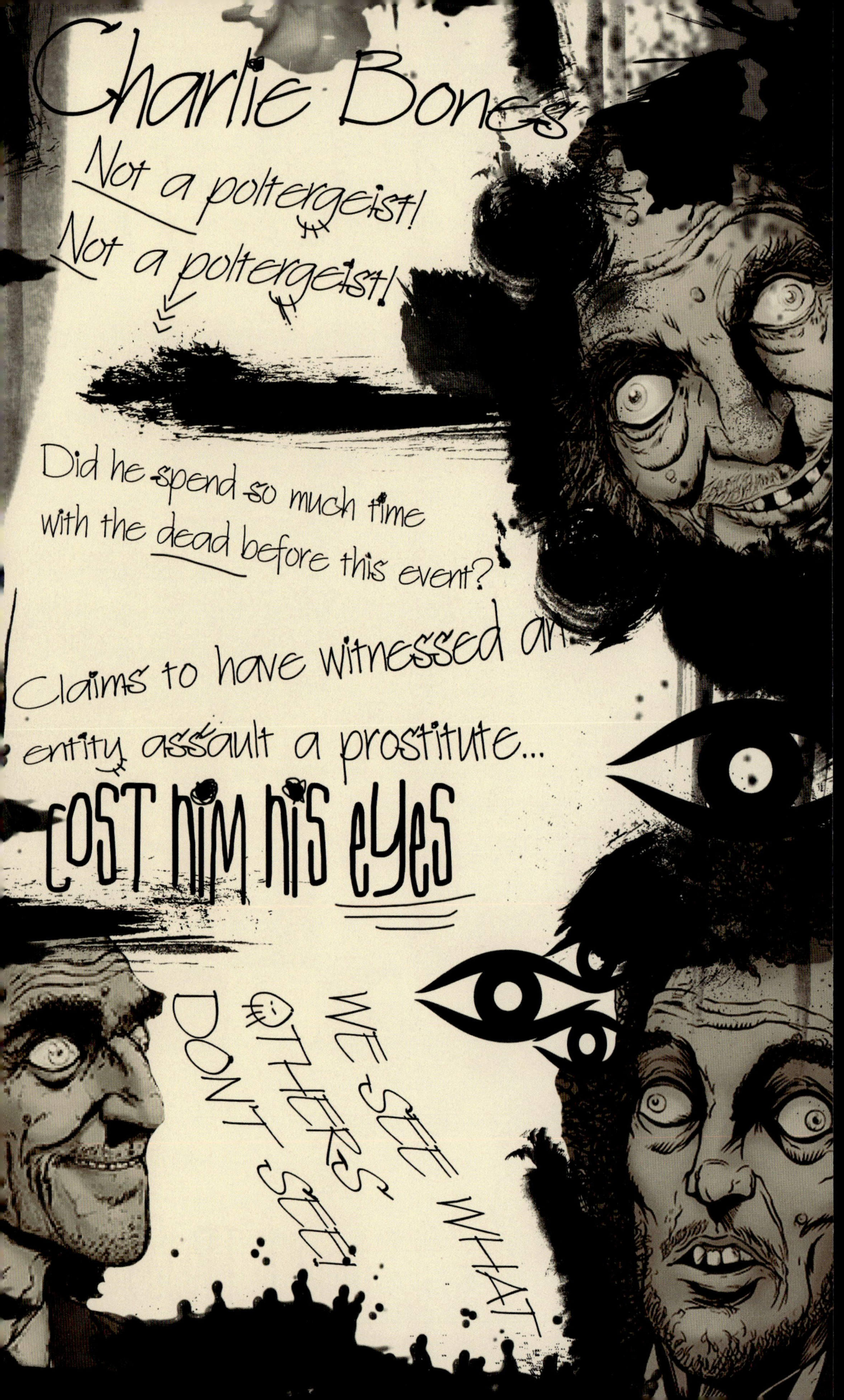
Charlie Bones
Not a poltergeist!
Not a poltergeist!
Did he spend so much time with the dead before this event?
Claims to have witnessed an entity assault a prostitute...
COST HIM HIS EYES
WE SEE WHAT OTHERS DON'T SEE!

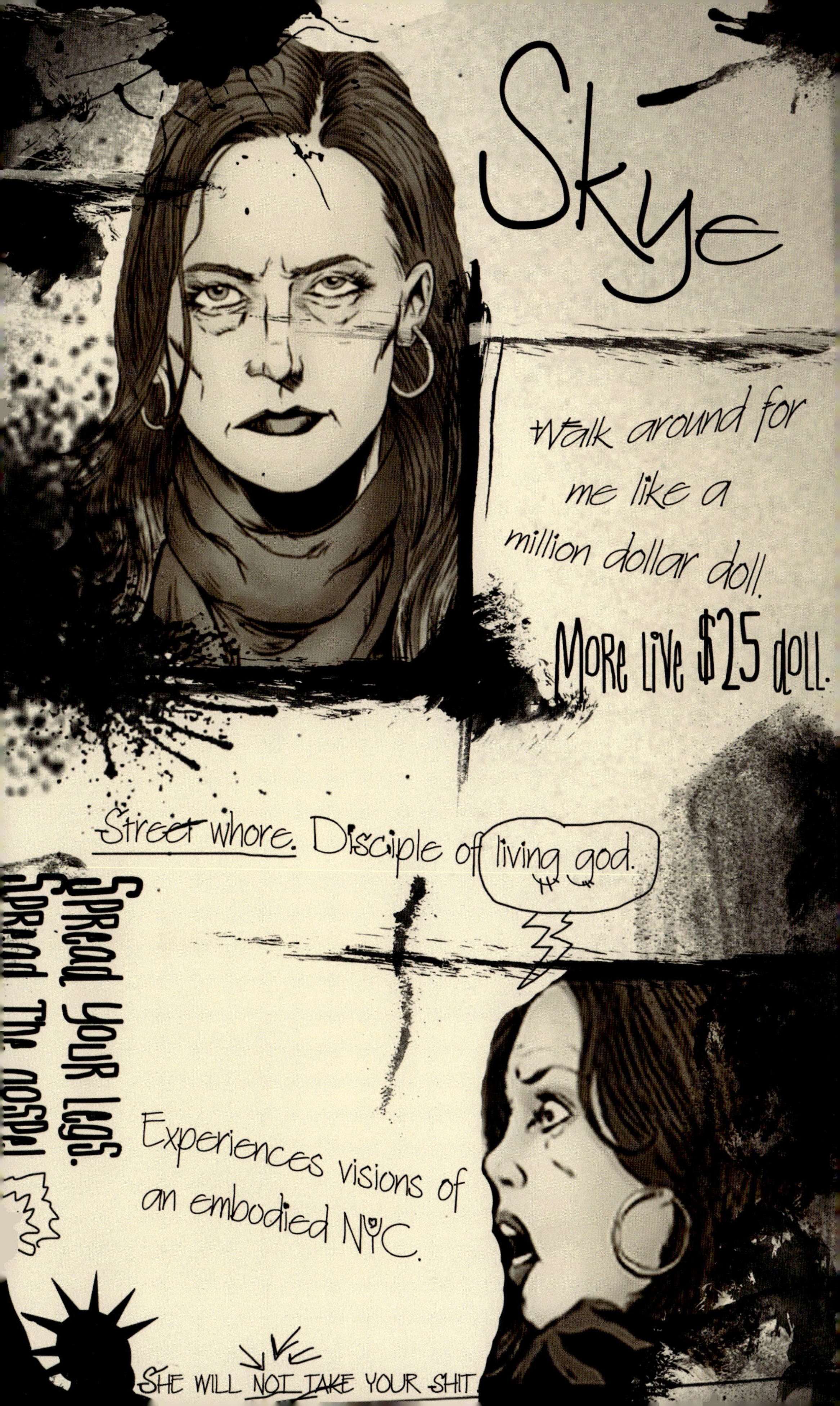
Skye
walk around for me like a million dollar doll.
More live $25 doll.
Street whore. Disciple of living god.
Spread your legs. Spread the gospel
Experiences visions of an embodied NYC.
SHE WILL NOT TAKE YOUR SHIT

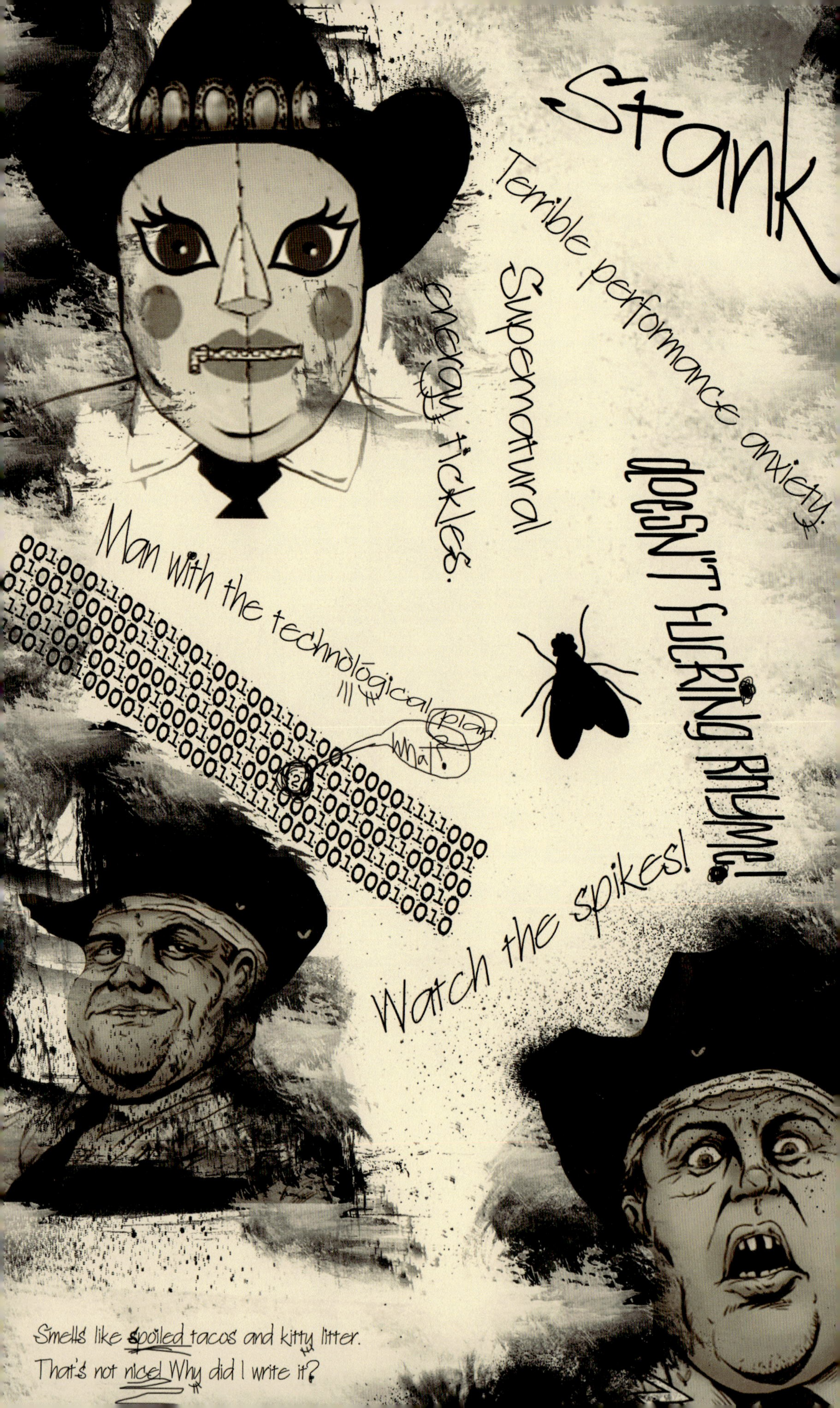

Stank
Terrible performance anxiety.
Supernatural
energy tickles.
DOESN'T FUCKING RHYME!
Man with the technological plan
What?
Watch the spikes!
Smells like spoiled tacos and kitty litter.
That's not nice! Why did I write it?

THANK YOU

1814
Yoho 4CD4LYFE
Fish)
cdharrison
JamesFerguson
ray_skinner
RossTheThird
SueKentAnt
ThatMattDickey
TheSethBerry
ThisAntHill
tor_tor0_0
Wahwahwahcosplay
% too much Q
13%Chris
3%er Kara
CDSeedoSteve
A. S. Rees
A.J. Head
"The 50ft Nerd" Mike Bell
Aaron B
Aaron Crampton
Aaron Edzerza
Aaron Fraser
Aaron Gebur
Aaron Graunke
Aaron Nail
Aaron R Carlin
Aaron S Bell
Aaron W.
Aaron Wayne Carr
Aaron Wolf
Abraham Delgado Román
AC Braevanov P.E.
Adam "Go Bears!" Sena
Adam Armstrong
Adam B. (FCD#1931)
Adam Bakow
Adam C. Brown A.K.A. Light Walker
Adam Crumpton
Adam G. Smith
Adam Gaines
Adam Mancuso
Adam Marquez
Adam McGrade
Adam Meyer
Adam Michael Schmid
Adam Oxley
Adam Rabczak
Adam Rawlings
Adam Renninger
Adam Slaughter
Adam Ullery
Ade Carlyon
Adrian APM Mulloy
Adrian Broughman
Adriana Porras Perez
Adriel More
Aidan Easson
Aisha aka @UpYourIrishAss

Aiyana Moore
AJ Bush
Aj Samples 4CD#358
AJC
Al
Alan Brannan
Alan Caldwell
Alan Cowsill
Alan 'Ely Axe Murderer' Isaacson
Alan Lee Stepp
Alan W. Riggs
Alana Bonet
Alana Rice
Aleman
Alex "Off The" Hall
Alex Adame
Alex Adan
Alex Alexand
Alex Dierling 4CD#2916
Alex Eschbach
Alex Ferrer 4CD #5283
Alex Iero-Way(Frikey)
Alex Morton 4CD #7395
Alex Nicolescu
Alex Perretti
Alex Workman 4CD#6816
Alex, Autumn, Sage, Nicole Posniewski
Alexander B Grover
Alexander Germaine
Alexandra Davis- 13% for life!
Alexandra Emmenegger
Alexis Gimenez - Sumacarcer
Alexis Kerkh
Alfredo Torres
Algin Shaw
Alice Hughes 4CD #8679 and Chris
Breedlove 4CD #9031
Alissa Jesle
Allen Christian
Allie Wible (RB)
Allison DeGrushe
Allison E. Barton
Allison Evans
Allison Reed 4CD#8828
Allison Romero
Ally Doyle
Alun and Naila
Alycia Gilger
Alyssa Yohe
Amalia Hubal
Amanda
Amanda and Matt Sheaffer
Amanda Dale
Amanda Elizabeth Scott
Amanda Elkins
Amanda F. Clyne
Amanda Fortenberry
Amanda Goodloe
Amanda Greb
Amanda Harvey

THANK YOU

Amanda James
Amanda Montagne
Amanda Ricuito
Amanda Rosinski
Amanda Swinburn
Amazin' Grace
Amazing Larry
Amber Lynne Medeiros
Amber Marie Carlance 4CD #2351
Amy Edge
Amy Fiend
Amy Hassing-Pankoke 4CD #4421
Amy Hodgkinson
Amy Louise Margaret Fraser
Amy Skaggs
Amy Whittaker
"Rlaloc" Villanueva
Andrea DiGenno
Andrea Ferrell 4CD#988
Andrea M. Sica-Becker
Andrea Winiarski
Andres Oberheide
Andrew and Alayna Duffel
Andrew and Truman Holmes
Andrew Baskin
Andrew Brown
Andrew Dookie Brewer-Davenport
Andrew Gilhool
Andrew Laqua
Andrew Lopez @i_drew_andrew
Andrew M. Nichols
Andrew Molburg
Andrew Murphy
Andrew Roth
Andrew Szymczyk
Andrew Taam
Andrew Tillman
Andrew Ubert
Andrew Winthrope
Andrew Woelmer
Andrew Z
Andy "Shaggy" Korty
Andy "VaultsOfExtoth" Wears
Andy Glover
Andy Graham 4CD #1228
Andy Lane
Andy MacPhee
Andy Patch
Andy Pickrell
Andy R
Andy Rae
Andy Schmidt
Andy Smith
Andy T. Valle
Andy Vaughan
Ang K. 4CD#831
Angela M. Vega
Angela Merriman
Angela Seldomridge
Angeleah Hoeppner

Angelo DeSio
Ani W.
Aniecea Williams PHS c/o 1994
Ann Mitchell
Anna Bened
Anna Dolan
Anna Elizabeth
Anna Southerland
Anna Watson
Anna Zammit 4CD #1258
Anna-Marie Dadd
Anne Carty
Anne Scheel
Annie Cleary
Ant Ark Key
Ant #9427
Ant Boucher
Ant Toni
Anthony Banks
Anthony Carlo Rodarte
Anthony Carreto
Anthony Catenaro
Anthony De Lissio
Anthony Kauf
Anthony Laatsch
Anthony Oddo
Anthony R. Ponzio
Anthony Rivera
Anthony Striffolino
Anthony Thomas Michael
Anthony Tu
AntKoolaid
Antonio _OHLE'_ Alvarado
Antti Rask
Anya Cat Robertson
Archie
Archigan
Ariane M Racer
Arthur Nelson
Arwen
Arwen Patterson
Asger Jacobsen #1923
Ash Portelli
Ash Tombs 4CD #4620
Ash, Gravy and Bits
Ashley Candelaria
Ashley Carment 4CD# 9043
Ashley Edemann
Ashley Eubanks
Ashley Laspina
Ashley M. Vest
Ashley Melanson
Ashley Rae Grobe
Ashley T.
Ashley Taliercio
Ashling Fenton
Ashton Griffin
Ashton Wills
Ateen Patel
Aubrey Courville

THANK YOU

Audra 4CD#0935
Audrey G. Cunningham
Aug
Aur'lia Apiona
Austin Erickson
Austin Nadeau
Austin Pierce
Austin Wein
Austin Wills
Austyn Pigeon
Avalon Comics
Avery G. Chadha
Ayesha Burrows
Back Row Heckers Podcast
Badger Spurrier
Badon Delmotte
Bailea Ann-Marie Coffel
Bailey Hansmeyer
Barbara Bagley
Barbara Bermejo
Barbara J. Krasicki
Barbara 'Nuggalo' Lilburn
Barnaby Nickletoes
Baron Von Flanagan
Barry Johnson
Barry Oh
Bashdown
Bay Dariz
Baylee Sellers
Bays Holdren
Bea Kalsi
Bec Sokol
Becka Reed
Becki Thueme
Becky Ware
Becky,Kevin,Noah,Maddie Bliss
Beefcake
Beki Norder
Ben Aikey
Ben Bard
Ben Bonnett
Ben Crellin
Ben Dolbee
Ben Erickson
Ben kl
Ben Krise
Ben Ryan
Ben Salazar
Ben Szela
Ben Wagner
Benjamin Apuan
Benjamin B
Benjamin Cat
BenJamin Hewitt
Benn Lee
Bennett Lee Miller
Benton M
Bernadette jones
Bernardo De Los Santos
Beth Nizack

Beth Roach
Beth Turner
Betty RockerChic Saybe
Beverly Rose Thomas
Bex Johnson
Bezuul
Big Daddy Z
Big kylew
Big Red Deb 4CD 743 4C4L
Bill "Daddy Shark" Loulousis
Bill Codd
Bill Fleming
Bill Geiger 4CD #1341
Bill Hoelzel
Bill Longa
Bill Shearer
Billy Bone
Billy Clemons
Billy Kay Jr. #7620
Billy Stormont
BJ Applegarth
Blacky Shep
Blair Matheson
Blake Rodier
Blanca Gonzalez
Blue Juice Comics
Blue Ox Games & Geekery
Blue Rose Jewels
Bo Roberts aka King BIZ 4CD #7903
Bob Zerull
Bobbie Jean King
Bobby K
Bongka Vichaita
Bozena Lebed
Brad "Copper" Wells
Brad Chard
Brad jan
Brad Rowson
Bradd
Bradden Miles
Bradley Moore
Braeden Robak
Brakeman 55
Brandee Darby
Brandi Harper
Brandon "Cletus" Kuhens 4CD #9204"
Brandon Butler
Brandon Fraccalvieri #2787 4C4L
Brandon Kelley
Brandon Leonhardt
Brandon Lopez
Brandon M. Johnson
Brandon Metz
Brandon Swett
Brandon Tanimoto 4CD#2439
Brandon Vidler
Brandon Zagleski
Brandy Burgess
Brandy Eatmon
Brendan McMorrow 4CD #9178

THANK YOU

Brenden Laine
Brendon Conway
Brendon Gabriel
Brenna Anderson
Brent C.
Brent Johnson
Brent Rome
Brent V
Brett Downward
Brett Gauthier
Brett Hannon
Brett Miller
Brett Pick
Brian Bailey
Brian Bennett
Brian Billow
Brian Burgundy
Brian Conner
Brian D. Boyd, Esq.
Brian Distefano
Brian Gonsiorowski
Brian Haggerty & Kirsty McGuire
Brian Hartman
Brian Hodge
Brian Keith James Cate
Brian Keohan
Brian Lively 4CD #4121
Brian Lynch
Brian Mann
Brian Mann/Mitchell
Brian Maxwell
Brian Nielsen
Brian Paul 4CD #8371
Brian R. Brown - Inkyscholar
Brian Ray
Brian Ruppert
Brian Sherrill
Brian Steinbach
Brian Trevarthen
Brian Weibeler
Brian Young 4CD#3883
Bridge City Comics
Brit Laird 4CD #1162
Brittany Curtin
Brittany Hansen 4CD #5525
Brittany Jones
Brittany Kriz
Brittany L. Harshman
Brittany Smith
Brittiany Free
Brittney Love 4CD #8667
Bronson Paris
Brooke Andres
Brooke Roxanne Loving
Bruce Borer
Bruce Edward Moore
Bruce Schwering
Brucio McGuire
Bryan Ferguson
Bryan Gahres

Bryan Hatton 4CD# 7929
Bryan Jacobs
Bryan McKnight
Bryan Sadowski
Bryan Walker
Bryant Stewart
Bryce Flowers
Brycen Bertoch
BRYNE
Brzinski
Bud Sims
C. Wayne Meadows
Calvin Jarosz
Cambot
Cameron Geach
Cameron J Mathews
Cameron Shaw
Camille Renée Calabrese
Captain Dennis J. Ryan
Cara Diamond
Cara Rafferty
Carl Gunther
Carl Harris 4CD#2688
Carl Rypysc
Carlos L Ochoa
Carly Cassone
Carmen Frischkorn
Carmen Pora
Carol Ames
Carol Brake 4CD#867
Carol Erdmann
Carol Kolarik
Carol Pa
Carrieann Steeger
Carson Sexsmith
Casey Littlefield
Casey Luna
Casey Patrick Stewart
Cassandra Dodson
Cassie Campbell
Cassie Madonia
Cat Ster
Catherine Do
Catie Brewster (girloutofengland)
Cato Vandrare
Cayce Roach
Cea Parten
Celeste Rocha
Cerys Ziritt
cfp33pfc
Chad & PJ Miller
Chad Draper
Chad Givens
Chad Hale
Chad Joh
Chad M Becker
Chad Mohr
Chad Patrick
Chadwick Leger
Chanelle-Marie

THANK YOU

Charla Ellenbrand 4CD # 2792
Charlene Goetz
Charles Cannon
Charles David Meinzinger
Charles Massaro
Charles Wise
Charley Skira
Charlotte Coop
Charlotte Lowe
Charlotte Organ
Charlotte Taylor
Charlotte Wills 4CD #8578
Chase M. Kruger
Chase W. Crouse
Chaw Kim Choo
Chelsea June Crook
Chelsea Segovia 4CD #6383
Cheri Larkin
Cheryl B.
Cheryl Becker 4CD#830
Cheryl Cool Mint Jazz Smith
Cheryl Fagan
Cheryl L. DeVore
Chet Jordan
Chewbode
Chip Majetic
Chloe Lois Donnelly
Chris "Rhinne" Joyce
Chris Downey
Chris Alleman
Chris and Heather!
Chris Ashcroft
Chris Bas
Chris Beeman
Chris Blue 4CD #2306
Chris Brewer
Chris C. Rushing
Chris Call
Chris Cerda 4CD#1355
Chris Chavez
Chris Conley
Chris Davidson
Chris Flanigan
Chris Grove
Chris Harford
Chris Hinsz
Chris Inthiraj
Chris L. Goodwill
Chris Laverdiere 4CD#8396
Chris Loseke
Chris Morris & Coral Roseberry
Chris Ramos 4CD# 7211
Chris Rumery
Chris Salemi
Chris Sloan
Chris Thomasson
Chris Waller
Chris Wilburn #5304
Chris Williams
Chrissi Sepe

Christian "Torkdik" Davis
Christian K.
Christian Monsalve
Christian Poet
Christina Hillock
Christina Lockfaw
Christina Richard
Christine Antosca
Christine Kre
Christine Longo
Christine M Todd
Christine Pawlik
Christine Remington Strough
Christine Ruiz-Sample
Christina Weiss
Christine Woodward
Christoph K.
Christopher "TheMtVernonkid" Bennett
Christopher A. Bell
Christopher Brooks
Christopher Cordes
Christopher J. Moore
Christopher Maxwell
Christopher P Williams Jr
Christopher Perry
Christopher Pete
Christopher Rundt
Christopher Smith
Christy L. Harker
Chuck Alexander
Chuck Crawford 4CD #1970
Chuckyzombie
Chun Kit Lam
Ciaran "The Shep" Hurd
Cilly Putty
Cindy & Squish Bunn — Cullen's #1 Fans
Cindy Marshall
Cindy Potter
Cindy W.
Claire R. Pokornicki
Clare Ratto
Claude "Ibnuzar" Lacroix
Clay Adams
Clay Olah
Cleo
Clifford Miles Krinsky
Clint Benesh
Clint Brown
Clint Dale
Clint Harper
Cody Begley
Cody Courtois
Cody D Brown
Cody James Snyder
Cody Meyer 4CD #9026
Cody Shipman
Cody Sites
Cody Warren
Cody Wolfe 4CD #1149
Cohen & Lorelei Hatfield

THANK YOU

Colby Rogers 4CD#4497
Cole Bates
Cole Brunner 4CD #8874
Coleen Higgins 4CD#1473
Colin Archer
Colin Hetherington
Colin Murray
Colleen Dixon
Colonel Baron von Whiskahs
Comic Force in Branson, Missouri
Comic Paradise Plus stores
Connie Evans   4CD #769
Connie Landry Vatsa
Connor Shapiro
Conor Brown
Coraline Fox
Coreen Flanery-Williams
Corey Clouse
Corey Dinsmore
Corey Flavin White
Corinne Vegh
Cornelius Jenkins
Corrina Breann
Cortiny Peterson
Cortney Ellen Cole
Cory D. Denio
Cory VanMeter
Courtney Meizinger
Courtney Serumgard
Craig "Nest" Norton
Craig Brownlie
Craig LeBaron
Craig M. Kuczynski
Craig Norval 4CD #5648
Craig Sardone
Cranjis McBasketball Coffey
Cristian Herrera
Croze
Crystal Collasius
Crystal Danser
Crystal Lee Pons 4CD #7721
Crystal R. Lynne
Crystal Williamson
Crystal Wojcik
Crystal Wright
Curtis Felts
cyberferret
cyberspacecomics.com
D.Beesil
D.J. Ellio
D.Millz
D_XXVI
Dafydd Thomas
Dale Dawson
Daman Messenger (Ant)
Damien 1412
Damien Armstrong
Damien W
Dan & Lianne McLeod
Dan "Wolf SeanPatrick" Lyons 4CD#1060

Dan Czerpak
Dan Edwards
Dan Eveland
Dan Fishman
dan gibson
Dan Gillmore
Dan H
Dan Handy
Dan Kinem
Dan Lombardo, 4CD
Dan McKenna
Dan Poormon Jr.
Dan S. Due
Dan Schoeninger
Dan Steere
Dan Tana
Dan Weidman
Dan Wright
Dana Borgia 4CD 1379
Dane Breker
Dane Winton
DANHOO & ROBHOO
Dani Martin
Daniel "Pickle Juice" DiStefano
Daniel coffin
Daniel Crane
Daniel Desmond
Daniel H. Bennett
Daniel J Simpson
Daniel John Cunningham aka Honki
Daniel Judge (Feenicks) 4CD #4904
Daniel Nosk
Daniel Patrick O'Connor
Daniel Sanchez
Daniel Simoneau, TESD Ant
Daniel Subroski
Daniel Tan JC
Daniel Taylor
Daniel Tornow 4CD #2979
Daniel Whiddon
Daniel Wolfgod
Danielle C Morgan
Danielle W 4CD #9337
danielpbrown1981
Dara Arnona Lessard
Daren & Christina 4CD #6977
Darragh "Ganty" Murphy
Darrell 4CD #5602
Darrell Hanratty
Darren E.
Darren O'Neill
Darren P. Bennett
Darren Paye
"Darren Sneed"
Darren Wearmou
Darrick Adams
Darryl Reid
Darryl Stef and Dahlia
Daryl Schwartzwalder
Dave & Erin Morehead

THANK YOU

Dave + Tricia
Dave and Sarah Argrave
Dave Barkoot
Dave Barnes
Dave Burke
Dave Kalish
Dave Kastner
Dave Payne
Dave Sieffert
Dave Thomas, Founder of Wendy's
Dave Valdil
Davey B
David
David A Mendez
David A. bauer
David Ahumada 4CD #1540
David and Cassie Sword
David Bannister
David Binmore 4CD #2594
David Breuer
David Cheek
David Cox
David Farrell
David Gonzalez
David Gray
David Gutman
David Ham
David & April Holcomb
David Holloway
David James Beaucar
David Jeffreys
David KJ Vogt
David Lars Chamberlain
David Lizewski
David Longworth & Noemi Germani
David Lyons
David Morin
David Puente
David Rains
David Reynolds
David Sarch
David Shiffler
David Soto
David Sterk
David T Hackett
David W Walters Jr
David Woodcock
Dawn Mattingly 4CD #1437
Dawn McAvoy
Dawn McEachern
Dawns man
Daysha Jim
Deak Niro
Dean Campbell
Dean Ferguson
Dean G.
Dean Reid
Deb
Deb 4CD 743
Debbie Ple

Debora Welsh
Deeann Gilliam
Demmy DeGregorie
Dena Rodrick
Denitt Pe
Dennice Haslett
Dennis "kame" Flanagan
Dennis Reed
Dennis Strasburg
Dennis Walsh
Denver Gordon
Derek A. Benson
Derek J. Primont
Derick Winterberg
Derrick McCall
Desmond Conor Dear
Devan Slater
Devante Stokes
Devin Caitlyn McShane 4CD #8293
Devin Clancy -- Four Color Demon #806
Devon Camel
Devon L. Wright
Dhruv Patel
Dia Morehead
Diane Abbott
Diane L. Ko
Diego Martins de Siqueira
Dillon Armistead
Dillon Bilodeau
Dillon Hagan Bond
Dimitri Cat Robertson
Distant Planet Comics & Collectibles
DJ Slim
DJ Young
dMichael - F8photo
Dom Anderson
Dominic DeCosa
Dominic Duca
Dominic Iacuzza
Dominic Jones (Ebbw Vale)
Don Kunkel
Don Marta
Donald E. Claxon
Donald Herring
Donald Kurasz
DonaldC
Donato Pierro
Donna Atchison
Donna Vicars
Donnavantoft
Donnie Mathis 4CD#3752
Donovan A. DiPasquale
Dora Minutillo
Double Shoe
Doug Bernard
Doug Bissell
Doug Schultz
Doug Sheldon
Doug Spiller
Douglas Fabrication, LLC.

THANK YOU

Douglas W. McCratic
Dr Gustavo Gonzalez
Dr Jazzy Jaff
Dr. Gabriel Axarlian
Dr. Matt Lindsay
Dr. Remy Lebeau @X-Lair
Dr.Rev. Matthias666 Ph.D.
Drew Dierschke
Drew Ford
Drew Justice
Drew Parkinson
Drew Stevens
Drew-4CD #6837
Dustash Montgomery-Scott
Dustin and Crystal Smeltz
Dustin Malcolm
Dustin McKenzie
Dwayne Daniel Harrington
John "Bigjl98" Lauff
Jon Roberts
Dyan Booth
Dylan "5592" Bray
Dylan "Hawkeye" Jones
Dylan Bloyer
Dylan Crosby
Dylan T Cummings Sr.
Dylyn Shapiro
Eamon Merrigan
Earthworld Comics
Eben M
Ed Cox (Patron #2547)
Ed Obomsawin
Ed Schwebel
Edgar Johnson
Eduardo Ortiz #TESD
Eduardo Perez
Edward E Hall
Edward T. Yeatts III (ety3rd.com)
Edward Wellman
Eileen Murphy
Eilidh Louisa Steele
Eiluvthebolts
Eimear O'Connor
EJC
Elaine Baldwin McGrath
Elaine Richey
Eldgeth
Eldridge Bernard Gordon
Elegant Jesus
Elijah Elliott
Elizabeth Michelle Horsley Snider
Elizabeth Shurtliff
Elizabeth Wright 4CD #6591
elodin
Emily Ariadne Barnes
Emily Keith
Emily McCabe
Emily Shurtliff
Emma O'Donnell
Emma Rosenfeld

Emma Sampford aka Baby K
Emma Webster
Emma Wilshire
Emma Winter
Emmeline Olson
Emo Ant
ENGINE ANT 4CD #1122
Enzo Veloo
Eric Bonin
Eric Brown
Eric Cooper
Eric DH Smith
Eric DiBiasio
Eric Howard Mason 4CD#1749
Eric Knapp
Eric L. Smith of Astora
Eric Londaits
Eric Michael Mess
Eric Moree
Eric Perrier
Eric Robert E. (A humble Ant)
Eric S cripe
Eric Taylor
Eric Wright
Eric Zilli
Erica "Erie" Clethen
Erica Greil
Erica Luna
Erich S. Lehman
Erik Bin
Erik Lykke Mogensen
Erik W. Fortman 4CD 838
Erika Gwynn
Erika Reuter
Erin B.
Erin McAteer
Ernesto Barrera
Erwin H.
Esther Marie
Ethan Brooks
Evan Ausura
Evan Gillette
Evan Tyler Johnson
Evelyn Sabbag - The Lady Ev
Everett A Warren
Everybody's Got One Podcast
Evie Jappy
Excalibur Comics
F.C.D. 6223
Fairmont Greg
Famous Faces & Funnies
Fantasy Shop Comics & Games
Fascination Street Podcast
Fat Mike Odinson
Faye P.
FCD#1213 Ryan Larin Clark
Felipe Arambarri Camprovin
FENIX COMIX (USA)
Fermin Serena Hortas
Fernando Aguirre

THANK YOU

Finn Charles
Flame Pieman
Flip Fierro 4CD#9156
Four Color Demon 7464 - Steve Kmet
Francisco Escalante
Franck De Vita
Franco Bentley
Frank & Melissa Straker
Frank C. Noble IV
Frank Flores
Frank Powers 4CD2911
Frankie G - 4CD #2513
Frankie Murray
Frankie Torok
Frankie Zamorano
Franks 'n Beans
Fred Cardona
Fred Sather
Fredrik Bergstedt
Fudo Morris
Fuhrman
funkbrush
G Scott Roden
G. Wohlrabe
G.fry
Gabriel Alba
Gabriel D. Jimenez
Gabriele Wright
Gabriella Leone
Gabrielle Loney
Gaby Razo aka @gabymmit 4CD#8838
Gael Diaz
Gail Thompson
GaNiElAiLu
Gareth Case
GarJennings
Garret
Garrett May
Gary Alexander Linton
Gary Carmon
Gary Gaines
Gary McCoy
Gary Stinson
Gary Troiano, Jr.
Gaz Morgan
GBoog
Gemma Wenham
Geneva Conway
Gentz
Geoff Johnson
Geoff Smiley 4CD 3197
George C Kirchhoffer
George Filby IV
George Haddad
George John Wharmby
George S.
George Scoufaras
George Teate II
Georgina Bignell
Gerardo C.

Gerry Green @professorfrenzy
Gianni Paradiso
Giles A Anderson
Gillian Young
Gillybean
Gina and David Hernandez
Gina Brotsis
Gingervitus
Gioia Elizabeth Rizzo
Giovanna V.
Glen Lees
Glen Pappas
Glenn "the" Baker
GMAN9424
GMarkC
Gr'goire Beaudry
Grace Ilasi
Graham Faught
Grant Fried
Grant Kimbrough
GrANT Rolston 4CD#8537
Grasser Michael
Greg Ames
Greg Hannah
Greg JW Williamson
Greg McElvain
Greg Shelander
Gregg Sugimura
Gretchen Shimek
Griffin "Fate" L.
Hal J Neat
Halen Spiering
Hallie Pierce
Hannah Carlan
Hannah E Roberts
Hannah E. Radcliffe
Hannah J.Z
Hannah Perry
Hannah Ruhl
Harbingerr
Harold Stutz
Harpreet Miglani
Hayden Brooks
Hayden Kody Heye
Hayley Jeffery 4CD #759
Hayley Le-Anne Mortimore
Hayley Mahoney
hazardgaming.com
Heath Amodio
Heather Beachler 4CD #9199
Heather Dugan
Heather Green
Heather Mason
Heather McKinney
Heather Nellis
Heather Reinsel
Heidi Katzer(Redfraggle)
Heidi Welton
Helen Bray
Helen Galluzzo, 4CD #9277

THANK YOU

Helen Morrison
Henchmen of Comics
Henry V. Fidler
Hev Axton
hn6
Holley Holran4CD#1856
Holly Chase
Holly Dixon
Holly M. Wright
Holly Smith
hoodyha
Hope Shevchuk
House Crane
Howard Tucker
Ian Britton
Ian Browne
Ian Corrao
Ian 'E' Barkley
Ian Edwards
Ian Holmes
Ian Nuessle
Ian Wells
Idc.
Idox
Imagine If You Will pod
inconsequential
Innovators
Irving Roca
Isabella Nesbit
ismickisgood
J Sargent
J Vasiloff 4CD #2046
J. Angelli
J. Cole Sheese
J. Jasper Remington
J.R. Murdock
Jørgen Pedersen
Jack "One Dog" Layzell
Jack E Simmons
Jack Hasson Esq.
Jack Lacey
Jack Leonard Smith
Jackie Dill
Jackie Pearson
Jackson Gage Burns
Jackson Peng
Jaclyn Alysse Arre
Jacob Bravard
Jacob Cuglewski
jacob derrick
Jacob Doukas
Jacob Harrison
Jacob Herczeg
Jacob Lorett
Jacob McCulley
Jacob McPhail
Jacob Stout
Jacob Valk
Jacob Velasquez #2378
Jacob Welch

Jacqueline Sauve
Jade Marsh
Jade 'Nuggalo' Swain
Jadron
Jaime Lino
Jaime M Garmendia III
Jake "TESD Ninja Ant" Oller
Jake & Jo S. (4CD# 4869, #9272)
Jake Eisenporth 4CD #2296
Jake Hughes
Jake Mecchi
Jake Saunders
Jamaal "Ryyudo" Graves
James C. Strachan
James casha
James Clark
James Clubb
James Cockrum - 4CD 2225
James Dalton
James Haakinson
James Henry IV 4CD #5361
James Holland
James Iver Meredith
James Macri
James O'Callahan
James O'Donovan
James P. Stimpson
James Pare
James Pontifex 4CD9266
James price 4CD #8924
James R. Crowley
James Sigman
James Sloan
James Tennant
James Timblin
James Turnbull
James Vincent
James Vincent Lane
James Wilton
Jameson Bell
Jamie Barnes & Oliver Lincoln
Jamie & Holly Brackell
Jamie Bromley-Nerdpool Podcast
Jamie Coon 4CD #1261
Jamie Erwine
Jamie F. McIntyre
Jamie G.
Jamie Hale
Jamie Harris
Jamie Kreis
Jamie Meecham
Jamie Phelps & Ava Christensen
Jamie Sanford
Jamie Sedlmayer
Jan Ohrstrom
Jan Roger Henden
Jane Fos
Janelle Howard
Jannie Gru
Jarblon FCD #6343

THANK YOU

Jared Folds
Jared Gunthorpe
Jared Martin
Jared Watterworth
Jarrett Bowen
Jason & Elizabeth Becker
Jason & Laura
Jason Anderson aka Stormms, 4CD
Jason Beckner 4CD #6814
Jason Bourne
Jason Chenoweth
Jason D Schmit
Jason D. Davis
Jason DeSanti
Jason G
Jason Gemmell
Jason Knol
Jason Madsack
Jason Massey
Jason McQuirns
Jason Murrell
Jason nitcholas
Jason Sessler
Jason Solis
Jason Tate
jason3k
Jasper Clement
Javi Barria 4CD #5690
Jay and Silent Bob's Secret Stash
Jay Cassidy
Jay dela Chevrotiere 4CD #2714
Jay Doom Desert Doom
Jay Quinn
Jaymi Morris 4CD#9087
JD Nelson
Jean Pelosa
Jeanette Zynthia Lopez
Jeanie C. Davis
Jedidiah Smith
Jeff "...Why Fat?" Kinsey
Jeff "Sweet Cheeks" Davis
Jeff Cutuli
Jeff Gibson 4CD #1047
Jeff Hartman
Jeff Hotchkiss
Jeff King
Jeff Leiboff 4CD#1310
Jeff P. Nelson
Jeff Ritzmann
Jeff Srack
Jeff Stephens
Jeff Stine
Jeff Talbot
Jeff Waldron
Jeff Weiss
Jefferson Mills
Jeffrey Allen Morris
Jeffrey Beschta II
Jen
Jen Backer

Jen Davenport
Jen Glatz-Zelek
Jen Hertzog
Jen Pellizzari
Jen Richardson
Jen Tunaitis
Jenifer Vazquez
Jenn
Jenn Bustillos 4CD#8419
Jenn Knapp
Jennie Sanchez
Jennifer Deasy
Jennifer Georges
Jennifer J Minton
Jennifer K Arnold
Jennifer L. Albert
Jennifer Marlowe-Rogers 4CD #9170
Jennifer Maudlin
Jennifer McKinney
Jennifer Peters 4CD #8136
Jennifer Pitts
Jennifer Robertson
Jennifer Yantes
Jenny Shapiro
Jennyfer
Jeoff Din
Jeramey Henson
Jeremiah "Solo" Beene
Jeremy Beason
Jeremy Hervey
Jeremy Howson
Jeremy L. Skeens
Jeremy LaForest
Jeremy Mace
Jeremy Schmidt
Jeremy Soers
Jeremy Sokol
Jeremy Stewart
Jeremy Teflon Scott
Jeremy Viteka 4CD #1237
Jeremy Walkama
Jeroen Meijering
Jerrad Billington
Jerri Birkofer
Jerry Driscoll
Jerry Goodridge
Jerry Mudd
Jerry Willoughby
Jess Kreamer
Jess Monning
Jess Yunker 13% 4CD #1712
Jesse Chuckry
Jesse Goldberg
Jesse Hahn
Jessica "M.J." Everett
Jessica Abelia
Jessica Chedore
Jessica Chernega
Jessica D'ANTonio 4CD #8729
Jessica Embacher

THANK YOU

Jessica Fritz
Jessica Lima (Jess)
Jessica Lomupo #4301
Jessica Natasha McEachern
Jessica Pounds
Jessica Rice
Jessica Selinger
Jessie and David Stockton
Jessie C. Hornberger
Jessie Dorsch 4CD#1586
Jewelia R. Hernandez
Jill Harland
Jill Kinlin
Jill Tasei
Jill Waite
Jillian Hooker
Jillian Vian
Jim DeCoyote
Jim Long
Jim Neal
Jim Warburton
Jimmy George
Jo Kates
Jo Pay #1440
Jo Pussinabox
Joanie Jane Burton
JoAnn Rosenmund
Joanna Balon
Joanne Robertson
Jodie Mac Intyre
Jodie Spencer
Jody L. Sellers
Joe Bolanos 4CD#1208
Joe Carter
Joe from Scio
Joe Gardner
Joe Hall
Joe Irwin
Joe Leinberger
Joe Stinn
Joe T.
Joe VanSchaick
Joe Webb
Joel Baldwin
Joel Burns
Joel Gulberti
Joel Herr
Joel M. Scinta
Joel Motta
Joel Scully
Joey Aulisio
Joey Brymer
Joey Lach
Joey Mills
John A. Vincent IV
John Abarca
John B Robertson
John B Rogers 4CD#9157
John Bussard 4CD#2721
John Christy

John Costello
John Dropchuk
John Duke Haller
John Duncan
John Engelman - @heavynuggets
John Fink
John Greenacre
John Heise
John Hourihan
John J Ostrosky Jr
John Jasinski
John l
John Litchford
John Lued
John M. cunningham
John MacLeod
John Manning
John Mercer
John Michael Burkett
John Minsung Kim
John Patton
John Paul DeLeon
John Reynolds
John Robert Wickham
John Royce
John Stephens and Desiarae Fisher
John Taylor
John Vernon Bedor
John Ward
John Worrall
John-Stuart PLANT
Jon Campion
Jon Lipscombe
Jon Trainer
Jonaas Sevilla
Jonas Lidstrom
Jonathan Adao
Jonathan and Bonney Thomas
Jonathan G. Hernandez
Jonathan Gibbs
Jonathan Gutheinz FCD #4020
Jonathan Hawker 4CD#8148
Jonathan JayLando Dipratna
Jonathan Pilmer
Jonathan Smith
Jonathon Ellis
Jonathon Macri
Jordan B Williams
Jordan Fuller 4CD #9013
Jordan M Cortes
Jordan Samuel Fleming
Jorunn Akselsen 4CD #1560
José Andrés Calderón A.
Jose Aguilera
Jose N Castro
Jose Pereira
Jose Villareal
Joseph A. Sahagun
Joseph Bradascio
Joseph Capewell 4CD#1897

THANK YOU

Joseph Corti
Joseph Crimarco
Joseph Hoffmeyer
Joseph John
Joseph Palen
Joseph Patrick McCarthy Tracey
Joseph Ramsey 4CD #1103
Joseph Sander
Joseph Stanton
Joseph Whyte
Josh and Jennifer Hurst
Josh Butzin
Josh Cabrera 4CD #4046
Josh Flickinger 4CD#1871
Josh Glossop
Josh Hillary
Josh Hogan
Josh Landsman
Josh Murphy
Josh Orenberg
Josh Picard
Josh Rader
Josh Rountree
Josh Sandoval 4CD #1946
Josh Trombley
Joshua BigBear Kapaun
Joshua C. Griffith
Joshua D. Bair
Joshua Fryar 4CD #7741
Joshua Joye
Joshua Pinson
Joshua Proctor
Joshua Reedy
"Joshua Stapleton"
Joshua Terrell1259
Josiah Street
JP Burke
JP Cutter
JPD
Juan "Boogie" Torres
Juan Carlos Castellanos
Juan Ramon Ramirez
Juan Stubbs
Judd & Kristen Morse
Judi Mark
Judy
Judy Goldsworth Petranek
JuJuBee
Juliana Brier
Juliana Tessaro
Julianna Mazzola
Julie Jarman
Julie McMonagle
Julie Reardon
Justin Ashley Powell
Justin Belant 4CD #1447
Justin Bianco
Justin Brouwer
Justin Car
Justin Christensen

Justin Cook
Justin Crawford
Justin Hargett
Justin Ingram 4CD#3867
Justin Krapf
Justin Kyle 4CD No. 8122
Justin Naff
Justin Paul (#3496)
Justin Power
Justin Prine
Justin Smith
Justin White
Justin Williams
Justine Cannon 4CD #1599
K Robb
k@mil
Kai Flannery
Kaila Riley
Kaitlyn Mccallister
Kaity McManus
Kami Cluff
Kaname Izki
Kane "Big Wiffy" Miller
Kanimozhi Sarah Jayaseelan
Kara J
Karen
Karen Cheema
Karen Frankaitis
Karen Moreau 4CD #8090
Karen Nicholds
Karen Verescak
Karen Wise
Karim Ghoul & Heba Afyouni
Karina Arlind
Karina'a
Karl Kesel
Karl Koch
Karlina & Adam Williamson
Karrie-Ann Versace
Kasey Williams - 4CD #1178
Kat Nobile
Kate Malcolm
Katelynn A. Smith
Kateri Arends
Kathleen Alfaro
Kathryn Ga
Kathryn Luznicky
Kathy D
Kathy J. Fink
Kathy Templeman
Katie Konig
Katie Stockwell
Katie Vannoy
Katja "Queen" Englund 4CD#790
Kay Manherz
Kayla Alishia Dolan
Kaylee Jo Wolff
Kayleigh Marie Watson 4CD #9186
Kaz #2080
Kaz Tomlinson #1480

THANK YOU

Ke
Keeley Brister
Keewatin Bird
Keith
Keith A. Wood
Keith Bowers
Keith Coffey
Keith G! Baker
Kelley A. Tolck
Kelley Miltier
Kelli Camuso
Kelli Hedges
Kells Dean
Kelly Corr
Kelly Grace Spruyt
Kelly Hutton
Kelly Krug
Kelly Mills
Kelly Quigley
Kelly Standridge
Ken Jensen
Ken Manderscheid
Kenneth
Kenny Carmon
Kenny Duncan
Kenny E
Kenny Hutton
Kerri Atwood
Kerri Williams
Kerry Pech-Kortbein
Kerryann Allen
Kev Shore
Kevin & Jori Behland
Kevin (Van) Clancey
Kevin and Alicia Remington
KEVIN BEST
Kevin Callan
Kevin Cileli
Kevin J. Rapp
Kevin Jones
Kevin Kerby Kleinhans
Kevin Kuell
Kevin Lawley
Kevin Lee Becton
Kevin McConnell
Kevin Quill
Kevin Reape, 4CD#4850
Kevin Seldomridge
Kevin Watkins
Kevira (TankTopAnt) and Corey Voegele
Kiera C. Perkins
Kieran Jason Lee
Kieran O'Sullivan
Kieth Freeman
Kim Blum
Kim Clements
Kim Fritz
Kim Hubscher
Kim Kirk 4CD#9071
Kim Stoltz

Kimberly Arcila
Kimberly Carr
Kimberly Elaine Hebert
Kimberly Theresa Schmidt
Kimberly Wilkerson
Kimble Wicker
King Dan Swan
Kirk Amico
Kirsten Sowden
Kischer Ma
Knoz
Kool-Aid Eads and Mrs. Buttertots
Kortny Clair #2435
Krimso
Kris Konkel #8640
Krista and Mike Costello
Krista Twinky McSugarNips
Kristen Sarno
Kristin Krause
Kristina Carmela 4CD #8379
Kristina M
Kristopher Volter
Kristy Gammon 4CD #9075
Krystal Bailey-Gauze
Krysten "KJ" Jablonowski
KT Wright
KUILAN
Kurt Crozier
Kurtis Hacker
Kurtis Redden
kwm7
Kyle (Keylime) Pryor
Kyle Dalrymple
Kyle Griner
Kyle Gustafson
Kyle Haner
Kyle MacDonald
Kyle Marcus
Kyle Phillips
Kyler Jaye
Kylie Wells
Kym O'Neill
Kyra Lennon
kza
L Jamal Walton
L Weakland
L. D.
L. Del Rosso
Lance "Thay" Queton
Lance H. Masse
Lance Kennamer
Larissa Hermanns
Larissa Hoskins
Larry G. Reed Jr.
Lascelles M Haughton
Latanya Williams
Laura "LG" Gentile (Boston)
Laura B. #857
Laura Bennett
Laura Davy-Thomas

THANK YOU

Laura Guinan 4CD#822
Laura Joyce
Laura L. Herron
Laura Prieto
Laura SchANTz 4CD #1766
Laura-Anne Sloan
Laurel Vores
Lauren
Lauren Alvarez
Lauren Buchenhain
Lauren Burdo 4CD #4848
Lauren Donofrio
Lauren Ezell
Lauren Furlonger
Lauren O'Neill 4CD #9269
Lauren Poyser
Laurie Zito 4CD #917
Lawrence R Visbisky
LD3
Ldbadseed
Leah G. Huckaby
Leah Hoffman
Leanna Tallett
Leanne Silverthorne
Lee Chappell
Lee Doyle
Lee Parr
LemonHead
Lena "The Elf" Dwire
Lena "Wellsy" Corley
Leo Gallofin
Leon Glaser
Leon Scorpius
LEON W
Leonard David
Leonel Caldela
Leroy Scott
Lesley & Paul Clarke
Leslie Terry
LethalZero485
Lewis Reece
Liam J. Sala
Lila Muri
LIM Cheng Tju
Linda Fell Peterson
Linda Lovell
Linda Lowe, Glendale, AZ
Linda Vetere #TeamQ #TESD
Lindsay E Fowler
Lindsay Enoch
Lindsay Musselman 4CD #2137
Lindsey Clayton (4CD #1649)
Lior Zafrir
Lisa "JerseyGirlAnt" 4CD #2579
Lisa Al
Lisa Blair
Lisa C. Janes
Lisa Caszatt
Lisa Chance
Lisa G.

Lisa Herman from JT, PA
Lisa Mott 4CD #9030
Lisa Osborne hois
Lisa Rafalko
Lisa Ritchie 4CD#2663
Lisa 'Taters' Clarke
Lisandro Gutierrez
Lissy
Liv Thomas
Liz Woods
LN
Logan "LD" Davis
Logan Russell
Lois and Tyler
Lolly Maute
Lord Cardenas
Loren and Travis Jennings- 4CD 8542
Lori Kelter
Lori Lee Boynton
Lori Oliver 4CD#6554
Lorna Pa
Lou Ann a Brian Quinn fan!!
Louis
Louise Charlton
LP_85
Lucas Crain
Lucas Devine
Lucas Vermillion
Lucy Caton
Lucy Cox
Lucy Spotswood 4CD #1378
Luis OCBrakeless
Luke Abramson
Luke Carceller
Luke Emery
Luke 'GOOEYBOY' Illes
Luke H. Brown
Luke Mathes
Luke W
lydia
Lynn B Wixted
Lynsey Snell
M
M. Erno
M. H. Burkett
M.Argentina Arias Gómez
Maddie M. White
Madelyn Jackson
Madison and Jayden Craig
Maevegan
mag. Rajko Jerenec
Magdalena Erlandsson
Maggie #885
MAGGIE BOILERBABE40 ROCKWELL
Makenzee Bruce
Malcolm & Islay Hintz
Mallory Leonard
Man
Mandy K. Eads 4CD #8358
Mandy Toftner

THANK YOU

Marc Bergeron
Marc Colombina
Marc Seatter
Marc Storrs
Marc Wolfgram
Marco A Cunalata
Marcus Ant
Marcus Zimmer 4CD# 3413
Maria Bainbridge
Maria Massey
Marianne England
Marie & Onyx #8205
Marie Day
Mariella Mercado
Marina Gustafson 4CD #1755
Marina Olympidis
Mario B.
Mario Pineda
Marizol Galv
Mark "BoomBoom" Bloom
Mark Andrew Roberts
Mark Arend
Mark Brandel
Mark Cornelius Lafferty
Mark DePippo
Mark G. Rayburn
Mark Green
Mark Hanratty 4CD #2285
Mark Herbrechtsmeier 4CD#3693
Mark Hollingsworth 4CD #1224
Mark Horton
Mark J. Western
Mark Jowett
Mark Live @ChunderToons
Mark London
Mark R.
Mark Tyas
Mark Whitehead
Mark Wilkinson
MarkTrain FCD #5533
MarkusM
Marnie and Ellie Harris
Marquett Spitznagel aka MarquANT #945
Marsha Black 4CD #7521
Marshall Carr
Marshall-squishynosinc
Martin Cameron
Martin Perez
Martin Smith
Martin Vittands
Mary Alice Finley Davis 4CD #8440
Mary Ann Palmiotti
Mary Anne Cachola
Mary E. Bobenmoyer
Mary Gray
Mary Kasten - WI
Mary Lee
Mary-Kate Anthony 4CD #2652
Mat Stafford
Mathew Bridgeman

Matrix
Matt "The Canadian Ant" Murray #3674
Matt and Stacey Draper
Matt Beccaria
Matt Bolyan
Matt Bruce
Matt Cambridge
Matt Cunliffe
Matt Davenport aka Fenn101
Matt Elkins
Matt Filip
Matt Flanagan
Matt Garcia
Matt Gervasi
Matt Goodwin
Matt Graves
Matt Hodges
Matt J. Miller
Matt Johnson
Matt Nemec
Matt Ortiz
Matt Peebles
Matt Robichaud
Matt Roohr
Matt Smith @Dayoldpizza
Matt Spence
Matt Strobelt
Matt Wiley 4CD:4794
Matt, Joy & Ryan Lewis
Matthew & Julie Ann Hood
Matthew A. Lettich
Matthew Berger
Matthew Byrne
Matthew Carrasquillo
Matthew Dawson
Matthew Deane 4CD#3657
Matthew H. Smith
Matthew Isak
Matthew J Rothblatt
Matthew Jappy
Matthew Lee Venner
Matthew McGregor
Matthew Mistalski (@mango666)
Matthew Parry
Matthew R S Taylor
Matthew Randall 4CD #1495
Matthew Repp 4CD #924
Matthew Salleo
Matthew Stalker
Matthew Van Houten
mattjmorrison
Matty Watson
Max Calhoun
Max Livingston
Maya Merth
MC Cross
Mccrae olson
Meesh Marsh
Meg Hughey
Megan & Tyler Hewitt

THANK YOU

Megan A. Jones
Megan Bedford
Megan Hermolle
Megan Malcolm
Megan Williams
Melinda Nankivell
Melinda Whitaker
Melissa Armenia 4CD# 860
Melissa Casey
Melissa Castorena
Melissa Daigle 4CD #1636
Melissa Flores
Melissa Hayes
Melissa M.
Melissa Rogers
Melissa Swinconos 4CD #1563
Melissa Thomas
Mercedes Martin 4CD #8376
Meredith K
meredith miller
mgc_starwarsij
Micah Casebeer
Michael Alamillo
Michael and Kathy Kassab
Michael Belfiore
Michael Benevento
Michael Beverage
Michael Bobenmoyer
Michael Cruz
Michael F. Gusella
Michael Finn
Michael Fox
Michael Grimshaw 4CD #8804
Michael Haner 4CD #8685
Michael Harry Allen
Michael Hodgson
Michael Holtry
Michael Hunter
Michael J. Skvarla
Michael Józef Adach
Michael Jack Jensen!
Michael Jefferson
Michael Joslin
Michael K. Kaye
Michael K. Wade
Michael Lett
Michael McIsaac
Michael Milgate
Michael Moore
Michael Myers
Michael Olson
Michael Peden
Michael Pettersen
Michael Pilapil
Michael Reid
Michael Roslen
Michael Schofield
Michael Shanholtz
Michael Silva
Michael Stevens

Michael T. Lowenthal
Michael Tyson
Michael V. Donahue
Michal Janowski
Michele Fetzer
Michele Manuk
Michele Speckman 4CD#6963
Michele Timbro
Michelle Brunetti
Michelle Lepore 4CD#1251
Michelle Levens
Michelle Nicolato
Michelle Porwoll Bramsen
Michelle Stafford
Michelle Tickle
Mickey & Jed Crandall
Miguel Aguilera
Mika Koykka
Mikasaraus
Mike
Mike "Black Pete" Robinson 4CD #930
Mike and Susan Sullivanz
Mike Betterelli
Mike Bultsma
Mike Chronister
Mike Drimones
Mike Drumm 4CD #6520
Mike Evans
Mike Frias 4CD #8800
Mike Hoffman
Mike Horst
Mike King
Mike Krol
Mike Lendi
Mike Madryga
Mike Marlow
Mike Martin
Mike McLaughlin
Mike Moring
Mike Newhouse-Bailey
Mike O'Brion
Mike Phillips (Ottawa, ON)
Mike Quattrochi
Mike Scerra
Mike Scott
Mike Svonavec
Mikey Warczak
Mila Joy Cole
Miles Watterson
Milouche La Mouche
Mineemowse 4CD #1320
Minh Nguyen
Miranda Crum
Miranda D. Lawson
Mischief
Miss Retro SJKG
Missy Bancroft (4CD #2111)
Missy Sollars
Misty Crain 4CD#8106
Misty Trann

THANK YOU

Mitchell McRoy
Mitchell Smith
Mogero
Mollie Gann
Money Matt Lou
Monica Baron
Monica Johnson
Monkey McGee
Monte St Aubyn
Morgan DuShane
Morgan Stuart Eastwood
Morris De
Mortimer C. Spongenuts III
MR RUSSIA
Mr Whiskers
Mr. Kevin Conroy (Batman)
Ms Michele
My wife can't know
My wife Nicole
mystady.com
Mystyc Star Metrik
N8
Na
nader rafieyan
Nancy Diem
Nancy E Escobedo
Nancy Slusar
Nancy Verlander 4CD #2802
Nat Dodd
Natalie Brown
Natalie Simon
Natalie Slechta
Nate Isaac
Natedigad Townsend
Nathan "DeadOneWalking" W
Nathan Brynley Shepherd
Nathan C. Vincent
Nathan Heinrich
Nathan Lacey
Nathan R.
Nathanial Walker
Neeter G
Neil Beigie
Neil G 4CD #762
Nestor Deleon III
Nic Gordon
Nic Orizaga
Nicholas Barroga
Nicholas Iacovou
Nicholas M. Himann
Nicholas Ruffing
Nicholas Schubert
Nicholas William John Armstrong
Nicholle Moreci
Nick
NICK ADRIAN
Nick Bauder
Nick Butcher
Nick Crist
Nick Danks

Nick FCD#4954
Nick Franco
Nick Giordano
Nick J
Nick Maggio
Nick Mikoleit
Nick Moniak
Nick Shafir
Nick Steiner
Nick Stevenson
Nick Suite
Nick W
Nick W. Adkinson
Nick Woltring
Nicky Branco
Nicky Nove
Nico Garcia
Nicolas B Newsome
Nicolas Solban
Nicole DaSilva
Nicole L. Chapman
Nicole Paxson
Nicole Toscano
Niki Faletufuga
Nikki 4CD #9167
Nikki Nykamp Foss 4CD #1705
Nikki Sanchez
Nikki Zwart (Lipke)
Nikolas Coffey
Ninasean Murphy
Nineite
Noah Foss
Noah YOURno1HERO Phillips
NoelDarling
Noemi Monge
Nolan D
Norma Jean Bullard
Norma Lockman
Nurul Aqilah Pauzi
Olivia And Phil
Olivia Eve Briskey
Olympic Cards and Comics
OmahaBound
Omar Pineda
Outland Entertainment
P_Hizz
Pacer B, Esq MOTHER FUCKERS!!!
Paden Smith
Paige Seuferling
Pam Wallace
Pamela Hughes
Pat & Jenn
Pat Callahan
Pat dunne
Pat Vice Wennekamp 4CD #4862
Patricia Davis
Patricia wisch
Patrick Conley
Patrick Dileo 4CD #6452
Patrick Donohue 4CD #1365

THANK YOU

Patrick M Grobe
Patrick McClain 4CD #5575
Patrick McHugh
Patrick Mulkerrins
Patty Loudon 4CD #9171
Patty Mienko
Patty Ottavi 4CD # 8572
Paul @GGmBrand
Paul Bailey
Paul Buchanan
Paul Cottrell
Paul D Smith
Paul Everingham
Paul Frarey
Paul Harvey Jr
Paul Mallon
Paul Maynard Jr.
Paul Munn
Paul Oliver
Paul Rowland JR 4168
Paul Sansone
Paul Saunders 4CD #2121
Paul Sherrick
Paul Stallbaum
Paul Tracy 4CD #4314
Paul Was
Paul y cod asyn Jarman
Paulie Dunn 4CD #6369
Paulina H.
Pedro Shing Rosa
Penny Lee
PENNY WATERS   4CD $9169
Pernille Orum
Perry Iaquinto Jr
Pete Dancer
Pete Korcynski
Pete Manchester
Pete Naylor 4CD #1006
Pete_Passion
Peter A. Cammarata
Peter Bahrenburg
Peter Reed
Peter W. Gacek
Peteypops
Peyton Damon Parr
Phil & Cari R.
Phil "OG18" Belch
Phil Slack
Philip Cochran
Philip Giles
Phill Hall
Phillip (PhillWill) Williams 4CD#7700
Phillip Hupp
Phillip Lewis
Phillip Theis-5178
Philly Krueger
Pierce O'Connor
Pippa Hawkins, Marstan Hotel
Plucky Hero
Pooja Kumari Prashar

Poop Office
Pop Goes The Culture Podcast
Poppa Wheelie
Porl Taylor
Portergraphic Podcast
Potsoyi (Adrian Potter)
Pug Riley
PyrosPlayhouse
Rachael L. Howell
Rachel H Sanders
Rachel Plowman
Rachel Podraza 4CD #7361
Rachel Yarger
rachellynnFTW
Ramsey
Randumb Thoughts Podcast
Randy Allen Lowery
Randy Anderson
Rayna Louise Spencer
Rebecca Ann Miller
Rebecca Carroll
Rebecca Collins
Rebecca Kirsch
Rebecca R Kline
Reemi Hautas'ki
Regan
Renayle Fink
Rene "nizz" Kaiel - 4CD 8670
Rene Garcia
Rene Harnois Jr
Renee Beckley
Rev. Chris Hudson
Rich "ArieAy" Arbo
Rich Humes
Rich Mendoza
Richard "Doc" Nocella
Richard beckett
Richard Botto
Richard Brown
Richard Ferguson 4CD #1669
Richard Foreman
Richard StJohn
Richard W. Pace
Rick & Gina Maynard
Rick Burwell
Rick Houlihan
Rick Mantilla
Rick Whiting
Rivol
RLecuyer
Rob Hettinger 4CD#3040
Rob Lambeth
Rob Leonard
Rob Linley
Rob Rogers
Rob Scaffidi
Rob Tanzola
Robbie W
Robert Ohler
Robert C Erickson

THANK YOU

Robert Capps
Robert Codd
Robert Dalbo
Robert DeCambra
Robert Draeger
Robert Jac
Robert Goral Ant 4266
Robert Iwataki
Robert Johnson III
Robert N Pohlman
Robert Nelson
Robert R. Joyce Esq.
Robert Rothschild Rochelle
Robert Spagna
Robert Zagami - 4CD #749
Robin Knapp
Robin Starn
Robyn Louise Goodchild
Robyn Noble
Rochelle Pinon
Ron Bonno
Ron Wheeler
Ronnie Barron
Rory Angus
Rosaline Gajeski
Rose June Burns
Rose Mintrone
Ross Williams
Rowan Marie Weiss
Roxfan00
Roz Gill #763
Rudy rodr
Rui Martins
Russ Thorn
Russell Hess, aka "H" #hh5art
Rusty ant. James Steele
Ruth Jack
Ryan "Tweet" Burk
Ryan and Ben Antemann
Ryan Arneson
Ryan Beagley 4CD #5153
Ryan Champion
Ryan Cox
Ryan Cregan
Ryan Croland
Ryan Dowell
Ryan Drews
Ryan Franks 4CD #8363
Ryan Fre
Ryan Frick
Ryan Goins
Ryan Hosner
Ryan Johnson
Ryan Kelbel
Ryan Keplinger
Ryan Moody 4CD#9160
Ryan Myers
Ryan Nolen
Ryan Pettit
Ryan Quint

Ryan R
Ryan Sauer
Ryan Smith
Ryan Smoley
Ryan Stokes
Ryan Supple
Ryan Tomcko
Ryan Wilch
Ryley Day
S W
Sabra Bunger 4CD #9027
Sabrina Marie DeFilippe
Sak
Sally Abelia
Sally Pett
Sam (Sgt. Pilko) Pilkington
Sam Andrews
Sam Batt
Sam Batten
Sam & Naomi Buckingham
Sam Connick
Sam Finney
Sam Levine
Sam McCoy
Sam McDonough
Sam McMillan
Sam Nimble Danger Fairhurst
Sam Pass
Samantha And Collin Randle
Samantha Arin Minier
Samantha Gaglione
Samantha Lee
Samantha Leigh
Samantha Pistell
Samantha Ripka
Samantha Staycer
Sami J
Samm Scherer
Sampaige
Samuel Loveridge
Samuel N. Lovejoy
SamuHappoldt
Sandra Zupancic 4CD#2939
Sandy Bellucci
Sandy Saati
Sandy Scott
Sara Digi
Sara Fischer
Sara Goodman
Sara Majetic
Sara Vogel
Sarah (Sonic) Jarratt
Sarah Anderson
Sarah Kachellek
Sarah Lebowitz #8758
Sarah Marksberry
Sarah Osborn and Hannah Osborn
Sarah Plocki
Sarah Poole
Sarah Rosenmund

THANK YOU

Sarah Szmyt
Sarah Todd
Sarah Vega 4CD #8837
Sarah Wilson
Sarah Wydner
Sasquatch Ate My Baby podcas
Savannah Bird and D.J. Boatman
Savannah Miller
Scarlett Letter
Scott Alder
SCOTT and SETH MILLER
Scott Bertucci
Scott Hamlin
Scott Hopkins SYR
Scott James Baker
Scott K. Petersen
Scott Koblich
Scott Krohn
Scott Lamont
Scott M. Adams
Scott Marrotti
Scott McKay
Scott Morrison
Scott Steubing
Scott Sunders
Scott Taylor
Scott Thomas
Scott Tolbert
Scott Waters
Scott Westerman
Scout & Cleo
Scuba-Steve Jones
Sétor Spaghettihead
Sean & Megan DeJean
Sean "@vacaboca" Hogarty 4CD #3231
Sean Anthony Smith
Sean Burke
Sean Chavan supports single moms
Sean Guymon
Sean Heatherley
Sean Knowles
Sean McCarthy
Sean McGraw #3226 4 Colors 4 Life
Sean O'Dell
Sean P. Aune
Sean Prouty
Sean Quinn
Sean Robinson 4cd#8704
Sean Smith
Sean Stacy
Sean Starke
Sean T Pedersen
SeanDoesComics
Secret Agent Randy Beans
Sergio Lugo II
Sergio Vidaurre
Seth Armstrong
Seth Morris
Shaad Schubert
Shana Potter

Shane Doh
Shane Rehder
Shanna Haid #8744
Shannon Blohm FCD #1541
ShannyCupcakes 4CD #1339
Shano D
Sharon Dornan
Sharon Gatchell 4CD#2140
Sharon Rose Powell
Sharon stmartin
Shaun Carr
Shavedbird
Shawn Dean
Shawn Dillon
Shawn Gabborin
Shawn McDaniel
Shayne Jones
SheedyX
Sheila Conner
Sheldon Tounzen
Sheri Izzo
Sheriff Scabs
Sherry Hall (a "Q" fanatic)
Sheryl Hale
Shivam Kumar
Shogun Pumba of Dem
Shohn Greer
Sid Sondergard
Sierra Marie
Sierra&Joe
SilverVulpes
Simo Suonio
Simon Gallacher
Simon hogg
Simon Mudrak
Simon Tanner
Siobhan Trinnaman
Skimbosh
Sky Brown
Skylar Maloney
SModBuddyChrist
SModfan 4CD #835
Smokey 4cd#1125
Sonia Carvalho
Sonia Sohappy
Sonica Ellis
sonky
Sophia Haddad
Sophie Doolan
Spencer Church
Spencer Cl
Spencer Self
Spider Jerusalem
Spiffykates
Stacey and Christian
Stacey Bell
Stacey McGuire
Stacey Thompson
Stacie Cole Patterson
Stacy and Estelle

THANK YOU

Starli L Bartlett
Steffany "Stella" Stine 4CD #2643
Steph & Lance
Steph Worwood
Stephanie & Charles Cascio 4CD #8774
Stephanie Boardman
Stephanie Estrada
Stephanie Nichole Hughes
Stephanie Rose
Stephen Andrews
Stephen D. Kayota
Stephen Erdman
Stephen Gris 4CD #6360
Stephen Lee
Stephen Meinhardt
Stephen Murphy
Stephen Peddigrew
Stephen R. Hicks
Stephen Regan 4CD #7691
Sterling
Steve "The Bard" Latour
Steve Barrass #1126
Steve Delap
Steve Green 4CD #1400
Steve Hain
Steve Kesler
Steve Morrison
Steve Pattee
Steve Storino
Steve Tiseo
Steve Vincent
Steve w.
Steve Wills - Newcastle
Steven Farwell
Steven Greathouse
Steven Hoveke
Steven J Hanson
Steven J. Feki
Steven Laity
Steven Ortlieb 4CD#2159
Steven Stark
Steven Stone
Steven Trout 4CD #4388
STEVEN TSAI
Steven Vande Vyvere
Steven Walker
Steven Young
Stuart Cornelio
Stuart Glenn Malone
Stuart Hayter
Suann Row
Sue Greene
Sunday Jeff Tattoo Guy
Susan Cavanaugh Boronczyk
Susan Fowler
Susan Murphy
Susan Nelson
Susane Berger
Susie Rando
Susy Coffey

Suzanne Butler
SuzyAnn
Swantopia
Sweet Cheeks Kari
SweetVAant
SwordFire
Sydney Hajek
Sydney Price
T. Hill 4CD #7858
T. Self (Ant)
T.A.
T.J. LaVere
Tah
Takeo 4CD 4036
Talking Codswallop Podcast
Tamara Tarbell 4CD #8772
Tammy Corrado
Tammy Stonelake
Tank McCarl
Tanya Gaona
Tara & james rath
Tara (Very) Dark Haubert
Tara Fronczkowski 4CD #8570
Tara Taddeo
Tatiana X. Dayers
Tavo Reyes
Taxes
Taylor "Chippy" Sadlowski
Taylor Blair
Taylor Sexton
Taylor Sigler
Team Cline
Ted Langstaff 4CD #3715
Teej
Tehnysha Moore
Tell Em Steve-Dave!
TellEmGwarth
Tema O'Brien
Tera Lewis
Teresa Grubb Chapman
Teresa R. Constancio
Teri Hackmack
Terri Currie 4CD #1287
Terri Spincken 4CD #1846
Terri Stritzel
Terry Austin
Terry Tilley
TESD
TESD Viking
Tess judge
Tess M. Anketell
ThatJoser
The bearded one-Frank Nixon
The Blanchards
The Bobeckerrella's
The Chronicles of Rachel Strand
The Comic Cave
The Goo 4CD#1293
The Lamplugh's SKOL!
The Leaman Family

THANK YOU

The McCollom Family
The McSwain Clan
The Meldrum Family
The Mr Matt
The Nerd Blitz w/ Doom & Fitz
The one and only LeeAnn Pedersen!
The Pirate Cats
The Queen of Serotonin Failure
The Stoker 4CD #1. Snoogans.
The TESD Ants
Theo Stathis
Theodore Alexander
Theresa B
Thinking Outside the Longbox
Thomas Allie 4CD #2582
Thomas Bosch
Thomas Clampitt
Thomas Earnest 4CD#2880
Thomas Hickam
Thomas Joseph Helget
Thomas M Bock
Thomas Murray
Thomas P Ehrig
Thomas Pauley
Thomas Stark
Tia Daniels
Tia Raines
Tierry M. Laforce
Tiffany & Tyler Clark
Tiffany Karol
Tigris Stark
Tim Dawson
Tim Fong
Tim Gallan
Tim Gardner
Tim Harris
Tim L
Tim Pitoniak
Tim Von Cloedt
Timothy Ripka
Timothy S Brennan
Tina Bra
Tina Omega Scoopreme Smith
TiredPirate
TJ Weaver
Toby Lockwood
Toby Martin
Toby Schofield
Todd Reichert
Todd Stephens
Todd Storm
Tom A. Hobson
Tom Anderson, 4 Color Demon #1571
Tom Barnes
Tom Cottrell
Tom F.
Tom Kristufek
Tom McGowan: 4CD #1205
Tom Michael
Tom Milo 4CD #2749

Tom Philpott
Tom Roushey
Tom SKOL TESD Jensen
Tom Vogel
Tom Woodward
Tommy J Marr
Tommy Lincoln
Tommy Lombardozzi 4CD #2147
Tommy Ramsden :)
Tommy Stratis
Toni 4CD #2925
Tony (Dabonetone) Rickard
Tony Baker
Tony Cap 4CD #1096
Tony D'Urso
Tony G.
Tony Johnson
Tony Lambiris
Tony Medcalf
Tori Behm
Tracey Baker
Tracey Baker
Tracey McCollum 13%er 4CD #1380
Tracey Spencer
Tracie Lockwood
Tracy Hixson
Tracy Rahn
Travis "Pillowtalk" Christy
Travis and Ashlie Post
Travis Crocker
Travis Jennings FCD#7811
Travis Nuckolls
Travis Pruitt
Travis Walston
Travis Wesley
Travis Witt
Travis Worley
Trent W
Trent Weldy
Trevor Boyd
Trevor Meisinger
Trevor Smith 4CD #5535
Trevor Talbott
Trey Terbay 111
Trinity Noia
Tristan
Tristyn Akbas
Trozzbozz
Tull Perry
Tuns2G
Tydanosaurus Rex
Tyler Bass "DarthAldered"
Tyler "The Foraner" Foran
Tyler A Staples Ant #9117
Tyler B. Orlando
Tyler Feldhege
Tyler Lassinger
Tyler Reguly
Tyler Trent
Uroš Stanič

THANK YOU

V
Val
Valene Carissa
Valerie Studnick
Vance Perez
Vanessa Cordell
Vanessa Espinosa 4CD #8879
Vanessa Garza
Veda Lee
Vicki ale
VickyS.07035
Victor Amato
Victoria Annie Griffiths
Victoria Lilith
Victoria O'Day
Victoria Teschner
Vincent Chen
Vincent Mak
Vincent S Salamon
Vincent Zawmek
Virginia & Jon Weaver
Vorpal Ladel
wabewalker
Walt Flanagan's Dog
Wascally Rabbit
Wastehound-am
Wayne Dwyer
Wayne Rae
Wayne Winsett
Wendy Beaver
Wendy Mongillo
Wendy Renee 4CD #1530
Wes Butler
Wes Hales
Wesley Benjamin
Whitney Danger Thompson-Harner
Wil and Liam's Mom
Wile E. Young
Will Allen
Will Ball
Will Brewster
Will Childs
Will Lewis
Will Pittluck
Will Rogers
William Brooks III
William Carranza
William D Dunlap
William Dixon
William F. Hogan
William John Green
William Kaplan
William Manis
William Withers
WNxCrab
Yazmin Darlow
yeti the ant
Yvonne Thomson
Z
Z.G.C.

Zac Cachia
Zac Pelkowski
Zach Davis- Bull Moose Entertainment
Zach Harris
Zach Long
Zach Lyman
Zach Steubing
Zach Wampler
Zachary Leeman
Zachary Oakes 4CD #8870
Zachary Paul Stewart
Zachary Williams
Zack Ailstock 4CD #1090
Zack Alfred
Zack Parkerson
Zack Pellichero
Zack Turner
Zafirah A. Alli
Zak Roddey
Zeehan Shaikh

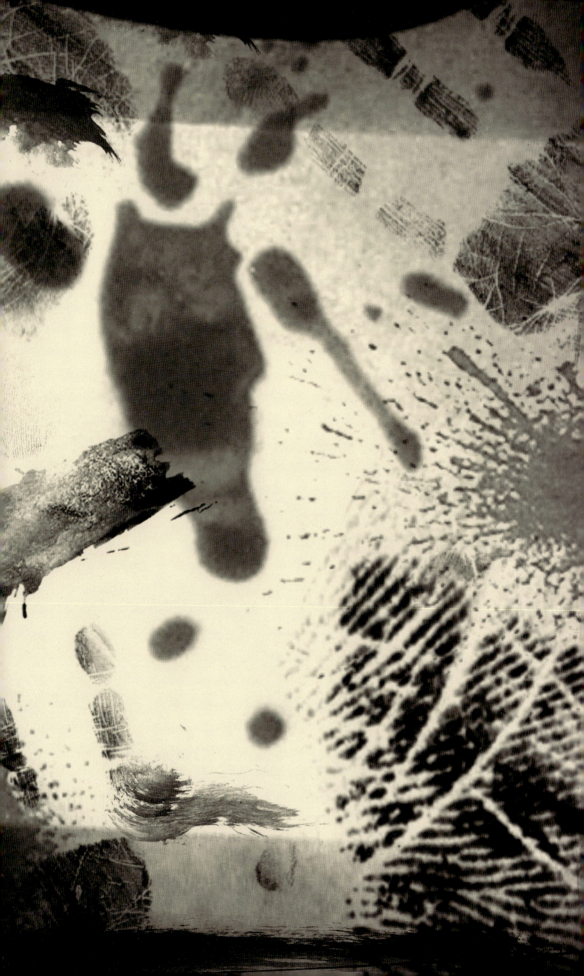

METRO

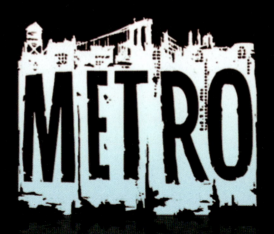

there is power in three.